Walks of a Lifetime
in America's National Parks

(opposite) Glacier National Park

FALCON®

An imprint of Rowman & Littlefield
Falcon and FalconGuides are registered trademarks of Rowman & Littlefield.

Distributed by NATIONAL BOOK NETWORK

British Library Cataloguing in Publication Information available

Library of Congress Cataloging-in-Publication Data

Names: Manning, Robert E., 1946– author. | Manning, Martha S., author.
Title: Walks of a lifetime in America's National Parks : extraordinary
  hikes in exceptional places / Robert and Martha Manning.
Description: Guilford, Connecticut : Falcon, 2020. | Includes
  bibliographical references. | Summary: "A guide to the nation's great
  national parks and their best hikes, ranging from short day hikes to
  backpacking treks and featuring scenic vistas, waterfalls, and
  information on lodging opportunities. Includes color photographs
  throughout."— Provided by publisher.
Identifiers: LCCN 2019049260 (print) | LCCN 2019049261 (ebook) | ISBN
  9781493039258 (paperback) | ISBN 9781493039265 (epub)
Subjects: LCSH: Hiking—United States—Guidebooks. | Trails—United
  States—Guidebooks. | National parks and reserves—United
  States—Guidebooks.
Classification: LCC GV199.4 .M36 2020 (print) | LCC GV199.4 (ebook) | DDC
  796.510973—dc23

LC record available at https://lccn.loc.gov/2019049260
LC ebook record available at https://lccn.loc.gov/2019049261

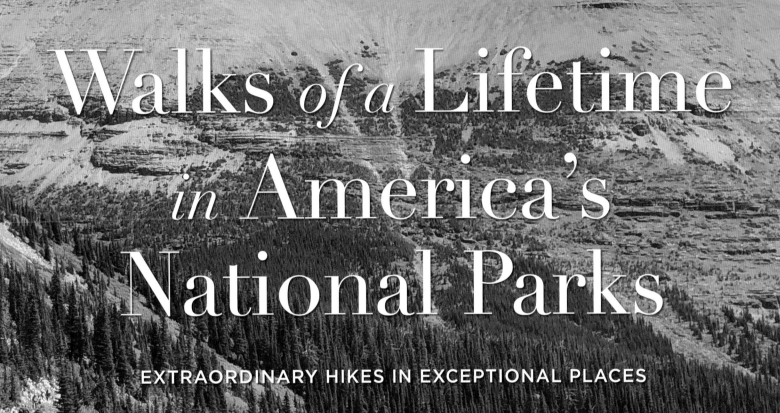

Walks *of a* Lifetime

in America's National Parks

EXTRAORDINARY HIKES IN EXCEPTIONAL PLACES

Robert and Martha Manning

FALCON®

GUILFORD, CONNECTICUT

We're pleased to dedicate this book to our extended family of hikers. We started our daughters, Amy and Molly, hiking very early in life and realized they were gifted walkers when they hiked to the bottom of Grand Canyon and back up, every step of the way, when they were just 5 and 7. (The only incentive was the promise of an ice-cream cone at the rim.) Their husbands, Nick and Mike, respectively, are the sons we didn't have. They were both city kids, but we've been delighted at the way they've become accomplished hikers as well. Our grandsons, Carter and Lucien (Junior Rangers at a growing number of national parks), are just 8 and 10, but they've proven to be prodigious hikers, walking 100-mile trails. For most of our adult lives, we lived in beautiful, peaceful Vermont, where hiking is in the culture, and our circle of hiking friends brought great joy to our lives. Now we live in lively Prescott, Arizona, where there are parks, public lands, and trails in all directions, and most are accessible year-round. We hike regularly with our friends in the Healthy Hikers and others as well, and this is an important part of our lives.

Thanks and love to all of you!

Grand Teton National Park

Petrified Forest National Park

Contents

Mammoth Cave National Park

Saguaro National Park

Big Bend National Park

Shenandoah National Park

Glacier National Park

Channel Islands National Park

Foreword

My wife and I were recently hiking a trail in a grove of giant sequoias deep within Sequoia National Park when we paused to absorb the soothing quiet. The only sound was a soft rustle from the branches of these ancient sentinels that were standing long before the fall of Troy. "Natural quiet," the sounds of nature uninterrupted by human-caused noise, is one of many benefits that walkers can appreciate in the national parks. More than a hundred years ago, early conservationists such as John Muir and President Teddy Roosevelt walked these old-growth forests and crafted a legacy of conservation. Today these forests are protected as part of Sequoia National Park, and we've built on that legacy by establishing many more national parks—and our National Park System continues to grow in number and diversity.

America's national parks are my passion and I was fortunate to spend forty years helping to manage and protect them, including eight years as Director of the National Park Service. Our national parks represent the best of our nation's landscape, history, and culture and are important expressions of American democracy. We all share in their ownership and in the responsibility for their stewardship to ensure they are appreciated and preserved for future generations. There's no better way to develop that appreciation than hiking along a park trail.

In this book Bob and Martha Manning—two people especially well qualified—describe the national parks and lead readers along their favorite national park trails. Bob was an award-winning professor in the Rubenstein School of Environment and Natural Resources at the University of Vermont, where he taught the history, philosophy, and management of national parks and conducted a long-term program of research for the National Park Service. He and his wife, Martha, have lived and worked in several national parks and hiked extensively throughout the National Park System, and they bring this expertise and experience to help guide readers through our remarkable national parks. Bob and Martha encourage us to take a hike for our health, to experience the national parks at pedestrian speed, and to reconnect with our national parks on a personal level. Follow them and you can walk in the footsteps of all who have devoted their lives to protecting the national parks and the planet we call home.

—Jonathan B. Jarvis, eighteenth director of the National Park Service

Sequoia National Park

Introduction

It's been a joy to prepare this book, a labor of love and a manifestation of two of our deepest passions: America's national parks and walking. For most of our adult lives, we've been fortunate to make regular visits to the national parks, returning often to many of our favorites, even living in some for a year at a time. While most of the national parks can be seen from the dramatic roads that travel through them, we're convinced that walking is the way to appreciate them in the richest, most intimate and fulfilling way. Our commitment to walking in the parks has helped us keep a promise to ourselves to appreciate them in the most meaningful way and to help preserve them in the process.

We prepared this book to invite you to join us in walking the national parks and to help guide you in the process. Part 1 of the book explores the question of why we should consider walking in the national parks. We begin by presenting our thinking about why the national parks are such a vital part of our American heritage and why we should celebrate them. The parks include hallowed places like Yellowstone, Yosemite, and Grand Canyon, as well as dozens more that, while they might not be as well-known, all warrant our attention and consideration. We implore you to take the time to visit and appreciate the national parks, as many as you can, when and where possible. We also consider the history and philosophy of walking, the oldest form of transportation, but the most rewarding as well. Indeed, walking is making a comeback in contemporary America because it has so many potential benefits. We finish Part 1 by noting the powerful synergy between walking and the national parks.

Part 2 of the book is its heart—descriptions of all sixty-two American national parks, one chapter devoted to each park. We present a map showing the location of all the national parks at the beginning of Part 2. If past is prologue, the number of national parks will continue to grow and diversify; we look forward to adding these new parks to our personal hiking agenda and including them in future editions of this book. Of all the national parks, we shine our light most brightly on the forty-seven that are the best hiking parks for most people. Each of these forty-seven chapters describes the park's natural and cultural history, catalogs its major attractions, and offers firsthand descriptions of the very best trails. All of these walks (and many more!) have been trail-tested by us and will allow you to enjoy and appreciate the importance of each park and how it contributes to the diversity of the National Park System and the American landscape more broadly. We've been deliberate in choosing only a handful of hikes in each park; our pact with you is that if you hike

Walking is the most intimate way to enjoy and appreciate
the national parks. (Capitol Reef National Park)

Deep canyons and towering cliffs are found in many national parks. (Kings Canyon National Park)

these trails, you'll come away from each park with a deep sense of why it's so important and how it contributes to our shared natural and cultural landscape. The hikes we recommend range from short nature trails to half- and full-day hikes; we couldn't resist including some iconic multiday hikes as well. Chapters also include photographs that illustrate what you'll see and vital logistical information.

Our criteria for selecting the parks to feature are that they must be reasonably accessible (i.e., not involve heroic travel and associated costs) and that they include substantial trail systems. Of the fifteen national parks that do not meet these criteria, three are quite small and have few trails, four are large but primarily water-based, six are found in Alaska and are difficult to access and have few or no maintained trails, and two are on US territories outside the continental United States.

Part 3 of the book offers guidance on how to best visit the national parks (when and where to visit, finding accommodations, appreciating the richness and diversity of each park, etc.) and how to walk the parks' trails (protecting park resources, avoiding crowds, exercising appropriate hiking etiquette, ensuring safety and well-being, etc.). The principles we outline are based on our years of experience in the parks; these are the practices that work for us and for the parks, and we're confident they'll work for you too.

The book concludes with an appendix and references. We call the appendix a "Table of Trails," a listing of all the trails we recommend and their vital statistics: name of the national park, name of trails, length of trails, degree of challenge, GPS coordinates of trailheads, and the page number where the trail description can be found. In "References" we include books, films, and websites that address the history, philosophy, and management of the national parks, information on walking/hiking, guidelines for preparing to visit and hike the national parks, and national park guidebooks.

Part 1
Why Walk the National Parks?

"America's Best Idea"

National parks are "America's best idea." So writer and conservationist Wallace Stegner famously wrote, noting that we were the first nation to preserve large areas of our land for the benefit of all, not just a privileged elite. In this way, national parks are a foundational expression of American democracy. Our national parks are also called America's "crown jewels," shining symbols of our national landscape and character. The national parks tell much of the story of our natural and cultural history—the underlying geology, biology, and ecology that have shaped our remarkable lands, and the history, values, and issues that have helped define our society. It's no wonder our National Park System attracts hundreds of millions of visits each year, from our own citizenry and from around the world.

There are more than 400 parks in the US National Park System, but only some carry the magical title "National Park"; the others are called "National Historic Sites," "National Monuments," "National Seashores," and more than a dozen other titles. All of these more than 400 parks are fully worthy of preservation and exploration. However, the national parks are the most famous places in the National Park System, parks such as Yellowstone, Yosemite, Acadia, Grand Canyon, Great Smoky Mountains, and Everglades. While most people have heard of many of these places, they may not fully appreciate their significance and diversity. And there are many lesser-known national parks that demand the attention of all national park–goers, places such as Kenai Fjords, Great Sand Dunes, Pinnacles, Capitol Reef, and Badlands. Scan the table of contents of this book to pique your imagination.

The first national park was established in 1872, but it was preceded by a nascent conservation movement. In 1832 ethnographer and painter George Catlin saw America's Great Plains disappearing before his eyes and called for a "nation's Park" to protect the landscape that supported herds of bison and the Native Americans who depended on them. In a similar vein, writer and philosopher Henry David Thoreau "wished to speak a word for nature" in his 1862 essay "Walking" and

The Roosevelt Arch at the entrance to Yellowstone National Park is inscribed with the words "for the enjoyment and benefit of the people," signaling the foundational democratic character of the national parks.

The magnificent scenery of the Yellowstone River Canyon helped convince Congress to establish the first national park in the country (and the world).

later asked, "Why should not . . . we have our national preserves"? Just two years later, President Abraham Lincoln signed legislation granting Yosemite Valley and the Mariposa Grove of giant sequoias to the State of California to be protected for the benefit of the nation, "inalienable for all time." Frederick Law Olmsted, America's great landscape architect and park pioneer, asserted that "establishment by government of great public grounds," such as Yosemite, "for the free enjoyment of the people" is "an essential responsibility of a democracy."

In response to this social movement, Congress established Yellowstone National Park in 1872, more than 2 million acres in what would become the states of Wyoming, Montana, and Idaho. Yellowstone is widely recognized as the first national park in both America and the world. Over the next several decades, thanks to conservationists such as John Muir, Theodore Roosevelt, and many others, more of the great western parks—Glacier, Yosemite, Mount Rainier, Rocky Mountain, and Sequoia—were established. These are celebrations of America's grandest and most sublime landscapes: tall mountains, ancient forests, expansive glaciers, wild rivers, exquisite valleys, and iconic wildlife, wilderness resources our ancestral European countries had lost long ago. These are the places that helped define our nation and the values to which we subscribe.

Shortly after the turn of the twentieth century, the country became more conscious of its remarkable prehistory and associated antiquities, especially Native American sites in the Southwest and elsewhere. To protect these areas from looting and vandalism, Congress passed the Antiquities Act in 1906, allowing the president to quickly create national monuments as a way to safeguard the archaeological, scientific, and other values of these places. (Only Congress can establish national parks, and this can be a lengthy process.) President Theodore Roosevelt swiftly set aside several national monuments, including Grand Canyon and Mesa Verde; these and other monuments were eventually elevated to national park status by Congress. American presidents continue to create national monuments under the auspices of the Antiquities Act, and many national monuments eventually achieve national park status.

Given the growing list of national parks, Congress created the National Park Service (NPS) in 1916 to manage these areas. Prior to this time, the US Cavalry kept order in the national parks, protecting them from unauthorized use and related denigration. The Buffalo Soldiers, regiments of the

US Army composed of African Americans, were instrumental in protecting the parks prior to establishment of the NPS. (Native Americans who fought in the Indian Wars bestowed the name "Buffalo Soldiers," possibly referring to the soldiers' characteristic curly black hair, the bison coats they wore in winter, or their fierce fighting ability; regardless, the term became a source of pride among the soldiers.) The 1916 Organic Act creating the NPS eloquently and presciently stated the mission of the agency: "to conserve the scenery and the natural and historic objects and wild life [*sic*] therein and provide for the enjoyment of the same in such manner and by such means as will leave them unimpaired for the enjoyment of future generations." Striking a balance between conservation of these areas and their use for recreation is an issue the NPS has wrestled with ever since, and this conundrum has become more urgent as the National Park System now accommodates more than 300 million visits a year.

The first director of the NPS was Steven Mather, who worked with the railroad and automobile industries to promote access to the parks as a way to build a constituency for them. During the Great Depression, President Franklin Roosevelt orchestrated creation of the Civilian Conservation Corps (CCC) to engage unemployed men in great public works projects, a large number of them in the national parks. Many of these artfully crafted facilities—roads, trails, picnic shelters, and campgrounds—are still in use.

After World War II, the National Park System began to expand more rapidly. Dramatic growth in US population, leisure time, and transportation led to steep increases in visits to the national parks that threatened to overwhelm park facilities and services, and the National Park System grew accordingly. More national parks were established and park infrastructure was expanded, including visitor centers, campgrounds, and trails. In addition, more national parks were established for their ecological and biodiversity values in response to the growing understanding and public appreciation of ecology and biodiversity. Everglades was the first of these parks, in 1947. The ecological values of existing parks began to be more widely recognized and emphasized as well.

The largest expansion of the National Park System occurred in 1980 when the long-standing national debate over the status of the vast Alaska public lands was finally settled. Congress passed the Alaska National Interest Lands Conservation Act that year, incorporating 47 million acres of public land in Alaska into the National Park System, more than doubling its size. Some of the new and previously created national parks received the title "National Park and Preserve"; the word "Preserve" formally acknowledges the subsistence rights of Alaskan Natives to hunt, fish, and gather

The Antiquities Act of 1906 led to preservation of the nation's most important cultural resources. (Mesa Verde National Park)

as vital elements of their traditional way of life, as long as these activities don't jeopardize the integrity of the park's natural resources.

Since then, the National Park System has continued to expand and evolve, and national parks can now be found in most states and even two US territories. This process is sure to continue, as the national parks are a reflection of our evolving natural and human history as well as the changing values of American society. For example, many units of the National Park System celebrate the expanded civil rights of underrepresented racial and ethnic groups, provide for the inclusion of more diverse ecosystems and historical periods, and help address the need for more open space and recreation opportunities in urban and metropolitan areas. Still more parks address the value of science in the National Park System, the role of national parks in public education, the provision of vital ecological services (such as sources of clean air and water and carbon sequestration), and as partners in the conservation of local communities. The national parks included in this book are the very best of the National Park System. We trust that public appreciation of the national parks will lead to continued expansion of the National Park System.

(above) The Alaska National Interest Lands Conservation Act of 1980 more than doubled the size of the National Park System. (Denali National Park and Preserve)

(below) Everglades National Park was the first to be preserved for ecological reasons.

Walking the Talk

We believe that walking is the most intimate way to experience the national parks; there's no better way to enjoy and appreciate them than by hiking their remarkable system of trails. When you travel at the human scale of 2 to 3 miles an hour, you appreciate the parks through so many of the senses: You can see the tracks of elusive mountain lions at Glacier National Park, hear the iconic call of the canyon wren as you hike through Grand Canyon, smell the sweetness of ponderosa pine bark warming in the sun in Yosemite, taste the salt air as you walk the Ocean Path at Acadia, and feel the solid granite beneath your feet as you explore the trails of Isle Royale. So many of these experiences are inevitably missed when traveling by car. Walking also offers a more personal way to appreciate the parks; step out of your vehicle and onto the trail, leaving the crowds behind. Walking also contributes to human health and happiness and has little impact on the environment (when walkers embrace the principles of the Leave No Trace program, which we describe later in this book).

Walking is the oldest form of transportation, but, ironically, history can be read as a millennia-long struggle to free ourselves from the need to walk. However, many people are rediscovering the manifold benefits of walking. At the most fundamental level, walking on two feet over long distances is a vital attribute of being human, an evolutionary adaptation that sets us apart from other animals. Moreover, walking is a miracle, a symphony of our skeletal, muscular, and nervous systems that allows us to place one foot in front of the other for miles on end over all sorts of terrain with

little conscious thought and without falling (at least not very often!). Walking also stimulates our thinking, as it did for Aristotle and his philosopher colleagues, who often walked as they thought and taught in the Lyceum of ancient Athens. More recent examples of the intellectual power of walking include William Wordsworth, Henry David Thoreau, and John Muir, some of the many poets, philosophers, and writers for whom walking was inspirational. Let walking inspire you too!

However, in an appropriate turn of contemporary phrase, we must walk the talk, and walking in the national parks is an ideal way to express this commitment. Please note that we use the words "walk" and "hike" interchangeably in this book. Some have tried to parse the difference between the two, but we don't think this is productive. We tend to like "walk" because it sounds less intimidating. Most of the walks we recommend in this book can be done by anyone who is reasonably fit and properly prepared. The National Park System has been made for walking: It includes tens of thousands of miles of marked and maintained trails that feature many of the most beautiful and important places in the National Park System. In this book, we're pleased to lead you to and along the very best of these walks.

Part 2
Walking the National Parks

Part 2 is the heart of this book— descriptions of all the national parks and the walks we recommend. The national parks are listed in alphabetical order, and each chapter is devoted to outlining the natural and cultural history of the park, an inventory of the park's major attractions, a personal narrative of the walks we recommend, an accounting of vital logistical information for visiting and walking in the park, and representative photographs of what you'll see in the park. We suggest you scan through the list of national parks in this section, as well as the map of all the national parks below, and select the parks you're most interested in visiting and walking. Then read these chapters to help you decide the parks you'll visit and when and the trails you'll walk. Use Part 3 of the book, "How to Visit and Walk the National Parks," to help guide this decision making and put your plan into action.

Acadia National Park's Ocean Path follows the shoreline to several of its most popular features.

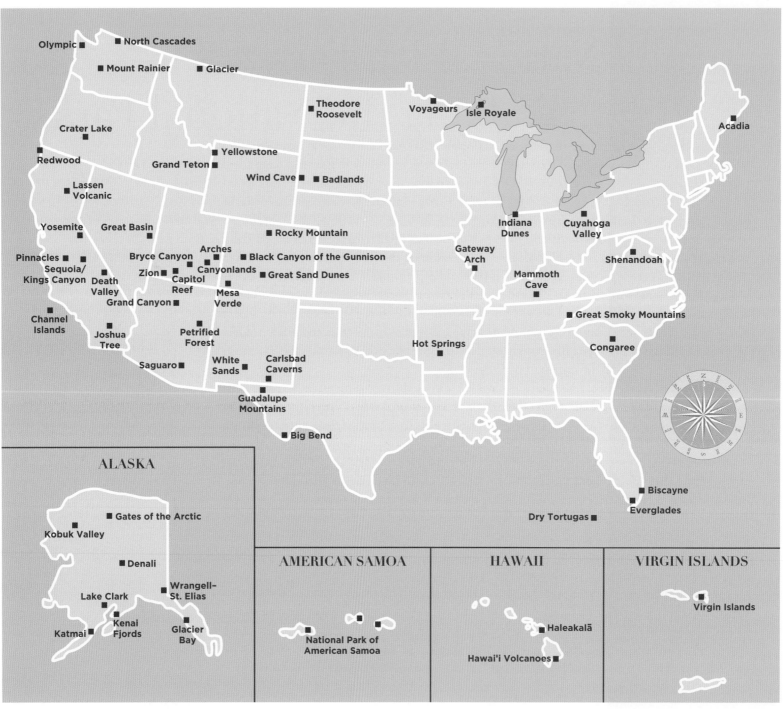

Olympic ■ North Cascades

Mount Rainier ■ Glacier

Theodore Roosevelt ■ Voyageurs ■ Isle Royale

Acadia

Crater Lake

Yellowstone

Redwood

Grand Teton Wind Cave ■ Badlands

Lassen Volcanic

Yosemite Great Basin Rocky Mountain

Indiana Dunes Cuyahoga Valley

Pinnacles Arches Black Canyon of the Gunnison Gateway Arch Shenandoah

Sequoia/ Kings Canyon Bryce Canyon Canyonlands Great Sand Dunes Mammoth Cave

Zion Capitol Reef

Death Valley Mesa Verde

Grand Canyon

Great Smoky Mountains

Channel Islands Joshua Tree Petrified Forest

Hot Springs Congaree

Saguaro White Sands Carlsbad Caverns

Guadalupe Mountains

Big Bend

ALASKA

Biscayne

Dry Tortugas ■ Everglades

Gates of the Arctic

Kobuk Valley

Denali

Wrangell– St. Elias

Lake Clark

Katmai Kenai Fjords Glacier Bay

AMERICAN SAMOA

National Park of American Samoa

HAWAII

Haleakalā

Hawai'i Volcanoes

VIRGIN ISLANDS

Virgin Islands

The National Parks of the United States

Acadia National Park

Maine | nps.gov/acad

Big things sometimes come in small packages, and Acadia National Park is a great example. At less than 50,000 acres, Acadia is among the smallest national parks, but its combination of natural, cultural, and recreational resources places it among the "crown jewels" of the National Park System. Visitors clearly agree, flocking to the park by the millions each year, making Acadia what may be the most intensely visited national park in the nation.

Acadia protects the finest remaining examples of Maine's rocky, rugged, undeveloped shoreline, and it's located in the vast Gulf of Maine and its associated archipelago, which includes nearly a thousand islands. Although the park is spread among nineteen islands and the mainland, the heart of the park is Mount Desert Island. The 27-mile Park Loop Road, partially designed by famous landscape architect Frederick Law Olmsted Jr., is one of the most iconic park features and connects many of the island's scenic and recreational attractions, as well as many of its trailheads. Cadillac Mountain is the highest point on the East Coast and is the first place the sun strikes the continental United States from late fall through most of the winter.

Geology has had the most dominant and obvious effect on the landscape; glaciers have sculpted the massive granite-domed mountains and the distinctive U-shaped valleys with plentiful lakes and wetlands. Evidence of the glaciers is everywhere; look for glacial erratics (large rocks carried by glaciers and deposited far from their origin—Bubble Rock is a jumbo-size example) and glacial polish, striations, and chatter marks on the park's bare granite summits. Somes Sound divides the eastern and western halves of the island and is the only fjord-like feature on the East Coast of the United States. Plant and animal life is rich and varied, as the park is in a transition zone where land meets the sea and the southern deciduous and northern coniferous forests intermix. Iconic wildlife include harbor seals, bald eagles, and peregrine falcons; moose and black bears occasionally visit. The park's rocky shorelines offer rich tide pools that harbor a multitude of marine life, and the Wild Gardens of Acadia feature more than 400 indigenous plant species.

The park's human history is just as significant. The small visitor center at Sieur de Monts and the larger Abbe Museum in Bar Harbor feature the vital Native American presence; these indigenous people lived on what are now park lands for at least 6,000 years, leaving shell mounds as evidence of their presence. Mount Desert Island takes its name from its treeless granite summits; Samuel de Champlain called it *I'Isle des Monts Desert* or "island of the Barren Mountains" on his voyage of

Acadia's "crafted trails" were built by village improvement societies in the late 1800s and early 1900s.

discovery in 1604, and the name "Acadia" reflects the history of the French Maritime Provinces and settlements in this part of the New World. In the early 1800s, Hudson River School painters Thomas Cole and Frederic Church celebrated the region's wild, "sublime" landscape. The park was established in 1916 thanks to conservation-minded residents, particularly George Dorr, who donated land to the park and successfully encouraged others to do so as well (Dorr is rightly considered the "father" of the park), and Charles Eliot, president of Harvard University, who worked to establish the park. John D. Rockefeller Jr. donated thousands of acres to the park and funded development of the park's carriage roads. Acadia was the first national park in the eastern United States, and the park is highly unusual in that it is composed almost entirely of donated land. The park and surrounding area include picturesque lighthouses such as Bass Harbor Head Light, one of the most photographed on the East Coast.

Walking Acadia

The park's trail and carriage road systems offer 175 miles of varied landscapes, from seashore to valleys to mountaintops. Many trails have their origin in the local village improvement societies on Mount Desert Island in the late 1800s and early 1900s and display a remarkably high level of craftsmanship and stonework. The carriage roads were constructed at the direction of John D. Rockefeller Jr. over a period of three decades, beginning in the early twentieth century. Designed by landscape architects, they gracefully weave their way through the eastern side of Mount Desert Island, following the contours of the land, and include seventeen strikingly beautiful bridges crafted of local granite by Italian stonemasons.

Ocean Path

Hikers can jump-start their walking with the short but impressive Ocean Path. The 2-mile footpath parallels a portion of the Park Loop Road and connects several of the park's most popular features, including Sand Beach, Thunder Hole, and Otter Cliff, and provides direct access to what may be the most scenic section of the Maine coast. The trail is generally flat and well-maintained, making it an especially good walk for families. While the path is never far from the Park Loop Road, portions detour through small copses of trees, and there is ready access to the rocky shoreline with dramatic views, pocket beaches, and tide pools. Walk Ocean Path out and back for a total of 4 miles, or ride the Island Explorer shuttle bus (see the "Logistics" section below) to Otter Cliff and walk 2 miles back to Sand Beach.

Emery Path / Homans Path / Jesup Path

These three short, interconnected paths are only moderately challenging (steep in a few places) but are dramatic and historic, offering insights into both the natural and cultural history of Acadia.

(above) Walkers along the carriage roads can stop at Jordan Pond House for tea and popovers.

(opposite) Fall is a lovely time to walk the iconic carriage roads at Acadia National Park.

The view from the summit of Cadillac Mountain includes much of Frenchman Bay and its islands.

These trails were "crafted" and offer a series of beautiful rock steps built from native granite, short stretches of forest floor, dramatic rock ledges, and artful patches of multicolored lichens. Clearings along the trail offer fine views of Great Meadow. Access is from Sieur de Monts Spring, the original heart of the park, and you should ask at the nature center for a helpful map of the trails of the area. The Emery Path connects with the Homans Path, and we recommend turning right at this point onto the path. Two sets of steps descend through narrow crevices that are capped with granite slabs, and these add to the drama. Clearings allow dazzling views of Frenchman Bay, Bar Harbor, the Porcupine Islands, and Great Meadow. The trail descends to meet the Jesup Path, which quickly returns you to Sieur de Monts. The whole hike is just over a mile.

The Beehive Trail

The Beehive Trail is also short but more challenging—and that's part of the fun! The trailhead is off the Park Loop Road near Sand Beach. After a short walk you reach the base of a large dome-like granite outcrop that juts out of the side of Champlain Mountain; this is the Beehive. Here the trail climbs steeply up a 500-foot ascent, facilitated by a series of iron ladders and rungs reminiscent of the famous *via ferrata* hikes in the Alps. (The nearby Precipice Trail is another of the park's *via ferrata*-style hikes.) The Beehive offers a strenuous climb and is not for those afraid of heights, but the rewards are generous, with spectacular views of the Park Loop Road, Sand Beach, Great Head, and Frenchman Bay. After completing the ascent of the Beehive (don't climb back down and cause a traffic jam on the trail), continue for another half a mile to The Bowl (a mountain pond) and then left to return to the trailhead, making a total distance of about 2 miles. If you want a longer walk, return to the Park Loop Road via Gorham Mountain Trail, which is almost entirely above tree line and offers stunning views. You can then walk back to the trailhead via the Ocean Path or simply catch the Island Explorer on to your next destination.

Cadillac Mountain (South Ridge Trail)

Most Acadia hikers will want to climb the larger mountains of the park, and why not Cadillac, the highest? Hiking to the summit is richly rewarding and offers an intimacy with the mountain that is simply not possible by any other means. The summit of the mountain is just over 1,500 feet, and most hikers will start near sea level, so this is a substantive climb. We recommend the South Ridge Trail, which offers a long, gradual ascent. This is one of the longest trails in the park—roughly 4 miles one way, depending on where you start—but the terrain is not challenging; the occasional scramble up and over a rock ledge only adds to the adventure. Like most mountain trails in the park, hikers quickly rise above tree line to appreciate outstanding views of the surrounding area. Look for evidence of glaciers everywhere in this open, granite landscape that hasn't changed appreciably since the glaciers retreated 10,000 years ago. Be sure to notice the Bates cairns marking the trail above tree line; named for historic pathmaker Waldron Bates, they consist of a base of two or more rocks with a bridge stone connecting them and a pointer stone on top signaling the direction of the trail. Please don't disturb these or other cairns. The summit offers a short loop trail that you should walk, but be prepared for the crowds (a road leads to the summit) and be especially careful to stay on the maintained trail; the surrounding subalpine vegetation is very fragile. The views from the summit are the best in the park, and many visitors come here for sunrise or sunset.

We suggest you pick up the South Ridge Trail as it crosses ME 3, where there's roadside parking; this will shorten the round-trip hike from nearly 9 miles (if started at Blackwoods Campground) to 7 miles. Unfortunately, the Island Explorer doesn't serve the summit of Cadillac Mountain, so this has to be an out-and-back hike, unless you can find a ride one way. This trail could be hiked downhill if you prefer, starting at the summit. Most of the South Ridge Trail is exposed and offers extensive views, but it also means hikers may spend several hours in the sun.

Carriage Roads (Around Mountain Loop)

The park's 50-mile web of carriage roads offers many days of enjoyable and rewarding walking opportunities. We recommend the Around Mountain route (just over 11 miles), actually a loop around three mountains (Sargent, Parkman, and Penobscot); it's easy to shorten or lengthen the

Wayfinding along many of the park's trails is guided by a series of unique Bates cairns.

Acadia National Park offers the best views of the most photographed coastline in New England.

walk by choosing different sections. Around Mountain takes walkers to the highest point on the carriage roads, features seven bridges and offers outstanding views of Somes Sound, Jordan Pond, and Eagle Lake. In addition to the trail's big views, be sure to look closely at the features in the foreground—huge slabs of the park's distinctive pink granite sporting numerous species of lichens, artfully gathered pine needles in the eddies of the prevailing winds, dense forests of evergreens, and an understory of blueberry and other shrubs. There's a short spur trail to Jordan Pond House, where tea and popovers refresh weary hikers; the tradition started a hundred years ago with carriage riders, and we heartily endorse it. We like to start this walk at the Parkman Mountain parking lot, accessible by the Island Explorer. All intersections of the carriage roads are marked with numbers and directions to nearby locations, and this facilitates wayfinding (though we recommend using a map of the carriage roads as well). With their gentle assents and descents and carefully groomed surface, the carriage roads make easy and delightful walking.

Logistics

Summer is the prime visitor season at Acadia, so be prepared for crowds (though getting out on the trails is a good way to find bits and pieces of solitude). However, the park enjoys long shoulder seasons that extend well into spring and fall, an especially pleasant time to be in the park. Winter can be quite cold but offers lots of peace and an occasional blanket of snow. There is no lodging in the park, but surrounding towns (Bar Harbor is the largest) offer lots of lodging choices, including commercial campgrounds. The park includes three large campgrounds, Blackwoods (on the busier, eastern side of Mount Desert Island), Seawall (on the "quiet side" of the island), and Schoodic Peninsula (across Frenchman Bay from Bar Harbor), and five campsites on remote Isle au Haut. The park's main visitor center is at Hulls Cove, and there is a small visitor center at Sieur de Monts. The park's extensive Island Explorer shuttle bus system serves many attractions and trailheads, helping visitors escape the problems of traffic congestion and parking. Horses and bicycles are not allowed on trails, though both are allowed on most of the carriage roads. On carriage roads, bikers must yield to hikers, and both bikers and hikers must yield to horses (though there is little equestrian use today).

The Last Word

The first national park in the East, Acadia is a mecca of hiking for the people of New England, the nation, and even many international visitors. Its distinctive geology, rich flora and fauna, colorful history, and generous trail and carriage road systems offer many days of rewarding hiking.

Arches National Park

Utah | nps.gov/arch

Geologic time has created a remarkable collection of more than 2,000 stone arches in the high desert of southeastern Utah, the nation's (and perhaps the world's) richest collection of these improbable formations. The arches in their namesake national park range in size from a 3-foot opening (the minimum to officially qualify as an arch) to Landscape Arch, at more than 300 feet, the world's longest opening. And of course there's Delicate Arch, the world's most famous, its image stamped onto Utah license plates, and a scenic symbol of the desert Southwest. But this park offers so much more: a vast array of giant monoliths, hoodoos, spires, walls, pinnacles, impossibly balanced rocks, slickrock domes, and giant sandstone fins. Project this fanciful assortment of pink, red, and orange rocks against the deep blue Western sky, and Arches rises to one of the great crowd-pleasers among national park visitors.

Geologists tell us that the park sits atop a layer of salt, thousands of feet thick in places, deposited by a great sea that occupied this area 300 million years ago. Later, sand and other materials were deposited on top of the salt, and these materials were compressed into the rock that now composes the park. Surface erosion has removed some of this overlayer, revealing the iconic pinkish Entrada Sandstone and the lighter-colored Navajo Sandstone that now dominate the park. The underlying salt layer is unstable and has shifted, causing geologic faults that have created vertical cracks in the rocks. Subsequent natural processes, including weathering, chemical action (slightly acidic water weakening the cement that holds sand grains together), and freezing/thawing then shaped these cracks into the park's characteristic giant sandstone fins and formed the many arches we admire today. This dynamic geology continues, and you can see evidence of it everywhere, including the appearance of new arches and the crumbling remains of old ones; for example, a large section of Landscape Arch fell in 1991 (though it is still the largest arch in the park), and Wall Arch collapsed entirely in 2008.

Though less evident, the park includes interesting flora and fauna well adapted to this high desert. Elevations in the park range from about 4,000 to 5,500 feet, and the park receives an average of less than 10 inches of precipitation a year. Dominant trees include pinyon pines and junipers, with cottonwoods and willows in the larger washes. Mammals include mule deer, coyotes, and desert bighorn sheep; the latter are increasing in number since being reintroduced from nearby Canyonlands National Park. Golden eagles, ravens, and a variety of migratory birds grace the sky. Unnoticed by

(above) Iconic Delicate Arch is a symbol of both the park and the desert Southwest.

(below) Hikers follow the trail through unusual Double Arch.

many visitors, the ground is often covered by a dark crust that's called biological soil crust or crypto-biotic soil. This is a complex, living entity composed of cyanobacteria, lichens, mosses, algae, fungi, and other organisms, and it plays a vital role in the ecology of the park, fixing nitrogen in the soil and lessening soil erosion. It takes decades for this soil crust to form, but it can be destroyed by a few footprints. For this reason, visitors are asked to stay on maintained trails or walk on bare rock or in dry, sandy washes. The park also includes several miles of frontage on the Colorado River.

Native Americans used this area for thousands of years, though they may not have lived here due to the environment's harshness; several pictograph and petroglyph panels exist in the park. One of these panels, near the Delicate Arch Trailhead, depicts horses and dogs, reflecting early travels in this area by Spanish explorers. European Americans made sporadic attempts at prospecting and settlement in the nineteenth century, but most were not successful. John Wesley Wolfe, a Civil War veteran, established a small ranch on Salt Wash in 1898; his log cabin, root cellar, and corral still stand just beyond the Delicate Arch Trailhead. The area's scenic wonders became more well-known and appreciated in the first decades of the twentieth century, leading to designation of Arches National Monument in 1929 and the redesignation as Arches National Park in 1971. Perhaps the most famous person associated with the park is Edward Abbey, who worked for two years as a ranger in the 1960s. Abbey carried on the tradition of American nature writing as defined by Henry David Thoreau, John Muir, and others by keeping a journal of his activities, observations, and thoughts. He transformed his journal entries into the enduring book *Desert Solitaire*, published in 1966, which influenced the environmental movement of the time. We recommend that you read this book before, or perhaps while, visiting the park. In addition to the substance of this book, Abbey's sometimes irreverent writing makes for an entertaining read.

Walking Arches

At a little more than 75,000 acres, Arches is relatively small by national park standards (compare, for example, Yellowstone National Park's 2.2 million acres). While this means fewer trails, the park makes up for this with quality. Walk the trails we recommend below; they'll deepen your experience and appreciation of this park, one of our very favorites.

Park Avenue Trail

Many visitors rush along the park's main road in a hurry to get to its major attractions such as Delicate Arch and Landscape Arch. However, just 2 miles beyond the park's visitor center, there's a 1-mile-long trail through a dramatic open canyon with towering cliffs. You'll understand the name "Park Avenue" as you enjoy this underappreciated stroll. It includes fanciful rock formations like Queen Nefertiti, Three Gossips, and Queen Victoria, interesting vegetation, and, if you're lucky, the

(top) The backcountry hike to dramatic Tower Arch offers time for reflection.

(bottom) Hikers on the trail through Devils Garden walk along the top of one of the park's many sandstone fins.

(opposite) Landscape Arch, the longest arch in the park, is as long as a football field.

(top) The Three Gossips are among the park's many natural formations.

(bottom) Looking through Pine Tree Arch offers a glimpse of the park beyond.

distinctive call of the canyon wren. The walk ends at massive Courthouse Towers. This is a point-to-point trail, so you'll need someone in your party to pick you up at Courthouse Towers or retrace your steps to the trailhead where you started (making it a 2-mile out-and-back hike).

Delicate Arch Trail

The park's premier trail (in our humble view) is the 3-mile (round-trip) hike to Delicate Arch. In fact, we think this is one of the best day hikes in the National Park System. (Yes, that's a bold statement, but we stand by it!) Just beyond the trailhead, you'll find the well-preserved remains of historic Wolfe Ranch and the aforementioned rock art panel that was probably made by Ute Indians. Soon the trail climbs onto a vast expanse of red slickrock, the way guided by a string of cairns. You're walking uphill, but you'll hardly notice given the overpowering excitement of this place. The final leg of the trail is a scaffold of solid rock that's been cut from the walls of a cliff; don't worry about the exposure—this section is short, and your reward is right around the corner. Then there it is in all its absurd improbability—a massive, free-standing arch poised on the rim of a giant slickrock bowl, framed by the snow-covered La Sal Mountains in the background. Revel in the glory of this magical place. After you've taken your pictures, retrace your steps to the trailhead, vowing to do this hike again—at sunrise and/or sunset to get the best photos, or by full moon for a special effect. We read a review of this hike a number of years ago where the writer said that this is not a hike, it's a pilgrimage. Amen.

Fiery Furnace

The Fiery Furnace is a maze of sandstone fins and spires that requires challenging scrambling and detailed attention to wayfinding. It's wild and beautiful, and hikers are rewarded with two large arches, potholes, and rare plants. There are regularly scheduled ranger-guided hikes through the area, and we highly recommend this tour. However, you need to reserve a place on one of these hikes far in advance. Yes, it can be hot in summer, but the name comes not from the temperatures but from the "fiery" red glow of this area at sunset.

Devils Garden Trail

At the end of the park's main road, you'll come to the trailhead for the Devils Garden. This is the park's longest trail, a 7.2-mile lollipop route. The first part of the trail is paved and leads to famous Landscape Arch; the easy 1.6-mile out-and-back hike to this arch is a favorite of many park visitors. Landscape Arch, longer than a football field, is the longest span in the park. At its narrowest, this unlikely arch is only about 11 feet thick. Perhaps you should see it soon as the arch is eroding! Beyond Landscape Arch, the trail becomes rougher, changing character to a primitive trail with challenging wayfinding, narrow drop-offs, and delightful scrambling over rocks. If you complete the full length of the Devils Garden Trail, you'll see seven major arches and some of the park's most beautiful scenery.

Tower Arch Trail

The trail to Tower Arch will take you into a more remote portion of the park where you can expect wilder scenery and even moments of solitude. The trailhead is served by a nearly 10-mile unpaved road through starkly beautiful Salt Valley. The trail is a 3.4-mile out-and-back route that requires attention to wayfinding, traversing some patches of soft sand, and a little scrambling. Watch for the dramatic pinnacles along the way called the Marching Men. At the end of the route you'll find massive Tower Arch. Climb up under the arch and linger here in the shade before returning to the trailhead using the same route.

Logistics

The entrance station to Arches is 5 miles north of the colorful and tourist-friendly town of Moab, Utah. Just beyond the entrance station you'll find the park's visitor center; here you can check local conditions and get your questions answered by knowledgeable rangers and other staff. The visitor center marks the beginning of the park's 18-mile road that connects many of the park's major attractions; this is one of the most strikingly beautiful roads in the National Park System. (Yes, again, that's saying a lot!) This road and its spurs deliver you to nearly all the park's trails, including the ones we recommend so highly above. Don't be lured into simply driving the park—the "real" park can only be seen on foot.

Refreshingly, there are no commercial services in the park—none. However, there is a small campground near the end of the road at Devils Garden; if you hope to stay there, you should reserve a site well in advance. Otherwise, there are camping opportunities outside the park on other state and federal lands, as well as commercial campgrounds in and around Moab. There's an excellent multiagency visitor center in Moab that's a great source of information and help. In addition to campgrounds, Moab and the surrounding area offer many motels and other accommodations. The park is open year-round, but it can be quite cold in winter and very hot in summer; spring and fall are ideal hiking seasons.

The Last Word

Ed Abbey wrote: "You can't see anything from a car; you have got to get out of the god-dammed contraption and walk." (See, we told you he could be irreverent!) While we probably wouldn't have used these words, we endorse the sentiment. Channel your inner Ed Abbey, and walk the trails of this grand national park.

Improbable Balanced Rock is found near the site where writer Ed Abbey wrote the journal he later fashioned into *Desert Solitaire*, a classic book of the environmental movement.

Badlands National Park

South Dakota | nps.gov/badl

Don't let the name fool you—Badlands National Park is a wondrous place that suffers from an unfortunate name that can be traced back hundreds, perhaps even thousands of years. The Lakota people called it *mako sica*, and early French trappers referred to the area as *les mauvaises terres a traverser*; both are translated as "bad lands." Spanish explorers called it *tierra baldia*, meaning "waste land." All these names reference the area's rugged terrain and the difficulties posed in traveling through it. Celebration of the area as a national park is a manifestation of the ways our thinking about this area and the environment in general have radically changed. Badlands National Park features a diverse landscape that is starkly beautiful, ecologically significant, and culturally important. This is a land of multicolored peaks, gullies, buttes, and spires, and the park supports one of the last grassland prairies that once covered vast expanses of the nation. The park also includes iconic wildlife such as herds of bison and pronghorn and numerous groups of prairie dogs that live in fascinating "towns." One of the world's richest beds of mammal fossils is also an important park resource.

The distinctive Badlands landscape is the result of two foundational geologic processes: deposition and erosion. Around 70 million years ago, a thick layer of shale was deposited under a vast shallow sea; this is the dark layer seen at the base of many Badlands features. Additional layers deposited after this time include sandstone, volcanic ash, ancient soils, and siltstone; these manifest themselves in different geologic layers, colors, and textures. Then, about 500,000 years ago, a long period of erosion began, cutting through the underlying geologic layers to form the area's extensive system of canyons, buttes, cliffs, and spires. At the present rate of erosion (about 1 inch a year), the park will be fully eroded to a large flat plain in another 500,000 years. One of the most prominent features of the Badlands landscape is The Wall, a deeply eroded escarpment that is 60 miles long and several miles wide. This steep slope separates the two relatively level regions of the park, which are at different elevations.

Over the last century or more, nearly all the vast prairie lands that covered much of the United States have been developed or converted into agricultural lands, so the remaining grasslands at Badlands make a vital contribution to the biological diversity of our country. About half the park is primarily a mixed-grass prairie that includes nearly sixty species of short- and tallgrasses. The remainder of the park is deeply eroded rock with patches of forests and shrubs. The diverse habitats of the park support an assortment of wildlife such as mule and white-tailed deer, coyotes, pronghorn,

(above) A steep ladder of logs and cables adds an element of adventure to the Notch Trail.

(opposite) The banded landforms of Badlands National Park are manifestations of the layers of shale, sandstone, volcanic ash, ancient soils, and siltstone that have been deposited here.

The views along the Sheep Mountain Trail extend over much of the park's Stronghold Unit, including the Pine Ridge Indian Reservation.

prairie dogs, and more than one hundred species of birds. In addition, there have been several successful reintroductions of iconic animals into the park in recent years, including bison, bighorn sheep, and black-footed ferrets, the latter one of the world's rarest species.

The park's mammal fossils are found in the Brule and Chadron Formations, sedimentary rock deposited between 30 and 35 million years ago, and this trove of fossils is one of the most important in the world. Scientists have found prehistoric animals such as sheep and deer-like creatures, a distant relative of pigs, an early saber-toothed cat, and ancestors of horses and rhinoceros.

Native Americans traveled and hunted in the Badlands area for an estimated 11,000 years, leaving behind charcoal, arrowheads, and tools that erode out of the area's streambanks. By the mid-eighteenth century, the Sioux, or Lakota people, became the dominant tribe, using horses they obtained from Spanish explorers. By the end of the nineteenth century, white settlers began to flow onto the land and Native Americans were forced onto reservations such as Pine Ridge Indian Reservation. In 1890, US Army units encountered a large band of Indians near Wounded Knee Creek; the resulting infamous Wounded Knee Massacre caused the death of nearly 300 Indians and 30 soldiers.

Because of the harshness and aridity of much of the land, most settlers were unsuccessful in establishing profitable farms and ranches (which later became known as "starvation claims"). During World War II, the US War Department used the area around the present-day park, including a large part of the Pine Ridge Indian Reservation, as a gunnery range; unexploded ordnance is still found scattered about the area. After the State of South Dakota constructed a road through the area for visitors in 1939, Congress established Badlands National Monument; the area was greatly expanded and designated a national park in 1978. Half the park is on the Pine Ridge Indian Reservation, and the park is comanaged by the NPS and the Oglala Lakota Nation.

Walking Badlands

As with nearly all national parks, walking the trails is truly the best way to experience the many dimensions of the park—its prairies and canyons, its wildlife, and its history. Nearly all the maintained trails are in the North Unit of the park, and this is where most visitors will want to hike. The Stronghold and Palmer Creek Units are located to the south on the Pine Ridge Indian Reservation; consult staff at the visitor center before exploring these areas.

Fossil Exhibit Trail

As noted above, the park's shale layer is a treasure of mammal fossils, one of the richest in the world. The short (less than half a mile) Fossil Exhibit Trail features this resource on a fully accessible boardwalk trail that features replicas and exhibits of now-extinct creatures that once roamed the area. The trail, along with the working Fossil Prep Lab in the main visitor center, provides a fascinating introduction to this dimension of the park. If you find a fossil in the park (we saw a young woman find a piece of a small jawbone with several teeth), you're asked to leave it in place, take a picture of the item, note its location, and report it at the Ben Reifel Visitor Center; in appreciation, NPS staff will take your picture and post it in the visitor center.

Window Trail / Door Trail / Notch Trail

Just a couple of miles north of the Ben Reifel Visitor Center you'll find a large parking area that serves three appealing trails, all short, that offer striking views through the park's great Badlands Wall out to badlands and prairie that extend well to the east and south. As the name suggests, the Window Trail leads to a natural window in The Wall with great views of an intricately eroded canyon; the trail is about a quarter-mile long (round-trip). With a similarly suggestive name, the three-quarter-mile (round-trip) Door Trail leads walkers through a natural opening in The Wall to pleasant views beyond. The first 100 yards of the trail is a boardwalk that is wheelchair accessible. Beyond the viewpoint and the end of the maintained trail, walkers have the option of following a trail (marked with yellow posts) out into a large and attractive eroded canyon where we saw several male desert bighorn sheep. The Notch Trail is the most adventurous of these three options. Though not long, about 1.5 miles (round-trip), the trail includes a long ladder fashioned of logs and cables that ascends a steep cliff; it's great fun. After this ascent, the trail follows a series of metal posts to a dramatic viewpoint of the White River Valley that lies beyond the Badlands Wall. A few stretches of the trail include steep drop-offs; we found our hiking poles helpful. Be advised that the soil along this trail can be especially slippery when wet.

Saddle Pass Trail / Medicine Root Trail / Castle Trail Loop

This trio of trails offers one of the finest hikes in the park, a 4.5-mile loop in the heart of the park's trail system. Start by making a short climb up the quarter-mile Saddle Pass Trail. Be careful, the trail is steep in places; we suggest hiking poles, especially for the way down. At the top of your ascent, gaze out at the striking landscape of eroded badlands and extensive prairies. This short trail meets both the Medicine Root and Castle Trails, allowing hikers to make a loop that presents a nearly constant stretch of views through this astounding landscape of mixed-grass prairie and sharply eroded landforms. We walked the Medicine Root section of the loop first and returned to the junction with the

Prairie sunflowers soften the park's otherwise rugged landscape.

(top) The rugged terrain of much of the park was an impediment to transportation, thus the name "bad lands."

(bottom) Billions of sweet clover's yellow flowers light up the early-summer landscape.

Saddle Pass Trail via a section of the Castle Trail. (The Castle Trail runs 10 miles through the park.) The Medicine Root–Castle Trail loop is easy walking over gently undulating terrain, but can be quite wet after rains; the trail is marked with metal posts—follow them closely. We were fortunate to see several male desert bighorn sheep with their iconic curled horns on the day we walked this route. Return to your car by walking—carefully—back down the Saddle Pass Trail. This walk can be shortened by starting and ending at the park's Old Northeast Road, eliminating the need to walk up and down the Saddle Pass Trail.

Sheep Mountain Trail

Want a little solitude with your hike at Badlands? This will require a long but beautiful drive to the Stronghold Unit of the park, located on the Pine Ridge Indian Reservation. Before doing this hike, stop by the White River Visitor Center that serves this area of the park to check on local conditions. Note that many of the visitor center's signs are in both English and the language of the Oglala Sioux. We had an interesting conversation with two rangers there (both Oglala Sioux) about how the park is managed in cooperation with the tribe. The Sheep Mountain hike requires driving a short distance on a gravel road that ascends to a complex of mesas that rise to more than 3,000 feet. At a small parking area that offers great views, the road begins to deteriorate sharply (you'll know when you're there). The road continues for 2 miles, but you should now consider the road your trail. This is a pleasant, generally level walk that offers jaw-dropping views off the mesas in all directions.

Logistics

Badlands is open year-round, but weather can be extreme in both summer and winter. Summers can be hot and may include dangerous thunderstorms; winters can be very cold. Fall can be an excellent time to hike. The park has two visitor centers, one in the North Unit and a seasonal visitor center in the South (Stronghold District) Unit. There are two campgrounds, and backpacking is allowed in the large Badlands Wilderness Area. Cedar Pass Lodge offers the only lodging and food service in the park, but communities around the park offer commercial visitor facilities and services.

The Last Word

Cast off the outdated notion that the park's badlands are unwelcoming wastelands. Badlands features much of the best of the ecological and cultural diversity that once reigned across so much of the upper Midwest but has now nearly disappeared. Viewed through this new biological and social lens, this is a beautiful and substantive park that deserves your attention; walk it and you'll be a believer.

Big Bend National Park

Texas | nps.gov/bibe

Chances are you haven't been to Big Bend National Park—not that many national park fans have. Big Bend is off the beaten track, and that's putting it mildly. It's hundreds of miles from the nearest city, interstate highway, or major airport. You have to really want to go to Big Bend, but if you do, you may come back again and again to see more of this large, diverse park; it has a tendency to grow on you. (It did for us.) Big Bend's really three parks in one; it includes a huge expanse of Chihuahuan Desert, 118 miles of the Rio Grande River separating the United States and Mexico, and the tall, dramatic Chisos Mountains. The name "Big Bend" comes from the geography of the park as the Rio Grande makes its graceful, sweeping turn around this area of southwest Texas. As you might expect from a national park in Texas, Big Bend is big indeed, more than 800,000 acres. Plan to spend several days in the park to appreciate its scale and diversity by hiking its inviting trails. You may find this wild and remote corner of the country with its starkly beautiful desert, lush limestone river canyons, and sublime mountain scenery calling to you again.

Morning fog spills into the valleys surrounding the Chisos Mountains.

Descriptions of national parks often start with geology, the environmental foundation of landscapes. But Big Bend is complicated, and geologists are still working on it. Geologic activity in the park has been highly varied over at least the last 500 million years. Major periods of activity in what is now the park include the presence of a deep ocean trough and associated sedimentation; massive pressure on these sediments from tectonic collision (with what is now the South American continent) that forced up a chain of mountains; subsequent erosion of these mountains; invasion of a shallow sea and deposition of sediments that formed a large limestone layer including fossils of marine organisms; compression of the Earth's crust, forming a second period of mountain building; a long series of volcanic eruptions spewing massive amounts of lava across the landscape; a period

(left) Hikers ford Terlingua Creek to access dramatic Santa Elena Canyon.

(opposite) Hikers look south through the Chisos Mountains and on to Mexico.

of dramatic faulting; and a continuing process of erosion driven primarily by flash flooding that is characteristic of the park today. See, it's complicated!

The park's varied topography along with its wide range of elevations—from about 2,000 to nearly 8,000 feet—has given rise to diverse habitats and associated plant and animal life. Moreover, the park is a transition zone between tropical areas of Central and South America and more conventional colder habitats of North America, resulting in a rich and varied stock of plants and animals. The park includes an estimated 1,200 species of plants, 600 species of vertebrates, and 3,600 species of insects. Iconic animals include mountain lions (locally called panthers), white-tailed deer, coyotes, foxes, javelinas, beavers, and black bears. The park has a well-deserved reputation as a birders' paradise, with more than 450 documented species either native or migratory, more than any other US national park.

Human history in the area is also rich. Nomadic Native Americans hunted and gathered hundreds of desert plants for food and medicine and employed atlatls to hunt small animals. Apache and Comanche occupied the area during historic times. The Spanish explored the area beginning in the sixteenth century, searching for gold, silver, and fertile soil and converting natives to Christianity. Following the end of the Mexican-American War in 1848, American settlers moved in to farm and ranch the area where feasible. In the 1930s a movement started in Texas to preserve the Big Bend area for future generations. Big Bend native and state legislator Everett Ewing Townsend, the "Father of Big Bend," lobbied hard for a park starting in the 1930s and succeeded when Congress established Big Bend National Park in 1944.

(above) The geology of Big Bend is complicated and not yet fully understood..

(above right) The Rio Grande takes a mighty "big bend," which defines the park's southern border.

Walking Big Bend

The park includes more than 200 miles of trails that range from short nature walks to longer back-packing trips. We recommend hiking one trail along the Rio Grande and then concentrating the rest of your hiking in the Chisos Mountains. Here are our favorites.

Santa Elena Canyon Trail

Santa Elena Canyon is one of three major canyons of the Rio Grande in Big Bend, and the short trail that draws visitors into the canyon offers a lot of bang for the buck—1.7 miles (round-trip) into a colorful canyon with a little adventure mixed in. Here, the Rio Grande flows out through the dramatic Santa Elena Canyon between sheer 1,500-foot stone walls, Mexico on the south and the United States on the north. After a short walk to the confluence of the Rio Grande and one of its tributaries, Terlingua Creek, you must cross the creek, which may be dry or filled with water. Be careful here: If the water in the creek is high and/or swiftly flowing, come back another day. When we were there, the creek was about 50 feet wide, knee deep, and hardly flowing, so we took off our boots and socks and waded across the creek without difficulty—the bottom of the creek was gener-ally smooth, composed of sand and small gravel. The hardest part was mounting the steep riverbank on the other side, but a short fixed rope helped a lot. From there, the trail briefly climbs then fol-lows the shore of the river through the shady and cool canyon, lush with giant river cane, mesquite, and tamarisk. Contrast the views up and down the river: to the east, where the river spills out onto the desert floodplain with the Sierra Quemada Mountains of Mexico and the Chisos Mountains of the park in the background, and to the west, where the river disappears into the monolithic and mysterious canyon. The 30 river miles of Santa Elena Canyon are a favorite of rafters and include one major rapid; maybe you'll be lucky and see a group of boaters emerging from the canyon. Too soon, the trail dead-ends where it meets a sheer canyon wall. But there's the option to linger a little and listen to the graceful call of the canyon wren—a musical series of descending notes that fill the canyons of the Southwest—before retracing your steps to the trailhead.

Lost Mine Trail

This wonderful trail shows off the drama of the Chisos Mountains that rise in the center of the park, high peaks and ridges of volcanic origin that surround the Chisos Basin, the epicenter of hiking in the park. The trail climbs at a gradual pace through pinyon-juniper forest with a sprinkling of oaks. In about a mile you reach a saddle that offers outstanding views into massive Juniper Canyon and on to the mountains of Mexico. The trail continues to climb, finally reaching a dramatic ridge of open bedrock that's a highlight of the trail. A short walk takes you to a group of massive rock outcrops that mark the end of the trail. Here the views are some of the very best in the park, including Pine and Juniper Canyons, Mexico's Sierra del Carmen, and the East Rim of the Chisos Mountains. Lost Mine Peak, the trail's namesake, lies just across Pine Canyon; the name of the peak references the legend that Spanish explorers found a rich gold mine in this area, but modern geology doesn't support this version of history. We reached the terminus of the trail at about noon, so this made the perfect lunch spot. In the early 1940s the Civilian Conservation Corps constructed this beautifully sited and crafted trail, and it still reflects the elegance and artfulness of their craftsmanship. This is an out-and-back trail of 4.8 miles (round-trip) and about 1,000 feet of elevation gain, making it a modestly demanding hike.

Emory Peak Trail (Pinnacles Trail)

There's something about the highest mountain in each park that draws hikers—Mount Whitney in Sequoia, Cadillac Mountain in Acadia, etc. It's the same with Emory Peak in Big Bend, and getting to the top is a strenuous but very doable hike. Like all of Big Bend's highest peaks, Emory (7,825 feet) is in the Chisos Mountains, square in the geographic center of the park. There are two routes up the mountain, the Pinnacles Trail and the Laguna Meadow Trail; the former is the shorter, a round-trip of about 10 miles (depending on which guidebook you consult), so this is the trail we selected. The hike begins in Chisos Basin and climbs steadily, though not steeply, through a pinyon-juniper forest with scattered oaks and madrone trees. The views out over the Chisos Basin all the way to the vast desert that surrounds these mountains begin almost immediately and become more dramatic with every switchback. After a steady climb of more than an hour, you reach the junction with the trail to Emory Peak and leave the Pinnacles Trail. This 1.5-mile spur trail continues climbing, and the views are awe-inspiring. The trail becomes rougher approaching the summit, and the last pitch to the peak

(above) The Lost Mine Trail shows off the striking Chisos Mountains that dominate the center of Big Bend.

(below) Wildflowers brighten the desert landscape of Big Bend National Park.

Big Bend has a dramatic landscape of mountains and desert.

is a serious scramble that requires both feet and hands. We share a modest fear of heights, so this was a challenge, but the route's not nearly as scary as it might look. And the views are a staggering 360 degrees of the whole park and beyond, making this an important part of hiking at Big Bend. Simply retrace your steps to return to the trailhead; we were fortunate to see a bear along the trail and watched it (from a safe distance) feeding on some berries.

It's possible to make this hike into a more extended outing: Return to the Pinnacles Trail from Emory Peak, turning south and ultimately reaching the park's Rim Trail (the southern rim of the Chisos Mountains), which offers sweeping views to the south, over the desert, to the Rio Grande and on to Mexico. For more variety, return to Chisos Basin, where you began your hike, using the Laguna Meadow Trail. This could be done as a very long day hike of more than 16 miles or, better, as a short back-packing trip.

Logistics

In keeping with its size, the park has five visitor centers scattered across the area: Panther Junction, Chisos Basin, Persimmon Gap, Rio Grande, and Castolon. Chisos Mountain Lodge is the only in-park lodging, but the park includes three campgrounds: Cottonwood, Chisos Basin, and Rio Grande Village; the latter includes some RV sites with full hookups. A variety of commercial services are found outside the park, but they may be located at quite a distance. The park is open year-round; winters are mild, summers hot, and spring and fall ideal, with wildflowers and fall foliage, respectively. The park is remote, so be sure to buy gas and supplies wherever you can find them; in the park, gas is sold only at Panther Junction and Rio Grande Village. Some park visitors cross the Rio Grande by boat to visit the Mexican village of Boquillas; this requires a passport or other appropriate identification.

The Last Word

It's a long way and a lot of effort to get to Big Bend National Park, but, as the saying goes, you get out of life what you put into it. A big, diverse park like nothing you'll find elsewhere is waiting for you. We think you'll be glad you added Big Bend to your life list of national parks.

Biscayne National Park

Florida | nps.gov/bisc

Just south of the sprawling city of Miami lies Biscayne National Park—the blue-green expanse of Biscayne Bay and its associated coral reefs, islands, and mangrove forests. This rare natural preserve proximate to a major metropolitan area offers a striking subtropical environment that is also a coveted recreation area. Construction of power plants along the shores of the bay and proposals for more large-scale development created concern about the future of the bay and resulted in designation of Biscayne National Monument in 1968. An expanded national park was established in 1980. Because the park is 95 percent water, it's best enjoyed by boating, fishing, and snorkeling; there are only a few short trails on the park's limited land base.

(above) American crocodiles are frequently seen at Biscayne National Park.

(left) The extensive coral reefs of Biscayne National Park are a big attraction for park visitors.

Black Canyon of the Gunnison National Park

Colorado | nps.gov/blca

There are many impressive canyons in the American West, but none combine the depth, sheerness, and narrowness that you'll find at Black Canyon of the Gunnison National Park in western Colorado. The canyon is a massive slit in the Earth's surface, reaching more than 2,500 feet deep, yet the north and south rims narrow to only 1,100 feet across; at river level in The Narrows section of the canyon, walls are as little as 40 feet apart. As you can imagine from these dimensions, the canyon walls appear to be nearly sheer, and this verticality can be truly dizzying. The name "Black" is derived from the dark gneiss and schist that compose the canyon walls and from the limited light that filters into the canyon, especially in fall and winter. For most of the day the canyon is cast in its own shadow. Black Canyon is 48 miles long, and the park protects the deepest and wildest 14 miles of this impressive gorge. Fortunately, more of the canyon and river are included in the adjacent Curecanti National Recreation Area to the east and Gunnison Gorge National Conservation Area to the north.

The dark gneiss and schist that compose the near vertical walls of Black Canyon are metamorphic rocks formed nearly 2 billion years ago as a result of heat and pressure deep within the earth. These rocks are hard and highly resistant to erosion. Pinkish veins of pegmatite lace the canyon walls; this is an igneous rock formed from magma that cooled in the cracks of the rocks. These igneous and metamorphic rocks were eventually buried by ash from surrounding volcanoes. Like most of the massive Colorado Plateau, this area was uplifted several thousand feet between 70 and 40 million years ago. The early Gunnison River established its course millions of years ago to carry runoff from the surrounding mountains. At first the river quickly cut through ash and other debris that had been deposited, but then it reached the ancient and much harder metamorphic rock. The river, aided by the rocks and other debris it carried, continued cutting, but at a slower rate, an estimated 1 inch per century. The steepness of the canyon we see today is a result of the hardness of the gneiss, schist, and pegmatite; most of the softer material that covered the canyon's igneous and metamorphic rocks has been eroded away.

(opposite) Visitors peer into the depths of the Black Canyon of the Gunnison.

(above) The Gunnison River supports a Gold Medal fishery.

(above right) The North Vista Trail leads to Exclamation Point, one of the best place names in the National Park System.

The canyon and its rims support a variety of plants and animals. Pinyon pines, junipers, and Gambel oaks are the dominant trees along the 8,000-foot rims of the canyon, with some aspens mixed in. Douglas fir grows along ridges in the canyon, and box elders are found along the river's turbulent shores. Mosses and ferns thrive along the shady, moist canyon walls, and the park has poison ivy, especially near the river (wear protective clothing). A variety of mammals live here, including mule deer, bobcats, mountain lions, black bears, bighorn sheep, elk, beavers, and river otters. Interesting birds include golden eagles, peregrine falcons, dusky grouse, and American dippers. The Gunnison River supports a Gold Medal fishery.

Ute Indians surely were familiar with Black Canyon; evidence suggests that some used the rim areas seasonally, but most steered clear of this transportation impediment. Early fur trappers probably used the riparian areas. Expeditions were conducted in the region in the mid- to late nineteenth century, one led by Captain John Gunnison, the other the famous Hayden Expedition that explored the Yellowstone Territory; both deemed the canyon impassable. However, William Jackson Palmer and his Denver and Rio Grande Railroad had other ideas. In response to the demand for railroad service, mostly related to mining, a 15-mile section of narrow-gauge railroad tracks was laid in the canyon at great monetary and human cost. This became the overstated "Scenic Line of the World," eventually completed and opened in August 1882. Rudyard Kipling rode the train in 1889 and wrote

that "there was a glory and wonder and a mystery about the mad ride which I felt keenly . . . until I had to offer prayers for the safety of the train." Demand for narrow-gauge rail service ultimately declined as mining ebbed, standard-gauge railroad service became more common, and sales of automobiles skyrocketed. The "Scenic Line of the World" went out of business in 1949.

The Gunnison River was also explored for its irrigation potential for the nearby Uncompahgre Valley, and a nearly 6-mile diversion tunnel was constructed in the early twentieth century. However, the canyon's scenic beauty, geological significance, and recreation potential were broadly recognized over the next two decades, and it became a national monument in 1933. Congress acted in 1999 to provide further protection, establishing the present-day Black Canyon of the Gunnison National Park.

Walking Black Canyon

Since Black Canyon is a relatively small park with especially steep terrain, hiking opportunities are somewhat limited. However, there are wonderful short and moderate hikes along both the south and north rims of the park that offer outstanding views into the canyon (our hearts were often in our mouths as we peeked over the canyon rims) and lots of interesting information about the park. The "glory" hike is down the canyon to the river; this strenuous and challenging hike is described below.

Oak Flat Loop Trail

This pleasant trail was constructed by Student Conservation Association volunteers and runs from the visitor center through a thick forest of Gambel oak and other characteristic vegetation that

(above left) The Gunnison River has cut through the park's hardest rock layers at an estimated 1 inch per century.

(above) Groves of aspens can be found on the 8,000 foot canyon rims.

(above) A fixed chain helps hikers navigate the steepest section of the Gunnison Route leading down to the river.

(below) The Gunnison River appears much more lush than when viewed from the canyon rims high above.

thrives on the park's uplands. The trail then drops 400 feet down the south rim for a taste of life inside the canyon. Note the sign for the associated Gunnison Route (described below).

Warner Point Nature Trail

The Warner Point Nature Trail starts where the South Rim Road ends in the western portion of the park. It's a little longer (about a mile and a half) and a little more demanding (it follows the undulating terrain) than most nature trails. The trail honors Mark Warner, unofficial "father" of the park, and has an especially good interpretive booklet with interesting descriptions of the area's history and ecology—we learned a lot!

North Vista Trail

The world famous Grand Canyon has north and south rims, and so does Black Canyon. And just like Grand Canyon, the vast majority of visitors to Black Canyon see only the south rim, and that's too bad. Even though the rims at Black Canyon are as little as 1,100 feet apart, it's an 80-mile drive from one to the other. But it can be worth it for those who seek a refreshing dose of solitude and quiet, and the thrill (or panic) of peeking over the near-vertical face of the canyon as it plunges about 2,000 feet to the wild river below. Our favorite hike on the north rim is the North Vista Trail, which starts at the ranger station (which doubles as a visitor center when the resident ranger is there). There are two destinations to choose from, and we suggest both. The first is aptly named Exclamation Point, perhaps the finest appellation in all the national parks. The viewpoint is 1.5 miles from the trailhead and is directly on the north rim, offering its namesake views into the canyon. This is a moderate hike at most and is lined with attractive Gambel oak and other arid-land shrubbery. The second destination is 2 more miles along the trail to the summit of Green Mountain, affording an unusual, elevated, almost "aerial" view of the canyon. There are views in all directions that include Grand Mesa, the West Elk Mountains, the San Juan Mountains, and Uncompahgre Valley (irrigated by Gunnison River water). This section of the trail rises nearly 1,000 feet, but the trail isn't steep and is well maintained. The upper elevations of the trail pass through an extensive pinyon-juniper forest with large and ancient specimens that were well established when the Spanish first explored the Southwest. We saw no one else along the trail.

Gunnison Route

Okay, you've seen the river from the rim, heard its roar, and now it's beckoning. There are several routes from the south and north rims to the river. However, these are *routes*, not marked and maintained trails, and they're strenuous and challenging (and that's an understatement). A permit is required to hike to the river. The Gunnison Route off the south rim is the most popular and probably the least difficult (which is why we selected it!). The hike is only about 1 mile (one-way), but it

The Gunnison River is poised to drop through the steep canyon.

falls (and rises on the return) nearly 1,800 feet over this short distance. You should start early in the day and allow sufficient time; the NPS suggests an hour and a half down and 2 hours up, but it took us longer (and a few days after that to recover). Start the hike on the Oak Flat Loop Trail (described above), but you soon reach a sign that reads "River Access: Permit Required," and the steep descent begins. The route follows a series of drainage gullies with scree slopes and big rocks. We found ourselves doing controlled slides down the steepest sections. At one point we were thankful for an 80-foot chain that has been fixed by the NPS; it was useful to negotiate an especially steep pitch. We eventually reached the river, where the canyon seems lush and much more delightful than it appears from the rim; we enjoyed walking along the river's edge before beginning the long scramble back up to the rim. If you want to overnight (with a permit), there are campsites along the river. Think carefully about this hike before committing to it; read the NPS website, talk to a ranger, and make an informed decision.

Logistics

The park is open year-round, though the canyon rims are at 8,000 feet and collect substantial snow; summer is the prime visitor season. The north and south rims of the park are only about a quarter mile apart as the crow (raven, really) flies, but there is no bridge across the canyon in this area. Consequently, it's a 2-hour drive from one rim to the other. Most visitor services are located on the south rim, including a visitor center and campground. The north rim is closed during winter; in summer the North Rim Ranger Station is a good source of information, but it's open only intermittently. Nearly all visitors go to the south rim, but we suggest that you consider the north rim as well—it has a much more backcountry character and includes a small campground. Montrose (south rim) and Crawford (north rim) offer more visitor facilities and services such as motels, commercial campgrounds, restaurants, and stores.

The Last Word

Black Canyon is a relatively new national park, and visiting this magnificent natural gorge will convince you that it's a worthy addition to the National Park System. The park has the advantage of relatively low visitation (though this surely will change as the park gains deserved recognition) and can be a good place to escape the crowds of many of the more popular national parks. The canyon is breathtaking in more ways than one!

Bryce Canyon National Park

Utah | nps.gov/brca

Bryce Canyon National Park is one of five national parks draped across the extensive high mesas and deep canyons of southern Utah, an area that is every national park lover's dream come true. And for many visitors, Bryce is their favorite. The park extends for 20 miles along the eastern edge of the vast Paunsaugunt Plateau. (*Paunsaugunt* is Paiute for "home of the beaver.") The west side of the park is richly forested, but the eastern side is where the magic happens: Erosive forces over millions of years have carved a series of canyons, horseshoe-shaped bowls, and amphitheaters filled with colorful rock spires called hoodoos, some 200 hundred feet high. This "forest of stone" comes in shades of yellow, orange, red, and white, and many formations carry imaginative and fanciful names like Thor's Hammer, Alligator, Queen Elizabeth, Sinking Ship, Hat Shop, and even E.T. While the views of these legions of hoodoos, fins, windows, bridges, and associated formations from the park's 18-mile scenic drive are staggering, the park's trail system, which extends along much of the rim and then down among these geologic wonders, offers the very best views in the park.

Bryce represents the top of the "Grand Staircase," a geologic system comprising many distinct layers of sedimentary rock that runs from the Grand Canyon in the south to Bryce Canyon in the north. At Bryce, the exposed layer of reddish/pinkish limestone (called the Claron Formation) has eroded along vertical joints to form walls, or "fins." These fins are further eroded to form the hoodoos for which the area is famous. Cap rocks on the top of hoodoos are composed of harder rock that protects the softer rock layers beneath it. Erosion of the area is a function of flowing water to some degree, but it is also caused by freezing and thawing, a process that occurs daily during most of the year at Bryce. (The park's high elevation means that daily temperature fluctuations include both below- and above-freezing temperatures an average of nearly 200 days a year.) This type of erosion is called "frost wedging."

Elevations in the park range from about 7,000 feet to more than 9,000 feet. Spruce-fir forests are found at the highest elevations, ponderosa pine in the middle, and pinyon-juniper forests at the lower elevations. Notable wildlife include elk, mule deer, pronghorn, black bears, mountain lions, foxes, bobcats, and Utah prairie dogs. Notable birds include golden eagles, peregrine falcons, and California condors. (Condor sightings are rare; be careful not to confuse them with turkey vultures.)

All the national parks on the Colorado Plateau offer especially good stargazing, but Bryce may be the best of all. Its combination of remoteness from the lights of large cities, high elevation, and

(above) The park's iconic landscape is formed by the erosion of flowing water, as well as the freezing and thawing that occurs most days in the park.

(opposite) Bryce Canyon's more than 65 miles of hiking trails offer outstanding views of the area's exceptional array of hoodoos.

(above) In Wall Street, 200-year-old Douglas firs reach for the sun.

(below) Much of the park is wilderness with no roads or other development.

low humidity result in strikingly dark night skies where 7,500 stars may be visible to the naked eye (compared to about 2,500 in other rural areas). This "natural darkness" is vital to the park's many species of nocturnal animals. The park offers several interpretive programs on the night sky, including telescope viewing.

Bryce has an eventful human history. There was a Native American presence for 8,000 years or more, but the area's harsh environment—modest rain and very high elevation—suggests that it could not have supported large-scale habitation. Paiute legend says that the area's colorful hoodoos—called *anka-ku-was-a-wits*, or "red painted faces"—were bad people who had been turned to stone by Coyote God. Because this was such a remote and rugged area, European-American explorers didn't arrive until the mid-eighteenth and early nineteenth centuries. John Wesley Powell's 1872 exploration of the Green and Colorado Rivers surveyed part of the area, and the Mormon Church sent Scottish immigrant Ebenezer Bryce and his wife, Mary, to settle land in the nearby Paria Valley in 1875. The family grazed cows just below what are now park lands and Ebenezer famously stated that the area's hoodoos were a "helluva place to lose a cow."

The scenic reputation of the area began to reach a national audience in the early twentieth century, aided by the Union Pacific Railroad. Local residents, including Ruby Syrett (the "Ruby" for whom the current complex of visitor services just outside the park is named), began building modest lodgings and conducting tours of the area. This contributed to concern by conservationists that the area was being damaged by tourism, as well as by logging and grazing. In response, Congress established Bryce Canyon National Monument in 1923, elevating it to national park status in 1928. The Civilian Conservation Corps constructed the park's Rim Road, completing it in 1934, and this 18-mile scenic drive still serves visitors today.

Walking Bryce

Bryce has more than 60 miles of hiking trails that offer outstanding views of the area's exceptional collection of hoodoos, and many trails wander through this remarkable landscape. Because the park is relatively small, most of these trails are designed for day hikes. However, short backpacking trips are possible, though they require a permit from the park. We found the following trails to offer the very best of the park's diverse landscape.

Rim Trail

The 5.5-mile Rim Trail is an attractive alternative to the park's scenic road. The trail runs along the rim of Bryce Amphitheater, the heart of the park, connecting Bryce Point and Fairyland Point. The trail includes all the observation points accessible by car—Sunrise, Sunset, Fairyland, and Bryce Points—but has the great advantage of including all the vistas in between as well; think of it as one long viewpoint! The well-maintained trail softly rises and falls as it makes its way along the rim. Short stretches enter forests of juniper, ponderosa pine, Douglas fir, and bristlecone pine. The trail intersects a number of other trails that lead down into Bryce Amphitheater, and wooden benches are strategically located. This is a popular trail, but not many people take the time to walk its full length, and that's too bad; we saw few other visitors on the section of the trail between Sunrise and Fairyland Points. If time is short, consider walking the section between Sunrise and Bryce Points and taking the park's free shuttle bus back to your car. Unfortunately, the shuttle bus system doesn't serve Fairyland Point (at least not when we recently walked it), so to walk the full length of the Rim Trail, you must shuttle a car to one end of the trail or make this a long out-and-back route.

Bristlecone Loop Trail

The short Bristlecone Loop Trail offers an interesting change of pace at Bryce and introduces hikers to another important dimension of the park. The park's scenic road rises to more than 9,000 feet at its terminus at the southernmost extension of the massive Paunsaugunt Plateau. Here you'll find dense stands of white fir, Douglas fir, and ponderosa pine, with a sprinkling of bristlecone pine, an especially long-lived tree. Some bristlecone pines (in other parks and protected areas) are an astounding 4,000 years or more old; bristlecones in Bryce have been dated to more than 1,000 years old. The Bristlecone Loop Trail leads for a half mile to the very edge of the Paunsaugunt Plateau, where the namesake trees tend to grow on the open clifftops. The trail then closes the loop by leading another half mile back to the trailhead.

Queen's Garden Trail / Navajo Loop Trail

The Queen's Garden Trail is an approximately 2-mile (round-trip) out-and-back walk that winds down into Bryce Amphitheater from Sunset Point. This is the most popular of the park's trails that descend below the rim of the canyon and offers outstanding views from the perspective of being deep within the park's hoodoos and other geologic features, adding immensely to enjoyment and appreciation of the park's grandeur. The trail ends at the Queen Victoria formation, where only a little imagination is required to see the famous queen on her throne. You may retrace your steps back to the trailhead, which of course requires a substantial climb. As an alternative, we suggest taking a short connector trail to the nearby Navajo Loop Trail to return to the rim. Navajo Loop is a 1.3-mile trail that features up-close views of Bryce Canyon; popular features along the loop are Wall Street, Twin Bridges, and Thor's Hammer. The connector trail from Queen's Garden Trail joins the Navajo Loop Trail at about its halfway point, so you can return to the canyon rim by following either the north or south half of the Navajo Loop Trail. We especially enjoyed the south section of the loop, including the walk through the narrow canyon called Wall Street with its 200-year-old Douglas

(top) Several of the trails lead down among the park's "forests of stone."

(bottom) Bryce Canyon Lodge is an example of the historic inns in many national parks.

The blue skies at Bryce are magical, but at night the park offers some of the best stargazing in the nation.

firs reaching for the sun and the elaborate series of switchbacks near the canyon rim. Combining Queen's Garden and Navajo Loop Trails makes for an approximately 3-mile loop hike.

Fairyland Loop Trail

The Fairyland Loop Trail is an 8-mile circuit through stunning Fairyland Canyon and its amphitheater of colorful formations. This is an ambitious hike and our favorite. Named geologic features include Boat Mesa, Sinking Ship, Tower Bridge, and the Chinese Wall. The trailhead is the Fairyland Point Overlook, an often-missed spur road off the park's scenic Rim Road just north of the park's entrance station. The trail brings you through many smaller canyons and concentrations of hoodoos, along narrow ridges, and deep into the forested bottomland of the park's canyons. At the about the halfway point, there's a short side trail to impressive Tower Bridge, resembling its London namesake. The Fairyland Loop ultimately climbs back to the canyon rim and meets the Rim Trail south of Fairyland Point. Follow the Rim Trail north to close the loop. The trail can be shortened by turning south at the junction with the Rim Trail and walking a short distance to Sunrise Point; however, this will require shuttling a car to Sunrise Point before beginning the hike. Most park visitors focus their time and attention on Bryce Amphitheater to the south, but Fairyland Canyon is just as beautiful and also offers moments of quiet and solitude.

Logistics

Approach the entrance road and fee station from beautiful UT 12; the park's visitor center is just a few miles beyond. The park's scenic road takes visitors to many striking overlooks and serves most of the park's trailheads. During peak visitor season, a free shuttle bus runs along this road and connects with visitor facilities and services outside the park. Bryce has two campgrounds, North and Sunset; Bryce Canyon Lodge, an example of the historic lodges in many national parks, is located near the visitor center. A complex of commercial campgrounds, lodging, and related services is located just outside the park in an area called Bryce Canyon City. More lodging and visitor services are available in the small nearby towns of Tropic and Panguitch. The park is open year-round, but peak season is summer; spring and fall can be delightful, but winters are cold.

The Last Word

Bryce is a favorite among national park–goers and for good reason—its colorful amphitheaters of hoodoos and other formations are clearly world-class. But hikers more fully appreciate the park by inserting themselves into it—walking amid these remarkable "forests of stone."

Canyonlands National Park

Utah | nps.gov/cany

As the name suggests, Canyonlands National Park in southeast Utah is a seemingly boundless network of canyons carved into the vast Colorado Plateau. But it should really be called Canyonlands National Park*s*, because it's actually three parks (well, technically four if you count Horseshoe Canyon near The Maze), divided by two of the longest and most historic rivers in the American Southwest, the Colorado and the Green. Picture these two rivers converging from the northeast and northwest, respectively, and joining deep in the heart of the park, forming a giant letter "Y." To the north, in the yoke of the Y, is a massive, broad mesa called the Island in the Sky district. This mesa sits some 2,000 feet above the rivers. To the southeast lies The Needles, the park district known for its colorful Cedar Mesa sandstone spires rising out of the desert floor, along with a labyrinth of canyons, stone arches, potholes, remnants of Native American occupation, and vast expanses of slickrock. To the west is the mysterious Maze district, one of the most remote and wild places in the Lower 48, where, as the name implies, it's easy to get lost.

Expanses of slickrock surround a lovely canyon in The Needles.

As with all parks in arid lands, it's the geology that stares us straight in the face. Like much of this portion of the Colorado Plateau, massive salt deposits from an ancient ocean, covered with many layers of the sedimentary rock we see today, underlie Canyonlands. However, the Colorado Plateau was uplifted nearly a mile and then eroded by the Colorado and Green Rivers, rain and snow, wind, and freezing/thawing. The result is a land of canyons, buttes, pinnacles, and spires. In the Island in the Sky, the original giant mesa has been cut by water into a network of impressive and dramatic canyons. In The Needles, the geology has presented us with multicolored spires and hoodoos and smaller, entrenched canyons. As the name suggests, The Maze is a complex network of canyons that is a true walk on the wild side. Canyonlands averages only 8 inches of precipitation a year, and this lack of rain calls for flora and fauna adapted to these arid conditions. Pinyon pines and gnarled junipers are the dominant trees, with cottonwoods in some of the washes. Junipers survive extreme drought by focusing growth on some branches and letting

others die. Mule deer and rabbits are common, but desert bighorn sheep are the real prize sighting for lucky hikers.

Like much of the Colorado Plateau, the Canyonlands region accommodated Native Americans for 10,000 years or more. Their prehistoric presence is manifested in stone and mud structures (used for granaries and other purposes), as well as pictographs and petroglyphs, some of the most important in North America (see the hike through Horseshoe Canyon described below). These people hunted and gathered local plants and animals and cultivated maize, beans, and squash. European Americans—trappers and missionaries—explored the area beginning in the early 1800s. The area's most famous explorer, John Wesley Powell, floated the Green and Colorado Rivers in 1869 to survey the scarce water resources of the American Southwest; his experiences are one of the great American adventure stories. Later, ranchers used the area for pasturelands. In the 1950s Bates Wilson, the superintendent of nearby Arches National Park, began a movement to create a new national park in what's now Canyonlands. This became an increasingly urgent cause because the area was being explored for uranium. The campaign was successful; the park was established in 1964, and Wilson, now known as the "Father of Canyonlands," was appointed its first superintendent.

Walking Canyonlands

The three districts of Canyonlands offer an especially large and diverse set of hiking opportunities. We recommend three short walks in the Island in the Sky District that take advantage of the mesa's spectacular views into the heart of this land of canyons. The Needles is laced with an intricate network of trails, and we recommend two longer hikers that feature the area's characteristic hoodoos, spires, smaller-scale canyons, and great slickrock expanses. Finally we recommend the challenging hike through Horseshoe Canyon that, while not an official part of the Maze District (it's a smaller, detached unit of the park near The Maze), will give you a taste of this dramatic and less-explored part of the park.

Grand View Point Trail

The aptly named Grand View Point Trail is an easy, 2-mile (round-trip) route that hugs the rim of the Island in the Sky mesa. The trail begins at Grand View Point, where you'll find interpretive signs pointing out the primary geologic and geographic features. The trail offers stunning views into the huge canyons that have been carved into the landscape over millions of years by the Green and Colorado Rivers and their tributaries; the trail ends where it reaches the southernmost point of the huge Island in the Sky mesa. Take care not to wander too close to the clifftops, and watch carefully for cairns that mark the trail.

(top) The Needles section of Canyonlands is known for its colorful sandstone spires rising out of the desert floor.

(bottom) Lovely Chesler Park, a grassland ringed with multicolored spires, is one of the "must-do" hikes in the park's Needles District.

(opposite) The Green and Colorado Rivers have carved this landscape into a network of deep canyons.

Rock cairns guide hikers along the slickrock landscape.

Upheaval Dome Overlook Trail

Massive Upheaval Dome in the Island in the Sky is one of the most interesting and mysterious geologic features in the park and, more broadly, the Southwest. In this 3-mile-wide crater, the normally ordered sedimentary rocks of Canyonlands are deformed and displaced. Contemporary geologists have advanced two theories to explain this. The first suggests that this is a "salt dome"—a large bubble of the underlying salt layer in the park caused by the pressure and heat generated by the overlying rock—and this upheaval accounts for the distorted rock layers. The second theory is that this is an impact crater created by a meteorite about a quarter mile in diameter; the impact exposed the salt layer. Either way, the 1.6-mile (round-trip) out-and-back hike presents up close and personal views of this puzzling geologic phenomenon; you can decide for yourself which theory the evidence supports. There are two overlooks along the way; the second overlook at the end of the trail is worth the extra effort.

Big Spring Canyon Trail / Squaw Canyon Trail

The loop that connects Big Spring Canyon and Squaw Canyon Trails is quintessential Needles and highly accessible. The 7.5-mile route begins and ends at Squaw Flat Campground; the moderate hike offers a great introduction to the grand and varied Needles landscape. Highlights include walking over great expanses of slickrock, hiking along the bottoms of two alluring canyons that often have flowing streams (especially in spring), and enjoying great views of the surrounding, wondrous landscape. Fall offers the striking yellow foliage of cottonwood trees that grow in both canyons. Much of the route is marked with cairns, so pay attention to wayfinding.

Chesler Park Trail

Nearly everyone would agree that the lollipop route to and around Chesler Park is the glamour hike in The Needles. Chesler Park is a large (nearly 1,000 acres) grassy area ringed by The Needles' iconic multicolored spires, and the combination is especially appealing. The hike starts at the Elephant Hill Trailhead reached by a 3-mile dirt road easily passable by a two-wheel-drive car when the road is dry, as it usually is. For the first few miles, the trail rises and falls over expanses of slickrock and through a series of canyons, offering good views into dramatic Elephant Canyon and Big Spring Canyon. Then comes the iconic loop around Chesler Park. The Joint Trail forms part of this loop; it's a quarter-mile walk through a deep and narrow fracture in the rock; in places, you may have to squeeze your way through. As you loop around Chesler Park, look for the remains of cattle ranching in this area, before the national park was established. Even though this is a fairly long hike (about 11 miles), we recommend adding a short side trail to the Chesler Park Overlook, which offers an impressive elevated perspective of Chesler Park and the variety of sandstone formations around it.

If you'd like to do this hike as two-day backpack, there are several designated campsites in this area (a permit is required).

Murphy Point Trail

The Murphy Point Trail takes hikers to the western edge of the huge mesa that makes up much of the Island in the Sky. This is a 3.6-mile (round-trip) out-and-back walk. Most of the trail is on the remains of an old dirt road, and the walking is easy, though not especially interesting. However, the breath-taking views from the end of the trail are more than worth the walking. You look over the White Rim below and see the Green River as it flows toward its confluence with the Colorado River just a few miles downstream. We were so struck with this vista that we walked north along the rim to find some even better views of the river.

Horseshoe Canyon / Great Gallery

Sometimes you have to work a little harder to be richly rewarded, and Horseshoe Canyon, site of the Great Gallery, is a good example. The Great Gallery is part of the stunning collection of rock art sites in Horseshoe Canyon, a detached unit of Canyonlands in the vast wilderness northwest of the main body of the park. The trailhead is reached by a 30-mile graded dirt road from UT 24 or a 47-mile dirt road from the town of Green River (we chose the former). Both roads are passable by conventional two-wheel-drive passenger cars when dry. The 7-mile (round-trip) out-and-back hike into Horseshoe Canyon is rough in places and drops nearly 800 feet, requiring a steep climb back up to the trailhead. But hikers are rewarded with many significant rock art panels, including the Great Gallery—a panel that's 200 feet long and 15 feet high containing a series of about twenty exquisite but mysterious, larger-than-life-size anthropomorphic figures. This panel is thousands of years old. The canyon also offers beautiful scenery, including spring wildflowers, towering sandstone walls, and mature cottonwood trees along the canyon bottom. The NPS offers ranger-guided walks on week-ends in spring and fall; check with park staff about availability (and road conditions).

Logistics

Each of the three districts of Canyonlands has an entry point and associated visitor center. In addition, a multiagency visitor center is located in the heart of Moab, Utah, the primary gateway town serving the park's Island in the Sky and Needles districts. The park has two developed campgrounds, Willow Flat at Island in the Sky and Squaw Flat at Needles. A great variety of campgrounds and other accommodations are available in Moab. The small towns of Monticello and Blanding, Utah, can also be used as base camps for hikes in The Needles. Be advised that due to the remoteness of most of this park, it can be a long (but beautiful) drive to many of its trailheads. The park is generally

The Great Gallery is part of the stunning collection of rock art sites in Horseshoe Canyon.

(above) Sunrise at Mesa Arch in Canyonlands' Island in the Sky District is a dramatic treat.

(above right) The Green River, one of the longest and most historic rivers in the Southwest, winds its way through Canyonlands.

open year-round, but winter can be cold, even snowy, and summers very hot. Spring and fall are the ideal hiking seasons at Canyonlands.

The Last Word

On his epic float trip down the Green and Colorado Rivers in 1869, Major John Wesley Powell scaled the canyon walls at the confluence of these two mighty rivers. (It should be noted that Powell had lost an arm years before in the Civil War.) He wrote in his journal: "Wherever we looked, there was a wilderness of rocks." Thanks to Canyonlands, this wilderness of rocks is still waiting to be explored in this "three-in-one" national park.

Capitol Reef National Park

Utah | nps.gov/care

Capitol Reef National Park in south-central Utah is not well-known among national park–goers, even though they drive right through it as they rush to get to the better-known national parks just to the east (Arches and Canyonlands) and west (Bryce, Zion, and the Grand Canyon's North Rim). However, this is changing and visitation is sharply rising, and for good reason. Try to find time in your schedule to allow for a few days at this wonderful park of colorful canyons, massive rock domes, twisting slot canyons, buttes, monoliths, arches, and a rich collection of the region's historic and pre-historic artifacts. The great nineteenth-century western geologist Clarence Dutton described the area as "a sublime panorama . . . the extreme of desolation, the blankest solitude, and a superlative desert." All of these qualities and more can still be found here.

But first, what about the park's name? This long and narrow, north–south-oriented park focuses on a 100-mile geologic phenomenon called the Waterpocket Fold, a giant wrinkle in the earth's surface. This great fold (technically a mono-cline) formed a barrier to east–west travel and was therefore called a reef—a geo-graphic term that refers to a rocky barrier to travel—by early pioneers. Erosion of the reef has created great domes in the area's Navajo Sandstone visually remi-niscent of the old US Capitol dome in Washington, DC; thus the name "Capitol Reef." Erosion of the fold has left many depressions and potholes (called "water-pockets") in the sandstone where water collects; these pools can be lovely, but they are also vital sources of water for wildlife and thirsty hikers (if the water is properly treated). Maps and models of the park at the visitor center help you visualize the area's unusual geologic past and the present-day character of the park.

The park consists of three regions, or districts. The middle region through which visitors drive includes some of the park's finest geologic features, and is also the heart of its prehistoric and historic stories, including impressive petroglyph panels and the well-preserved remnants of the historic village of Fruita, where Latter-day Saint (Mormon) pioneers settled. The two regions to the north and south are more remote and can be explored via backcountry roads and trails.

This is an arid region, but many plants and animals have adapted to this high-desert envi-ronment. A few perennial rivers and streams help support a variety of plant and animal life. Trees

Capitol Reef is a long and narrow park that focuses on a 100-mile geologic feature called the Waterpocket Fold.

include pinyon pines and junipers, ponderosa pines, mixed conifer forests, and cottonwoods in wetter locations. Iconic mammals include mountain lions, mule deer, and bighorn sheep (which were extirpated from the park but successfully reintroduced in the mid-1990s), and there are more than 200 species of birds.

Like many areas in the Southwest, the park was home to ancient Native Americans. The Fremont People (a term widely used by archaeologists but rejected by most contemporary Native Americans), thought to be ancestors of the modern-day Hopi, Zuni, and Paiute, settled along what is now called the Fremont River in the heart of the park. They farmed as well as hunted and gathered local animals and plants for about 1,000 years, but left the area in the thirteenth century—the same time Ancestral Puebloans were leaving many traditional homelands in the Southwest, possibly because of extended drought. They had developed irrigation ditches, granaries, and pit houses, and left behind impressive rock art panels that often feature bighorn sheep and anthropomorphic figures. Later, Paiute and Ute occupied the area seasonally. Mormon pioneers settled here in the 1880s, building extensive irrigation systems and establishing a sustainable agricultural lifestyle; their historic settlement is at Fruita, an oasis at the confluence of two rivers in the heart of the park. Remnants of the settlement include a restored one-room schoolhouse, a barn, the Gifford House, a blacksmith shop, and extensive orchards of nearly 3,000 cherry, apple, apricot, peach, pear, and

(above left) The campground in the historic town of Fruita is one of the sweetest in the National Park System.

(above) The walk through Grand Wash is one of the most popular in the park.

(opposite) Erosion of Capitol Reef has created great domes reminiscent of the US Capitol dome.

(top) The NPS manages the historic orchards of Fruita, an early Mormon settlement.

(bottom) Walk along the Fremont River and see impressive rock art panels left by the Fremont People, thought to be ancestors of the modern-day Hopi, Zuni, and Paiute.

almond trees. Dewey Gifford was one of the last settlers to leave the area, in 1969. The NPS manages the historic orchards, and visitors are allowed to pick the fruit (check the park's website for an orchard hotline); this has been a favorite activity of ours for years. The harvest season generally runs from mid-June (cherries) to mid-October (apples).

Local Utah residents began to lobby for creation of a park in the early 1920s to protect the area, and Capitol Reef National Monument was established in 1937 by an executive order of President Franklin D. Roosevelt. Charles Kelley retired to the area and served as voluntary custodian; he was ultimately appointed the area's first superintendent in 1950. Congress established a much larger national park (nearly 250,000 acres) in 1971.

Walking Capitol Reef

Capitol Reef has nearly 40 miles of marked and maintained trails that range from easy to strenuous and an extensive system of unmaintained routes that penetrate the area's vast backcountry. Explore the interesting history and prehistory of the area, walk through majestic canyons, squeeze through tight slot canyons, enjoy striking viewpoints, backpack into the wilderness, and more.

Fruita Rural Historic District

Preservation of Fruita, a lush island of green in this otherwise arid region, helps visitors envision Mormon settlement in the park and elsewhere in the West. Here you'll find the park's visitor center and a network of short trails that allows you to tour the area on foot. Look at the park map and create your own route through the 200-acre Fruita Rural Historic District, listed on the National Register of Historic Places. The Gifford House sells locally made pies that beckon visitors to "Taste the pioneer spirt of Fruita"—we recommend them! Check at the visitor center for a schedule of free guided walks of this area. For a striking view of Fruita from above, walk the Rim Overlook Trail (described below).

Grand Wash Trail / Capitol Gorge Trail

The park's 8-mile Scenic Drive heads south out of Fruita and leads to two large and deep canyons, first Grand Wash and then Capitol Gorge, two of the most iconic and popular walks in the park. The trail through Grand Wash is 2.2 miles (one-way) to its confluence with the Fremont River at UT 24. The highlight is a dramatic half-mile narrows section where the canyon walls close to within 15 feet of each other. You'll also find the trailhead for a strenuous 1.7-mile (one-way) hike to Cassidy Arch, the name reflecting local lore that this was one of outlaw Butch Cassidy's hideouts. If you have two vehicles, Grand Wash makes an excellent shuttle hike. Dramatic Capitol Gorge served as the primary road through Capitol Reef until the early 1960s and offers an out-and-back hike of as much as 5 miles to the park boundary; most of the primary attractions are found in the first mile. Capitol

Gorge has petroglyph panels made by Fremont People, historic inscriptions of explorers and pioneers, and striking views of iconic Golden Throne. Look high on the south wall for the artfully carved names of six surveyors who worked here in 1911. Shortly after this inscription, a sign near the north wall points out a short but steep route to The Tanks, a series of natural waterpockets that are characteristic of the area.

Rim Overlook Trail

While many of the trails at Capitol Reef feature canyons (and there are some great ones), the Rim Overlook Trail goes *up* to offer striking views of the great Waterpocket Fold in the earth that is Capitol Reef, extending 100 miles along its north–south axis. This 4.5-mile out-and-back trail gains about 1,100 feet, and much of it is highly entertaining as it crosses great slickrock expanses, contours around small canyons, offers a peek down at Hickman Bridge (an impressive natural bridge), and presents ever more dizzying views. A sign marks the terminus of this section of the trail, and hikers are free to approach the edge of the viewing area—a 1,000-foot sheer drop—as closely as they like. (Be careful!) Directly below is a panoramic view of Fruita, and spreading out before you is a maze of geologic wonder. The trail affords moments of solitude that are hard to find on the nearby popular Hickman Bridge Trail. You can continue on the Rim Overlook Trail to its end at Navajo Knobs for more great views, but this adds another 5 miles (round-trip) and an additional 1,000 feet of elevation gain.

Pleasant Creek

Want a bit of adventure at Capitol Reef? Check at the visitor center about road conditions and then drive south to the end of the park's Scenic Drive. Bear right onto a 3-mile gravel road that passes the extensive corrals of the historic Sleeping Rainbow Ranch, and park just before the road makes a difficult crossing of Pleasant Creek. This is a stream that lives up to its name and more. There's no trail, but the route along the creek to the east is easy to find; it's best to stay on the existing social trail paralleling the creek to avoid disturbing any more of the area than necessary. Enjoy the sense of discovery as you wander along this unusual perennial stream with its glistening waters, lush vegetation, natural quiet, and abundant wildlife. Explore to your heart's content—the creek can be followed almost 4 miles to the park boundary.

Halls Creek Narrows

Want even more of an adventure? We did and found it in the remote southern section of the park—a short backpacking trip through spectacular Halls Creek Narrows. We saw no one else on this hike. The trailhead is a long drive down the partially-paved Notom-Bullfrog Road and the unpaved Burr Trail Road. The 22.4-mile (round-trip) hike is along a rough route, not a maintained trail, so maps

The walk along Pleasant Creek more than lives up to its name.

The Rim Overlook Trail skirts small canyons and climbs to offer views of a maze of geologic wonder.

and/or GPS and some navigation skills are essential. The route follows Halls Creek drainage and ultimately leads to a spectacular 3.8-mile deeply incised and sinuous narrows. Traveling through the narrows requires wading through a deep, cold stream and may necessitate swimming short sections. A permit is required; check with rangers on local conditions before attempting this hike.

Logistics

The park's visitor center is located in Fruita just off UT 24. Here you'll also find the park's Fruita Campground, one of the sweetest in the National Park System. There are also two small primitive campgrounds at Cathedral Valley and Cedar Mesa in the northern and southern areas of the park, respectively. There are few other visitor facilities or services in the park; commercial campgrounds, accommodations, restaurants, and other services are available in the nearby towns of Torrey and Bicknell, on the west side of the park. The park also includes an extensive system of backcountry roads that offer access to more-remote locations and associated trailheads; remember to check at the visitor center about the condition of these roads before attempting to drive them. The park is open year-round but experiences a brief, cold winter and a hot summer; spring and fall are ideal times to hike in the park.

The Last Word

We feel a little guilty spilling the beans about Capitol Reef. The other national parks scattered across southern Utah—Arches, Canyonlands, Zion, Bryce—are beautiful, but they're sometimes oversubscribed. Take the time to discover Capitol Reef on foot and enjoy the peace and quiet.

Carlsbad Caverns National Park

New Mexico | nps.gov/cave

The mysterious drawings on the cave walls near the cavern's entrance suggest that Native Americans entered what is now Carlsbad Caverns more than 1,000 years ago, but it's unlikely they explored its darkness. That was left to local cowboy Jim White, who was just a teenager when he entered the cave around the turn of the twentieth century. But few people were interested in the tours White offered to lead because exploring the cave was considered too dangerous. Not until the US Department of the Interior dispatched a staff member and photographer to the cavern and members of the National Geographic Society toured the area over the next two decades did the world begin to take notice of the immense and elaborate Carlsbad Caverns in the Guadalupe Mountains of New Mexico. President Calvin Coolidge established Carlsbad Caverns National Monument in 1923. Congress established an expanded Carlsbad Caverns National Park in 1930, and in 1995 the park was recognized as a World Heritage Site.

Excitement over Carlsbad was driven by the size of the caverns—a series of huge subterranean chambers (often called rooms) connected by a maze of passages that measure 30 miles in total—and their extensive decorations and fanciful cave formations. Carlsbad Caverns is only one of more than one hundred caves in the park. Cave formation on this order is unusual and complicated. The origin of the caverns was a 400-mile-long reef on a great inland sea that covered what's now southeast New Mexico and west Texas some 250 million years ago. Tectonic forces eventually lifted this limestone formation into what are now the Guadalupe Mountains. Slightly acidic rain and groundwater seeped through the limestone, dissolving it to create the cavern. This process was accelerated by sulfuric acid from large oil and gas deposits lying below the limestone formation. Over the past 500,000 years, groundwater filtered through the cave roofs carrying dissolved calcite from the limestone, and this material—drop by billions of drops—was deposited on the ceilings, floors, and walls of the cavern, creating magical, wonderful, and endlessly varied speleothems (structures formed in caves by the deposition of mineral-laden water). Water dripping from the ceilings formed stalactites and soda straws; water falling onto the floors created stalagmites. When stalactites and stalagmites met, impressive columns were formed. Elaborate draperies were created where water ran down a slanted ceiling, and flowstone formed where water ran over the surface of a wall or floor. Small cave pearls developed as layers of calcite built up around grains of sand, and lily pads formed on the surface of pools that collected in the caves. Rimstone forms a series of terraces or small dams on the floor of

Cave decorations take many fanciful forms, including the Darth Vader–like figure.

caves. Popcorn formed where water evaporated and left behind aragonite, similar to calcite but with a different crystal structure.

Carlsbad is home to several species of bats, the only species of mammals that flies (some mammals, such as flying squirrels, glide), including several hundred thousand Brazilian free-tailed bats, and they put on quite a show when they're in residence. Typically, bats call Carlsbad home from May through October; they migrate south to tropical areas in Mexico for the winter. During the day, the bats reside in great densities on the ceiling of Bat Cave, which is not accessible to visitors. But at dusk the bats fly from the cavern in great swarms to feed on insects in the nearby river valleys, where they may consume up to half their body weight in moths, mosquitoes, and other insects in a single night. Their nightly flight from the cavern may take up to an hour or more, and they return to the cave the next morning. A ranger-led program on bats is held each evening, culminating in the flight of the bats—it all makes great theater. The bats use a well-developed process of echolocation to find their prey (and avoid other objects), emitting ultra-high frequency sounds that are reflected back to guide their flight. During the day, the cavern serves the important function of maternity roost. Females typically give birth to one pup in June and rely on the darkness of the cavern and its location away from predators and other potential threats. Pups cling to their mothers or the ceiling for four to five weeks before they're ready to fly. As many as 300 bats may crowd into 1 square foot of ceiling space, which raises the question of how mothers find their pups when they return from the nightly hunt. Scientists think mothers can remember a pup's location, scent, and the sound of its cry.

Before Carlsbad was widely recognized for its scientific and tourism values, it was "mined" in the early 1900s for its extensive bat guano deposits. The guano was gathered and lifted 170 feet out of the cave and then packed in gunnysacks and sold to citrus growers in California. Jim White participated in this venture. The business was not profitable, however, and White went back to exploring the caverns and leading trips. Shortly after the area became a national monument, White was appointed its first chief ranger. Exploration continues in the park and is yielding sometimes astonishing finds. For example, recently discovered Lechuguilla Cave extends more than 140 miles (several times the length of Carlsbad Cavern). Given the pristine and fragile nature of this area, Lechuguilla is open only to exploration and scientific groups.

Walking Carlsbad Caverns

Of course all visitors will want to walk through the major portions of the cavern that are accessible to visitors—about 3 miles—and these trails are briefly described below. But there are other options as well, including other caves in the park and a network of 50 miles of interesting trails on the extensive surface of the park above the caves.

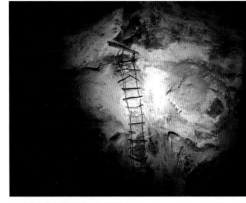

(top) A remnant of the old chain and wood ladders used to navigate the caves shortly after they were discovered in the late 1800s suggests how frightening early exploration must have been.

(bottom) On a "wild cave" tour in Slaughter Canyon, headlamps are the only source of light.

(opposite) Congress established Carlsbad Caverns National Park in 1930; it was recognized as a World Heritage Site in 1995.

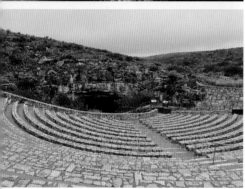

(top) Groundwater carried dissolved calcite into the caves and—drop by billions of drops—deposited this material on the ceilings, walls, and floors of the caverns.

(bottom) The park's large amphitheater sits at the mouth of the cave entrance and provides excellent viewing of the remarkable flight of the cave's bats at dusk.

Carlsbad Caverns (Big Room Trail / Natural Entrance Trail / King's Palace Tour)

There are three basic options for touring the attractions of Carlsbad Cavern. The Big Room Trail is a 1.25-mile self-guided tour of the huge, 8.7-acre Big Room, the most famous portion of the park. Here you'll see features such as the Bottomless Pit, Giant Dome, Rock of Ages, and Painted Grotto. This area can be reached by an elevator and is at least partially wheelchair accessible. The Natural Entrance Trail is also self-guided and eschews the elevator, descending 750 feet along a 1.25-mile paved trail to the Big Room. Highlights of this route include Bat Cave (which may not be entered), Devil's Spring, Green Lake Overlook, and the Boneyard. King's Palace Tour is a 1-mile, 90-minute ranger-guided walk through four scenic, highly-decorated chambers. At one point the ranger turns off all lights for a sense of the true blackness of the cave environment, a highlight of the tour! There is a fee for this tour, and it must be reserved.

Slaughter Canyon Cave

This is a "wild" cave in a different location in the park where there are no paved walkways or electricity; only headlamps light the way! This is a 5.5-hour ranger-guided adventure that roughly simulates the conditions under which caves were originally explored, and illustrates how this process continues even today. Hiking boots or shoes with an aggressive tread are required, as is drinking water. Participants in this adventure gather at the visitor center, where they are fitted with hard hats (with lights) and gloves. All participants then drive to more-remote Slaughter Canyon (named for an early rancher in the area) and climb a strenuous half-mile trail to reach the cave entrance. Rangers guide visitors through the cave and its expansive rooms and features. Walking can be slippery; fixed ropes offer welcome assistance in a few places. We found this to be a great adventure and recommend it.

Rattlesnake Canyon Trail

Yes, the main attractions at Carlsbad are underground, but of course the park includes a large surface area that offers a range of hiking opportunities. We found that there's something intriguing about walking in the park, knowing that there's a labyrinth of world-class caverns just below our feet. Our favorite surface hike is Rattlesnake Canyon, which departs from the park's Scenic Loop Road. This little-visited, shallow canyon features a diversity of Chihuahuan Desert plants and animals. (Yes, there are rattlesnakes. You're unlikely to see any—but always look before placing your feet and hands.) This is a 7-mile out-and-back hike (you can turn around at any time), or you can link to other trails to make it a 5-mile loop, which is what we did. The trail quickly drops into the canyon and then alternates between stretches of conventional trail and the bottom of the wash, which is marked with cairns. At about 1.5 miles the trail divides; the trail to the left continues in Rattlesnake Canyon to the park boundary, where you must turn around. The trail to the right heads up North

Rattlesnake Canyon (where you'll find the remains of a 1900s stone ranch) and then intersects the Guadalupe Ridge Trail. Turn right here and follow this trail through pretty Walnut Canyon (look for cairns where the trail is faint) back to the Scenic Loop Road. However, the junction with the Loop Road is about a mile farther along the Loop than where you started, so you must walk back to where you parked your car.

Logistics

The park's visitor center is located near the main cavern entrance at the end of the park road. The park is open year-round, though winters can be cold and summers hot. There is neither a campground nor other lodging in the park (other than backcountry camping, which requires a permit). There's a commercial campground just outside the park, and

Walking the above-ground trails at Carlsbad Caverns gives little hint of the vast underground caves below.

more visitor facilities and services are available in the town of Carlsbad, about 20 miles from the park entrance. The temperature in the caves is a relatively constant 56 degrees, so bring a jacket, and wear sturdy nonskid shoes. Cave formations are much more delicate than they might appear. Do not touch them; they are easily damaged, and oils from the skin permanently discolor the rock. Photography is allowed, though you may not step off the paved trails for this or any other purpose. A limited-service snack bar is located near the Big Room of Carlsbad Cavern, and there's a surprisingly good cafeteria in the visitor center.

The Last Word

Carlsbad is just one more example of the remarkable size and diversity of the National Park System; until relatively recently, Carlsbad was a huge but unknown and strange underground world of striking and improbable geologic formations. Accept the invitation this park now presents to walk intimately within this world, as well as along the starkly beautiful desert trails on the park's large surface.

Channel Islands National Park

California | nps.gov/chis

Just an hour or so boat ride from the megalopolis of Los Angeles lies a chain of eight islands often called the "Galapagos of North America"; five of these islands and their surrounding waters compose Channel Islands National Park. The park is also referred to as "No Where Else on Earth," signaling the Channel Islands' isolation from the mainland that has resulted in the evolution and adaptation of nearly 150 endemic species—plants and animals that are found naturally nowhere else on Earth. Though the islands have been occupied by humans for thousands of years, the land remains mostly undeveloped. Moreover, the islands are alive with an unusually diverse collection of plants and animals, including a rich variety of marine mammals and other sea life that are safeguarded by the park and an associated system of Marine Protected Areas. The name "Channel Islands" is derived from the deep ocean troughs that separate the islands from the mainland. Though Channel Islands is managed to study and protect this special place, much of it is accessible to visitors who are willing to accept it on its own terms: to hike and camp with few of the amenities that most national parks offer and to be especially careful to minimize their impact.

Santa Cruz is the largest island, though much of it is owned by The Nature Conservancy, the nonprofit organization that manages the land in cooperation with the NPS. The island's extensive system of trails and campsites makes it the most popular for visitors. Anacapa Island, actually composed of three small islets, is also popular, but hiking is limited to a short but striking network of trails. East Anacapa is open to visitors; Middle and West Anacapa are reserved for wildlife only. San Miguel Island, the park's westernmost island, is often subject to strong winds and poor weather, but it offers trails and many marine mammals. Santa Rosa Island lies between San Miguel and Santa Cruz; though it's the park's second-largest island, it's lightly visited. Santa Barbara Island, the smallest island in the park, is located quite a distance from the other four. Though it offers rich wildlife viewing, it's also lightly visited.

The Channel Islands emerged from the sea millions of years ago as a result of plate tectonics, volcanism, and sea levels that changed as a function of the rise and fall of ice ages. During the ice ages, ocean levels fell and several of the islands were joined; when the ice receded and the polar caps began to melt, ocean levels rose, creating the distinct islands we see today. Late Pleistocene animals became isolated on individual islands; the lack of resources forced them to adapt and become smaller. Fossil remains on Santa Rosa reveal a new species of pygmy mammoth. (Is this an oxymoron?) Similarly, the foxes that originally inhabited the islands evolved into present-day cat-size foxes.

(above) The lighthouse on West Anacapa Island was the last permanent lighthouse built on the West Coast.

(opposite) The dramatic archipelago of the Channel Islands is popularly known as the "Galapagos of North America."

(top) Foxes—about the size of a large house cat—are one of many species that have adapted and evolved on the isolated islands.

(bottom) A small cluster of Spanish Revival buildings was constructed to support operation of the lighthouse on West Anacapa Island.

Cold ocean waters from the North Pacific mix with a warm current from the south here, expanding habitat diversity and triggering an upwelling of nutrients. Vast kelp "forests" help support marine life, from microscopic plankton to giant blue whales. Marine life includes dolphins, seals, sea lions, sea otters, porpoises, and several species of whales. The islands provide important nesting and feeding grounds for most of the seabirds in Southern California. Inland areas of the islands are mostly open land that was once used for farming and grazing, but these areas are returning to their natural state since the islands' designation as a national park.

Several archaeological sites on the islands, including the remains of ancient campfires and middens, document a human presence that goes back at least 13,000 years. Sometime later, Chumash Indians settled on the northern islands and members of the Gabrielino-Tongva Nation settled on the southern islands. These tribes cooperated in a trading network that extended up and down what is now the California coast. They traveled among the islands and along the mainland in boats called *tomols*, built from redwood trees that had floated down the coast. In 1542 Spanish explorer Juan Rodríguez Cabrillo landed on the islands when he sailed into the Santa Barbara Channel. Hunters decimated the population of sea lions, seals, and sea otters in the 1800s. Most remaining Native Americans were moved to mainland missions by 1822; fishing and ranching enterprises developed in the latter half of the century. In the twentieth century, the US military established lookouts on Anacapa and Santa Barbara Islands and used San Miguel Island as a bombing range; of course these activities were damaging to the islands' ecology. Channel Islands National Monument was established in 1938 and included Anacapa and Santa Barbara Islands. The monument was expanded in 1980 to include Santa Cruz, Santa Rosa, and San Miguel Islands in the newly created Channel Islands National Park; the park now includes submerged lands and waters within 1 nautical mile of the islands. The waters extending 6 nautical miles from each island are protected as a National Marine Sanctuary.

Unfortunately, these protections did not shelter the islands from the massive oil spill in the Santa Barbara Channel in 1969 that traumatized the nation, helped galvanize the environmental movement, and was instrumental in the creation of the federal Environmental Protection Agency. Today the park is managed to rehabilitate areas affected by the oil spill and the historic commercial and military uses of the islands, to protect the park's natural and cultural resources, and to provide opportunities for visitors to enjoy and appreciate this remarkable area.

Walking Channel Islands

All five of the park's islands offer opportunities for hiking, though these are limited by the inherently confined size of the islands and logistical issues associated with traveling to and from the archipelago. However, walking along the islands' dramatic coastlines and interior spaces, learning their history, and seeing the interesting plant and animal life that resides there is a magical experience. The hikes we recommend are concentrated on Santa Cruz and East Anacapa Islands because they're closest to the mainland and have the most convenient ferry service.

Santa Cruz Island

This is the largest of the Channel Islands and has an extensive trail system. However, as noted earlier, much of the island is owned by The Nature Conservancy; hikers must respect that this is private land and cannot be accessed without special permission. Nevertheless, there is an appealing network of trails on the lands managed by the NPS. Ferries that serve the island land at two destinations, Scorpion Anchorage and Prisoners Harbor; we feel the best hiking is served by the former. The half-mile Historic Ranch Trail that begins near the dock tours the remnants of the ranch that once covered most of the island in the late 1800s. Take the time to visit the small but interesting visitor center that has been set up in a historic ranch house. We particularly liked the 5-mile (round-trip) hike to the overlook of Potato Harbor. The trail begins with a climb to dramatic Cavern Point, with views of the coastline from the island's steep bluffs. The trail continues directly along the tops of the bluffs all the way to beautiful Potato Harbor, a striking turquoise bay where we listened to seals and sea lions call. We suggest returning to the dock area by walking the unpaved Potato Harbor Road through a pretty inland valley. We also hiked the 8-mile (round-trip) trail to Smugglers Cove. This trail traverses the east end of the island and dead-ends at Smugglers Cove and its wonderful secluded beach. The trail includes some steep climbs, but it affords expansive views of the island's scenic hilly interior and nearby East Anacapa Island.

Anacapa Island

The trail network on East Anacapa totals only about 2 miles, so your time on the island (between ferries) will allow you to leisurely walk the full network. The trails include dramatic cliff-top views out over the ocean (the view from Inspiration Point is especially stunning, and we enjoyed Pinniped Point as well), the gently undulating hills of the island's interior, the last permanent lighthouse built on the West Coast (in 1932), the small cluster of Spanish Revival buildings constructed to support operation of the lighthouse, and the sights and sounds of lots of seabirds (including western gulls and pelicans) and marine wildlife (including sea lions and harbor seals). The adventure on East Anacapa Island begins as the ferry approaches Arch Rock, a dramatic natural feature on the east side of the island. After the boat deposits you on the island and you've climbed the ladders and 150 stairs, take a few minutes at the small visitor center to orient yourself and learn more about the natural and cultural history of this place. Be sure to pick up a copy of the excellent map and guide to East Anacapa.

(top) The trail to Potato Harbor on Santa Cruz Island runs along the cliff tops to a striking turquoise bay, where we listened to the calls of sea lions.

(bottom) A network of trails offers lots of hiking opportunities on Santa Cruz Island, the largest of the park's five islands.

(top) Hikers will find secluded beaches in the park.

(bottom) Arch Rock welcomes visitors to West Anacapa Island.

Santa Rosa Island, San Miguel Island, and Santa Barbara Island

These islands also offer hiking opportunities, with Santa Rosa having the largest network of trails. A centrally located campground at Water Canyon is close to Water Canyon Beach and serves as a base camp to walk the park's extensive road and trail system over several days. Several trails traverse San Miguel, but some can be hiked only when NPS personnel are available to serve as guides, and visitors to the island must know and obey all NPS rules and regulations. Much of the island is closed to protect wildlife and fragile plants. The ranger-led hike to Point Bennett leads to one of the largest concentrations of wildlife in the world—more than 30,000 marine mammals of several species. However, this hike is rigorous—16 miles round-trip. The island is owned by the US Navy but managed by the NPS. Santa Barbara has just over 5 miles of trails that feature outstanding coastal views and the gently rolling hills of the island's interior.

Logistics

The park includes a visitor center on the mainland (in Ventura) and a small contact station in Santa Barbara. The park is open year-round, but most visitors come in summer. Whale migration occurs nearly year-round, and wildflowers bloom from late winter through early summer, making these good times to visit as well. Transportation to and from the park is provided by Island Packers, a concessionaire that is contracted by the NPS. Ferries typically leave from the mainland (Ventura or Oxnard) in the morning and provide return service in the afternoon for day visitors, or you can stay overnight by camping on any of the islands (this requires a permit). Campgrounds are primitive, and campers on some of the islands must bring all the water they'll need. Campfires are not allowed. Santa Cruz and Anacapa Islands have the most frequent ferry service; service to other islands may be limited by season and/or day of the week. You may also visit Santa Rosa and San Miguel Islands by airplane service provided by Channel Islands Aviation. Private boats may access some of the islands: Check with the NPS for regulations and guidelines, as well as The Nature Conservancy for Santa Cruz Island. Weather in the park can be highly variable; it's often windy and foggy, so bring warm and protective clothing.

The Last Word

Remember, this is the American Galapagos, an archipelago that offers vital wildlife refuges and strikingly beautiful places where the land is surrounded by the sea. It's fortunate that their isolation has kept them in a relatively natural state and that they are now protected as a part of the National Park System. Take the ferry from the crowded mainland and hike where time passes on geologic and evolutionary scales. (But don't forget to catch the ferry back to the mainland!)

Congaree National Park

South Carolina | nps.gov/cong

Congaree is known as the "wild heart of South Carolina," where a vast floodplain supports a system of rivers, including the Congaree River, and forests that protect the astonishing natural diversity of the largest remaining expanse of old-growth bottomland forest in the southeastern United States. The park includes many champion trees, the tallest specimens of these trees in the world. A grassroots movement to save the area's forest began in 1969 and led to establishment of the national park in 2003. Notable wildlife includes bobcats, deer, coyotes, armadillos, turkeys, opossums, otters, turtles, and snakes. Several trails start from the Harry Hampton Visitor Center and lead to interesting destinations, but since much of the park is a massive floodplain, many portions of these trails are often underwater. The most popular trail is the 2.4-mile Boardwalk Loop that keeps visitors dry and protects the delicate plant life at ground level.

(top) Kayaking is a great way to see Congaree.

(bottom) Short sections of boardwalk are needed to keep walkers out of the water.

(left) Striking wood ducks are frequently seen in Congaree.

Crater Lake National Park

Oregon | nps.gov/crla

The dramatic landscape of Crater Lake National Park tells the magical story of how a mighty volcano became one of the most beautiful lakes in the world. About 420,000 years ago, a volcano began building in the southern Cascade Mountains; dubbed Mount Mazama (for the Pacific Northwest hiking and climbing club), this volcano ultimately reached 12,000 feet in height. Nearly 8,000 years ago, a cataclysmic eruption occurred that was a hundred times larger than that of Mount St. Helens in 1980. This was followed by development of vents at the mountain's base. These two events caused the volcano to collapse into itself, leaving a giant nearly symmetrical caldera 6 miles wide and about 4,000 feet deep. Rain and snow poured into the caldera, eventually creating what we now call Crater Lake.

For centuries the lake has maintained a relatively constant water level at an elevation of about 6,000 feet, precipitation nearly matching evaporation and seepage through the caldera walls. (This is what scientists call its "hydrologic budget.") The lake is nearly 2,000 feet deep, the deepest in the United States. It is also one of the clearest and purest lakes in the world. Many park visitors consider Crater Lake one of the most enchanting views in all the national parks, and the park's 33-mile Rim Drive offers views of the lake from every angle.

The park has robust populations of diverse plants and animals. Old-growth forests form the bulk of the park's vegetation, which includes ponderosa, lodgepole, western white, and whitebark pines; hemlocks; and Shasta red firs. Notable wildlife include black bears, mountain lions, bobcats, Roosevelt elk, mule and black-tailed deer, coyotes, foxes, pine martens, marmots, pikas, bald eagles, peregrine falcons, and spotted owls.

Archaeologists believe that Native Americans used the Crater Lake area for hunting, gathering, and religious purposes for at least 10,000 years. Oral traditions of contemporary Indians align with the scientific timeline of the eruption of Mount Mazama, suggesting that ancestors of present-day Native Americans witnessed the eruption and subsequent creation of Crater Lake. The first European Americans to see Crater Lake were three prospectors, in 1853; they were so taken by the lake's color, they named it Deep Blue Lake. William Steel first saw the lake in 1870 and devoted the next several decades of his life advocating for its protection. He participated in a government survey of the lake and surrounding area in 1886. The party carried a half-ton boat up the steep slopes of the crater and then steeply down to launch it in the lake (think about this when you see the steepness

(above) The trail to the top of Mount Scott starts with a gentle walk; hikers then ascend switchbacks to the summit, where the views are sweeping.

(opposite) Crater Lake National Park tells the story of how a mighty volcano became one of the most beautiful lakes in the world.

(above) Crater Lake as seen from the summit of Mount Scott, locally known as "Great Scott!"

(above right) Hikes along the rim of Crater Lake present many attractive perspectives of the park.

of the terrain). Using a section of pipe tied to a (very long) piece of piano wire, they determined the depth of the lake to be 1,996 feet, very close to the contemporary "official" sonar-based depth of 1,943 feet. Crater Lake National Park was established in 1902 as the nation's fifth national park.

Walking Crater Lake

More than 90 miles of hiking trails overlay the park, many focused on views of the lake, but others explore the park's backcountry. The park includes 33 miles of the Pacific Crest National Scenic Trail; walk a few miles of this 2,650-mile trail to get a sense of long-distance hiking. Here are our favorite walks in the park.

Garfield Peak Trail

This is a good place to start your hiking at Crater Lake. The trail leaves directly from popular Rim Village (which includes a visitor center) and climbs along a rocky ridge to one of the high points of the lake's dramatic rim. This is mostly an open landscape, and each turn in the trail seems to offer a better view of the lake. It's not unusual to see patches of snow in shady areas well into August and colorful wildflowers along the way. Linger at the summit to enjoy this bird's-eye perspective of Crater Lake, but don't forget to turn around and see the vast landscape of southern Oregon and northern California spread out before you. This is a moderate out-and-back hike of 3.4 miles (round-trip) with an elevation gain of 1,000 feet.

Cleetwood Cove Trail / Wizard Summit Trail

Though these are very different hikes, they almost always go together. Wizard Island is the large and distinctive cinder cone that forms the major island in Crater Lake, its name referencing the pointy hat of mythical wizards. A trail switchbacks up the cinder cone, climbing about 750 feet in elevation over about 1 mile for a round-trip hike of 2 miles. The 360 degree view of the lake from atop the caldera is unique; you're standing on the rim of a volcano (the cinder cone) inside a larger volcano (the caldera). A secondary trail encircles the rim of the cinder cone and a tertiary route drops to the floor of the cinder cone, about 100 feet below the rim. Now to Cleetwood Cove. . . . The only way to reach Wizard Island is to take a tour boat run by the park's concessionaire, and the only way to reach the boat dock (indeed, the only way to reach the shore of Crater Lake) is to walk down the Cleetwood Cove Trail, a 1.1-mile descent of about 700 feet. Shuttle boats (which must usually be reserved) run back and forth from Cleetwood Cove to Wizard Island a few times a day and allow for a stay on the island of about 3 hours. You'll want to allow most of a day for this adventure, one of the most unusual and enjoyable ways of experiencing and appreciating Crater Lake. (Don't forget that you have to walk back up the Cleetwood Cove Trail!)

(above left) Park lands that surround the lake offer opportunities for delightful hikes.

(above) The small island of Phantom Ship accents the vastness of Crater Lake.

(top) The Pinnacles are an interesting but little understood feature of Crater Lake National Park.

(bottom) The hike to the summit of the cinder cone known as Wizard Island is magical, featuring a volcano within a volcano.

Mount Scott Trail

Every park has a high point, and many become a favorite among hikers; Mount Scott (or "Great Scott!" as it's known among locals) is both of these at Crater Lake. At a little under 9,000 feet, the mountain is said to be just tall enough for most camera lenses to accommodate a photograph of the whole lake. The trail to the top is an out-and-back hike of 5 miles (round-trip) and about 1,200 feet of elevation gain. The first mile is a gentle walk through a large meadow and copses of trees, but then there's a series of long switchbacks that ultimately bring you up to a ridge and finally to the summit. Here you'll find awe-inspiring views of not only the lake but also the surrounding landscape of much of southern Oregon and northern California. You'll also find an old fire lookout station that is no longer in service (it's not open to the public). Most of the scattered trees at the summit are white-bark pines with limbs so flexible they can be tied in a knot. (This makes the trees more resistant to the strong winds on the summit.) Return to your car using the same trail.

Logistics

The park is open year-round, but winters are long and especially snowy; the park receives about 40 feet of snow on average each year. The main visitor season is July and August; September and October are less crowded but cool. The park has two campgrounds, Mazama and Lost Creek. The vast majority of the park is managed as wilderness where backpacking is allowed in most places but requires a permit. There's a lodge in the park and additional cabins at Mazama Village. Other visitor facilities and services are available at Mazama Village and Rim Village. Be especially careful around the rim of the lake; slopes are steep and unstable. Climbing anywhere inside the caldera (except the trail to the lake at Cleetwood Cove) is prohibited.

The Last Word

Crater Lake is one of the oldest and most venerable national parks, and the remarkable beauty of the lake and its context within an immense volcanic caldera make it a favorite for many visitors. Hike down to the shore of the lake and touch its cool water (go for a swim if you're up to it), enjoy the perspective of the landscape you gain from the surface of the lake, walk to the top of an ancient cinder cone, or hike to the summit of the park's mountains with their old-growth forests and remarkable views. Invest a few days at the park and you'll be rewarded with all it gives in return.

Cuyahoga Valley National Park

Ohio | nps.gov/cuva

Cuyahoga Valley National Park is not just one of the newest national parks (the area received national park status in 2000), it also represents a new model for national parks in America. Most national parks were established by setting aside large areas of uninhabited public land that featured monumental scenery. But Cuyahoga Valley lies between the cities of Cleveland and Akron, Ohio, and includes urban and suburban lands. Its proximity to urban populations is an important part of the genesis of this national park—bringing national parks to large and diverse metropolitan areas.

The park includes 33,000 acres strung out along 22 miles of the winding Cuyahoga River (*Ka-ih-ogh-ha* is Mohawk for "crooked river"). In the early 1960s residents of this area became concerned about the development that was beginning to sprawl into the historic and picturesque valley. Their efforts to save the area ultimately came to fruition in the form of this new model of national parks, one that has been successfully applied for years in densely populated areas of Europe and elsewhere. Rather than a large wilderness where virtually no one lives, key areas are owned and managed by the NPS and mixed with lands protected by other agencies and organizations, in this case Cleveland Metroparks and Akron's Summit Metro Parks. Even private lands in and outside the park are afforded some element of conservation through a system of incentives to landowners. The result is a vital layer of protection over the valley's key resources—lush farmlands, rolling hills covered in forests, a historic river, an abundance of waterfalls, narrow ravines, important wildlife habitat, and wetlands—managed by a coordinated group of public, private, and nonprofit partners. These natural resources are complemented by an array of cultural resources, including an almost 20-mile restored section of towpath along the 308-mile-long historic Ohio & Erie Canal, working farms, bed-and-breakfasts, the historic Hale Farm and Village, and a diverse system of more than 125 miles of trails. Rather than a wilderness, this is a place that has been occupied by generations of private landowners and has achieved a pleasing balance between nature and culture. Civilization is never far from the park, but that's the point!

The geography of the Cuyahoga River and its surrounding valley is unusual. The river rises in wetlands east of Cleveland, flows south toward Akron, then turns sharply north to empty into Lake Erie, only 30 miles from the river's source. Even to scientists, the underlying geology of Cuyahoga Valley is complex, partly due to massive glaciation that has largely obscured earlier geologic periods. The park's steep ravines—places such as Tinkers Creek, Furnace Run, and the Cuyahoga River

(top) A great blue heron enjoys a perch in the park's wetlands.

(bottom) The Cuyahoga Valley Scenic Railroad makes several regular stops in the park, offering rides for hikers.

itself—were caused at least partially by the varying water levels of Lake Erie as it was affected by glacial advances and retreats.

The park is in a transition zone between the Allegheny Plateau and the Central Lowlands; consequently, it includes a variety of land types, including wetlands, floodplains, and uplands in various stages of natural and human-caused succession. The result is an unusually rich variety of plants and animals. Trees include deciduous forests of oak, red maple, tulip tree, ash, hickory, and beech. More northern species of hemlocks and yellow birch are found in colder ravines, while cottonwoods, willows, Ohio buckeyes, and sycamores grow along the river. More than forty species of mammals inhabit the park, including deer, foxes, coyotes, river otters, and minks; beavers have recently returned. There are nearly 250 species of birds, including great blue herons, wood ducks, kingfishers, and a great variety of songbirds. Bald eagles have recently returned to the area in response to improving water quality in the Cuyahoga River.

The human history of the park is also interesting. People have lived in this area for nearly 12,000 years, leaving hundreds of archaeological sites scattered through the valley. The Cuyahoga River and its surrounding valley was an important transportation route and therefore considered neutral territory among the area's many Native American tribes. Prehistoric artifacts suggest that these people traveled and traded widely. European settlers moved to the area in the nineteenth century to take advantage of the agricultural potential.

But better transportation was needed to carry crops to regional and distant markets in the East. The Cuyahoga River had widely fluctuating water levels that made navigation difficult, so a canal was constructed along the route of the river. The 308-mile Ohio & Erie Canal was completed in 1832 and was a vital part of the nation's growing network of canals, connecting the Great Lakes region with the Gulf of Mexico via the Mississippi, Ohio, and Cuyahoga Rivers. Cleveland and Akron boomed, as did smaller towns along the river, such as Boston and Peninsula, both of which became canal boat-building centers and are now included within the boundaries of the national park. However, railroads soon replaced the canals with faster and more efficient transportation of both goods and people.

As early as the turn of the twentieth century, Cuyahoga Valley became a restful retreat for residents of Cleveland, Akron, and other towns seized by the Industrial Revolution. In 1929 the estate of businessman Hayward Kendall donated 430 acres of land in the valley to the State of Ohio, prescribing that it "shall be perpetually used for park purposes." During the Great Depression, the federal Civilian Conservation Corps constructed many recreation-related facilities that are still in use today.

The Cuyahoga River played a paradoxical role in helping foster the modern environmental movement. In June 1969, ongoing industrial activities along the river caused oil and other contaminants and debris to collect at a railroad trestle, where the river caught fire! This and related events throughout the nation convinced people that more environmental protection was desperately

(above) The towpath features several locks that have been preserved along the Ohio & Erie Canal.

(opposite) One of the park's many waterfalls spills into the historic Cuyahoga River.

The park is a cultural landscape that preserves the area's natural and cultural history.

needed, resulting in a suite of federal legislation, such as the Environmental Protection Act of 1970 and the Clean Water Act of 1972. The river has a strong record of improving water quality, though it is still not clean enough for swimming.

A movement to create a large reserve in the valley took shape in the 1960s, led by the Cuyahoga Valley Association (now the Conservancy for Cuyahoga Valley National Park). Public attention turned to the NPS and the establishment of a new unit of the National Park System. This idea had strong local support and a dogged advocate in US Representative John Seiberling, who had strong ties to the area. Congress acted in 1974, establishing Cuyahoga Valley National Recreation Area, elevated to national park status in 2000.

Walking Cuyahoga Valley

The park includes more than 125 miles of trails offering a wide variety of experiences, from short nature walks to the park's signature towpath trail. We recommend the following trails to appreciate this innovative national park and the historic and grand cultural and natural landscape it preserves and celebrates.

Blue Hen Falls Trail

This short trail (about a quarter mile) leads to one the park's many small but delightful waterfalls. From the trailhead parking lot, the trail drops quickly to Spring Creek. You cross the creek on a footbridge and follow the trail to where the long-distance Buckeye Trail branches off. Follow the trail to the right to the viewing area for Blue Hen Falls. Please stay behind the split-rail fence that defines the viewing area. If you're inspired to take a longer walk, return to the trail junction and follow the Buckeye Trail for as long as you wish (it's 1,400 miles!). Otherwise, retrace your steps.

Ledges Trail

The Ledges Trail is a favorite of many Cuyahoga Valley visitors and residents alike. The 2.2-mile loop trail passes beneath dramatically-eroded bluffs, through tight passageways and a number of other scenic spots, offering a cool microclimate where you'll find ferns, mosses, and hemlock and yellow birch trees. Along the trail, note the large graceful Ledges Shelter built by the Civilian Conservation Corps in the 1930s from native stone and American chestnut trees as well as the artful stone steps they strategically placed and occasionally carved into the natural bedrock outcroppings along the trail.

Brandywine Gorge Trail / Brandywine Falls Trail

This 1.4-mile trail encircling Brandywine Creek leads to one of the signature features of the park, 65-foot Brandywine Falls. It's a pleasant loop that can be significantly shortened by simply turning around and retracing your steps after you've reached the falls. An extensive system of boardwalks,

stairs, and viewing platforms offers visitors viewing options; we recommend walking both the lower and upper walkways.

Ohio & Erie Canal Towpath Trail

Boats were towed along the nineteenth-century Ohio & Erie Canal by mules walking the adjacent towpath; this towpath has been renovated into a 20-mile trail that is the heart of the park. Nearly all visitors walk at least a portion of the trail, but we encourage you to consider walking the trail in its entirety; this was the highlight of our visit. We walked the trail in two easy days, sharing the trail in places with bikers, and used the Cuyahoga Valley Scenic Railroad to return us to our starting point and a local B&B for our overnight. The trail is essentially flat and the surface hard-packed, making for easy walking.

The Towpath Trail is served by the local villages of Boston and Peninsula and the park's Canal Exploration Center. There are occasional benches, picnic areas, and interpretive signs, and a number of road crossings with vehicle parking that can be used as trailheads. Generally, the trail is located between the canal and the river. On its journey through the park, the trail includes access to many canal-related structures, including locks, aqueducts, feeder canals, weirs, sluices, and gates, offering lots of opportunities to learn the fascinating story of how historic canals were constructed and operated. The Towpath Trail also immerses walkers in the natural history of the valley, passing through forests, fields, and wetlands. The Cuyahoga Valley Scenic Railroad parallels the river on its route linking downtown Akron to the park's northern border and makes several regular stops in the park.

(above left) The park includes an extensive area of wetlands, accessible by a network of boardwalks.

(above) Sixty-five-foot Brandywine Falls is one of the park's signature features.

The towpath of the historic Ohio & Erie Canal has been converted into a 20-mile trail that runs the length of the park.

Logistics

The park is in northeast Ohio between Cleveland and Akron and is readily accessible by car. It's open year-round, but the primary season is March to October (winters can be cold and snowy). Spring and fall are especially nice. The Boston Store Visitor Center and the Canal Exploration Center offer interesting exhibits and helpful staff and volunteers. In-park lodging is available at Stanford House, a historic nineteenth-century farmhouse, and the more upscale Inn at Brandywine Falls, another historic home. Many other accommodations are available outside the park. Five primitive campsites are available near the Stanford House, but no backcountry or RV camping is allowed.

The Final Word

Many local people refer to Cuyahoga Valley National Park as "the green-shrouded miracle," a historic cultural landscape in an urbanizing area that has been preserved as an innovative and unlikely national park. As a guidebook to the national park suggests, "Since its founding in the 1970s, its landscapes, its nature, its history, and its culture have inspired those who live in it and the widening circle of those who visit." It represents a new model for national parks in America, one that's based on partnerships among public, private, and nonprofit groups, all committed to work together in the interest of preserving this unique cultural landscape. As always, the best way to enjoy and appreciate a national park is to walk it, and Cuyahoga's more than 125 miles of trails are made for just that.

Death Valley National Park

California and Nevada | nps.gov/deva

This park's unfortunate name is derived from a group of 1849 emigrants who mistakenly found themselves in what is now the park. Unprepared for this hot, dry landscape, they struggled for two months to find their way; in the process, one of them died and the others thought they might too. As they eventually found their way out of the valley through the park's Panamint Mountains, one of the party looked back and muttered "Good-bye, Death Valley." The name stuck.

Yes, you can perish in the park. This is one of the hottest places on Earth (a recorded temperature of 134°F, a world record) and one of the driest areas in North America (averaging less than 2 inches of precipitation annually), but you'll be fine if you're reasonably prepared. In fact, this is a remarkable national park with a long list of superlatives: extensive sand dunes, 11,000-plus-foot mountains, lovely canyons, spring wildflowers, a magnificent set of volcanic craters, ghost towns, extensive salt flats, colorful badlands, iconic wildlife, and vast reserves of natural quiet and dark night skies. It's also home to some of the most unusual attractions in all the national parks, including a strange castle, the lowest place in North America, plants and animals that are found naturally nowhere else, and rocks that move mysteriously across the desert. There's room for all this and more in the largest national park outside Alaska (nearly 3.4 million acres).

Much of the park is classic Basin and Range geography that characterizes vast swaths of the American West and Southwest, a series of deep basins (or valleys) bordered by mountains running generally north–south. The primary valleys are Death and Panamint; the primary mountain ranges are the Amargosa and the Panamint. The park is mainly in California but extends north and east into Nevada. The diversity of the park's topographic features suggests the area has a complex geologic history, much of it poorly understood. Forces that shaped the park include shifting tectonic plates that uplifted the mountains, a subsequent volcanic period, movement of large blocks of land along fault lines, and erosion of mountains and associated deposition onto valley floors. Over the past 3 million years, the area has experienced major climatic changes, including formation of large lakes during the most recent ice age and evaporation of these lakes during subsequent warmer periods. The current dry lake beds (called salt pans) are covered in salt and deposits of other minerals such as borax. The park is in a vast "rain shadow" caused by the westward-lying Sierra Nevada and other mountains, meaning that Pacific storms release most of their moisture over these mountains rather than in the park.

(top) The sand dunes at Mesquite are the park's largest, occupying more than 14 square miles.

(bottom) In the north of the park lie a set of spectacular interlinked volcanic craters. Feel free to walk around and even down in them.

The variation in elevations in the park is extreme—from nearly 300 feet below sea level to more than 11,000 feet above—and offers a great variety of habitats. Vegetation ranges from common desert plants such as creosote bush and cacti to pinyon-juniper and bristlecone pine forests. Iconic animals include desert bighorn sheep, mule deer, coyotes, bobcats, kit foxes, jackrabbits, desert tortoises, and the tiny, endangered Devils Hole pupfish. Many of these animals are primarily nocturnal to avoid the park's extreme heat. The geographic orientation of the Basin and Range topography creates a natural flyway for migratory birds, and the park's natural springs and scattered oases attract more than 300 species.

Native Americans occupied the Death Valley area as much as 10,000 years ago during milder climatic times. More recently, the Timbisha lived in the area and practiced a vertical form of migration, occupying the valleys in winter and the higher mountainous regions in summer. The area was heavily prospected in the late 1800s and early 1900s for precious metals, but without great success except, perhaps, for the Keane Wonder Mine. The boomtowns that sprang up then are today's ghost towns, scattered across the park and surrounding region along with an estimated 10,000 abandoned mines. But it was borax, a mineral deposited from the area's ancient lakes and used in soaps and industrial processes, that proved the most economically successful. Stephen Mather, named the first director of the NPS in 1916, became wealthy in this industry before he joined the agency.

Tourism became important in the 1920s based primarily on natural springs thought to have curative properties, and the area soon became a popular winter retreat. Scotty's Castle, a large Spanish Revival–style vacation home was built by a wealthy Chicago couple in the 1920s. The couple befriended Walter Scott (aka Death Valley Scotty), a local huckster and faux gold miner, who was invited to live at the mansion, thus the name of the home. The castle was later converted into a hotel and museum. A large national monument was created to protect the Death Valley region in 1933. In 1994 Congress passed the California Desert Protection Act, designating the area a national park and increasing its size to nearly 3.4 million acres.

Walking Death Valley

This is a vast park that would take years or even lifetimes to thoroughly explore on foot. Moreover, it's a park that's dominated by wilderness (more than 3.1 million acres of it, more than 90 percent of the park) and an associated ethic that eschews too many miles of maintained trails. But these trails—from easy to challenging—are carefully located so hikers can experience much of the diversity of the park.

(above) Striking beehive-shaped charcoal kilns stand at the trailhead for the hike up 9,000-foot Wildrose Peak.

(opposite) All visitors should walk at Badwater Basin, 282 feet below sea level, site of the hottest recorded temperature in North America. (Don't walk there in summer!)

Seeps, springs, and winter precipitation support a number of oases scattered across the park's landscape.

Badwater Salt Flats Trail

All park visitors should walk at Badwater Basin, 282 feet below sea level, site of the hottest recorded temperature in North America. The popular hike follows a short boardwalk onto the salt flats, but continue your walk out onto the extensive surface of the salt flats to gain an appreciation for this phenomenon of nature. Groundwater that carries dissolved salt to the surface evaporates quickly, leaving a complex of fascinating geometric patterns of salt on the flat surface of the ground; the area resembles an all-white jigsaw puzzle. Walk as long and far as you wish. The white surface of the salt flats reflects the sun, so wear sunglasses, and don't hike here in the heat of the summer.

Mesquite Flat Sand Dunes

The park has several areas of sand dunes, some of them quite extensive; the dunes at Mesquite Flat are the largest, occupying more than 14 square miles. These dunes reach 100 feet high and can be challenging to climb but fun to explore. There are no marked or maintained trails—just a giant sandbox to play in. Look for animal tracks in the dunes, especially in the morning before the wind washes them out, and notice the ways in which the dunes change color and character with the natural lighting patterns during the day—sunrise and sunset are especially dramatic. Consider a moonlight walk in the dunes for extra drama. Be sure to note a visual landmark on the surrounding mountains that you can use to find your way back to your car. You shouldn't walk on the sand dunes in the heat of summer when ground temperatures can reach 180°F.

Salt Creek Interpretive Trail

The name Death Valley suggests the extreme arid character of this park, but seeps, springs, and winter precipitation support a number of surprising oases scattered across the landscape. Salt Creek is one of these places and is one of our favorite walks, especially in the early-morning light. A boardwalk follows Salt Creek for a lovely quarter mile, featuring several steam crossings, masses of attractive pickleweed, and the chance to see the endangered Death Valley pupfish, found only in this park. The fish tend to dart about, thus their playful name. At the end of the boardwalk, consider walking farther by joining the obvious social trail that runs along the lushly vegetated creek through a gentle badlands. This walk offers a sense of adventure through a stunning landscape, all of it below sea level. The social trail eventually peters out at a series of small sand dunes; return to the trailhead from here for a delightful round-trip walk of about 4 miles.

Golden Canyon Trail / Gower Gulch Loop Trail

Deep canyons cut into the park's mountains and alluvial fans, making some of the most desirable hiking destinations. And if the number of hikers is a good measure, then Golden Canyon is one of the most dramatic and beautiful. The first mile of this hike is an interpretive trail that takes hikers on a walk through geologic time; see volcanic rocks that predate Death Valley, the tilted canyon walls that are a result of geologic faulting, mudstone deposits and ripple marks that are evidence of an ancient lake, and deep washes caused by flash floods and erosion. At the end of the interpretive trail, hikers can retrace their steps to the trailhead for a 2-mile round-trip outing or continue a short distance to the base of impressive Red Cathedral, colored by the weathering of iron in the rocks. For a longer adventure (and far fewer hikers), follow the trail markers through expansive badlands and over a pass that leads into Gower Gulch, a wide dry wash. A side trail leads to an overlook below Zabriskie Point. Follow Gower Gulch to its mouth and bear right to return to the Golden Canyon parking area. Look for small tunnels in the high canyon walls, evidence of early borax exploration, but don't enter these mines. This loop is 4.7 miles; the side trips to Red Cathedral and the lookout below Zabriskie Point add another 1.8 miles of wonderful walking. The golds of Golden Canyon and reds of Red Cathedral light up in the late-day sun.

Ubehebe / Little Hebe Craters

Why not add dramatic volcanic craters to the mix of trails you walk at Death Valley? In the north of the park lie a series of interlinked craters, perhaps a dozen of them, the most prominent of which are Ubehebe and Little Hebe, taken from the Shoshone word for "basket." These are what geologists call maar volcanoes, which have no cones; they are simply massive holes left from violent explosions of superheated groundwater. The largest is Ubehebe, nearly a half mile across and 500 feet deep; the explosion occurred recently in geologic time—perhaps within the last 1,000 to 2,000 years—and covered an estimated 6 square miles of surrounding desert with volcanic debris up to 150 feet deep. Little Hebe is a smaller crater, but it probably exploded even more recently, as its rim shows little signs of subsequent erosion. Walk the trails that sit directly on the rims of these and other craters for an otherworldly experience. Want more? Walk down to the bottom of Ubehebe Crater, though the walk back up is made considerably harder by the deep, loose cinders. The route around the craters and down in them is perhaps a couple of miles, constituting a hike you won't soon forget.

Wildrose Peak Trail

Arriving at Death Valley, you're sure to notice that the park includes several impressive mountain ranges, some rising to more than 11,000 feet. Maintained trails lead to the summit of two of these mountains, Telescope and Wildrose, both in the Panamint Mountains in the western part of the

(top) The park was prospected extensively for precious metals, but it was borax that made the most money. One of the twenty-mule-team wagons that carried the raw material out of the park has been preserved.

(bottom) The ridge near Dante's View may be the best place to witness sunrise in the park.

Deep canyons (Golden Canyon in this image) cut into the park's mountains and alluvial fans, making some of the most desirable hiking destinations.

park. Telescope is the highest mountain in the park, but it's a very strenuous hike, and reaching the trailhead requires a four-wheel-drive vehicle. We recommend the hike to Wildrose Peak, an 8.4-mile (round-trip) route with an elevation gain of about 2,200 feet to reach the 9,064-foot summit. The trailhead is a long but beautiful drive from Stovepipe Wells, and the last 2 miles or so are over a very rough road that can generally (but carefully) be negotiated with a standard passenger car (check at the visitor center for road conditions). At the trailhead stand ten striking beehive-shaped charcoal kilns that were used to help fuel silver mine smelters in the late 1800s. The generally well-groomed trail travels through a lovely pinyon-juniper forest characteristic of much of the southwestern United States but uncommon at Death Valley. At higher elevations look for long-lived bristlecone pines. Reaching the bald summit requires negotiating a short, steep pitch of trail, much of it above tree line. Look to the east to Badwater Basin, the lowest point in the United States, then turn around to see Mount Whitney to the west, the highest in the Lower 48. Remarkable! This high-elevation trail is a good choice in summer, when most of the rest of the park swelters.

Logistics

Most visitors arrive from late fall through spring (which sometimes features showy wildflower displays, depending on precipitation). The NPS manages nine campgrounds, one with RV hookups; there are also three private campgrounds, two with RV hookups. Three sites offer visitor information: Furnace Creek Visitor Center, the ranger station at Stovepipe Wells, and Scotty's Castle Visitor Center and Museum. There are several hotels/motels in the park, including the historic and luxurious Inn at Death Valley, and more outside the park in the surrounding small communities.

The Last Word

What a difference time has made in the public perception of Death Valley. Once considered an inhospitable, even dangerous, wasteland, it's now a vast national park of diverse superlatives that attracts a million visitors a year. As long as visitors prepare and exercise reasonable care, this large park offers memorable hiking on its trails and in its extensive wilderness.

Denali National Park and Preserve

Alaska | nps.gov/dena

Denali National Park and Preserve is a crown jewel of the National Park System. This is one of several vast national parks in Alaska, but it's unusual in that visitors can reach the park, even its interior, relatively easily by car, bus, train, and plane. The park is more than 6 million acres, larger than some states, and offers nearly unlimited hiking through its trailless wilderness. The dominating feature of the park is 20,310-foot Denali, the highest mountain in North America; *Denali* means "the high one" in the native Athabaskan language. When the park was established in 1917, it was called Mount McKinley National Park in honor of President William McKinley; however, the name of the park was changed in 1980 to Denali National Park and Preserve. The word "preserve" was added to note that portions of the park can be used for traditional subsistence purposes by native people. More recently, the name of the mountain itself has been changed to Denali, the name by which it has been generally known by Alaskans.

The park encompasses a portion of the 600-mile-long Alaska Range and surrounding areas. The distance from the base of the mountain to its peak (its vertical relief) is 18,000 feet, the highest of any mountain in the world. Views of the mountain are astounding—one has to look up as well as out to fully appreciate it. Unfortunately, the mountain is draped in clouds much of the time, at least somewhat obscuring the view; in local parlance, the mountain is "out" only part of the time. Spending several days in the area will increase your chances of seeing it.

Visitors can always appreciate Denali's remarkable wildlife; the park is sometimes referred to as the "Serengeti of North America." Iconic mammals include grizzly and black bears, herds of caribou, Dall sheep, moose, wolves, foxes, martens, Canadian lynx, and wolverines; visitors are sure to see many of these animals. Of course there are many birds as well, including golden eagles, a variety of hawks and owls, gyrfalcons, ptarmigan, and Arctic warblers.

Most of Denali is managed as a wilderness area; the objective is to provide hikers with a sense of discovery and self-reliance.

This large park is composed of several types of landscapes, including the Alaska Range with its glaciers and snowfields, vast expanses of tundra, forests, rivers and lakes. The mountains have a complicated and varied geologic history but result mostly from uplift caused by the collision of tectonic plates. Volcanic activity has also contributed to the underlying structure of some areas and is very evident where the Denali Park Road travels through colorful Polychrome Pass. Glaciers cover about 16 percent of the park and have been instrumental in shaping the landscape. Some of the existing glaciers are more than 30 miles long and nearly 4,000 feet thick. Classic manifestations of this glaciation include huge cirques (amphitheater-like formations near the summit of mountains), arêtes (narrow ridges), and cols (saddles) in the mountains; moraines (great piles of glacial debris) along the sides and at the terminus of each glacier; erratics (large rocks picked up by glaciers and deposited elsewhere) strewn across the valleys; wide, "braided" rivers (with multiple channels and much glacial debris); and "kettle" lakes (formed by the meltwater of large blocks of ice left behind as glaciers retreat). Large and serene Wonder Lake is a kettle lake that's about four miles across and nearly 300 feet deep.

Vast expanses of tundra and its low-lying vegetation occupy the middle elevations of the park, and the generally open character of these areas can make for good walking, allowing hikers to appreciate the scenery and see wildlife. The park's lower elevations feature a mix of forests; these forests are a classic example of taiga—a mix of usually stunted trees, dominated by white and black spruce but including some deciduous trees such as aspen, birch, poplars, and willows. Tree line in the park ranges from about 2,500 to 3,000 feet. More than 450 species of flowering plants grow in the park's extensive valleys.

Early indigenous peoples probably didn't use the area that is now the park because of its high elevation and long, harsh winters. Archaeologists have found relatively few prehistoric sites, and these are thought to be seasonal hunting camps. However, evidence from outside the park suggests that humans occupied this area of Alaska for 10,000 years or more. Charles Sheldon wintered in a cabin on the Toklat River in 1903 and witnessed the slaughter of Dall sheep to feed gold miners; in response, he successfully lobbied for establishment of the national park. Adolph Murie, an early NPS wildlife biologist, studied the dynamics of the wolf–Dall sheep relationship in the late 1930s and early 1940s. Based on his research, he encouraged the park to protect predators such as wolves to ensure an intact wilderness ecosystem; this helped change management policies of the entire National Park System. Murie also successfully opposed development in the park and is referred to as "Denali's Wilderness Conscience." In the early 1970s the first modern highway was built in interior Alaska, connecting the cities of Anchorage and Fairbanks and running near the entrance to Denali National Park. Anticipating an increase in visitation, the NPS closed most of the Denali Park Road

(top) The park's iconic animals include grizzly and black bears, herds of caribou, Dall sheep, moose, and wolves.

(bottom) Caribou are often seen in the park's valleys.

(opposite) The dominating feature of the park is Denali—at 20,310 feet, the highest mountain in North America.

(above) The park is composed of several types of landscapes, including the Alaska Range of mountains with its glaciers and snowfields, large glacial rivers and lakes, and vast expanses of tundra and forests.

(above right) The park's lower elevations are dominated by wetlands and taiga, a mix of stunted trees.

to automobile traffic and required visitors to ride buses to minimize potential disturbance of the park's iconic wildlife.

Walking Denali

There are three basic options for hiking in Denali. First, there are a few, relatively short maintained trails. Second, the vast trail-less portion of the park allows a series of day and overnight hikes, with the park's shuttle bus system (specifically, the green buses) nicely facilitating this option. Buses will stop anywhere along the road (with a few exceptions related to the presence of sensitive wildlife) to let hikers off and on. Walk into the wilderness portion of the park and return to the road to get a ride back to your origin (e.g., the park entrance, one of the park's campgrounds, lodging at Kantishna). A third option is to engage the services of an outfitter and fly into a remote portion of the park to do a guided or unguided hike.

Trails

There are only a few marked and maintained trails in the park, and several are near the Denali Visitor Center, close to the park entrance. The Denali Park Road travels over the Savage River at about mile 15, the point at which the road is closed to automobile travel. There's a parking lot there from which you can access the 1.7-mile Savage River Loop Trail and the approximately 4-mile (one-way) Savage Alpine Trail; you may see wildlife along both. The Savage River Alpine Trail connects with the Savage River Campground, and you can take the park's free Savage River Shuttle back to the trailhead. At mile 66 along the Denali Park Road, there are two marked trails around the Eielson Visitor Center. The Tundra Loop is about a third of a mile through alpine tundra, and the Eielson Alpine Trail is about 2 miles (round-trip) up Thorofare Ridge (this trail is steep in places). Wonder Lake is at mile 85 along the road, and the McKinley Bar Trail leads from the Wonder Lake Campground to the McKinley River, about a 5-mile round-trip.

Trail-less

Nearly all the park is a vast area without maintained trails. However, day hikes can be readily done in many places. Ranger-guided hikes leave from the Denali and Eielson Visitor Centers, and this is a good way to begin. You can also consult with staff at the Backcountry Desk at the Denali Visitor Center; here you'll get some good hiking suggestions based on local conditions. Another option is to ride the park's shuttle bus until you see an area that looks intriguing and ask the driver to stop. River valleys offer relatively flat terrain, and it's generally easy to find your way and return to the road (especially if you don't wander too far from it). River channels are often wide, and it may be possible to walk along open river bars. We've enjoyed Riley Creek, Upper Savage River, and Upper Teklanika River. Scout the terrain ahead to avoid "terrain traps" such as dense pockets of spruce forest and alder that are both hard to walk through and make it difficult to see bears and other animals you should avoid at close range. Of course you can always walk (with care) along the park road.

Denali National Park features wonderful multiday backpacking trips. In this case, you must consult with the Backcountry Desk at the Denali Visitor Center to receive a permit. Based on your objectives, experience, and abilities, rangers will suggest appealing options. The loop around Mount Eielson, the treks to Anderson and McGonagall Passes, and routes that include the Teklanika, Sanctuary, and Toklat Rivers are popular. Most hikers choose trips of 1 to 3 nights, although park rules allow trips of up to 30 nights!

Logistics

The park is accessible by car from Anchorage (240 miles) and Fairbanks (120 miles) and by train, with the Alaska Railroad delivering passengers to the park entrance area. There are two visitor centers, Denali near the park entrance and Eielson on the Denali Park Road, deep within the park. The park has six campgrounds, four accessible from the park's shuttle bus system and two by automobile, the latter closer to the park entrance. Commercial campgrounds, accommodations, and other visitor facilities and services are located outside the park, a short distance from the park entrance road; locals humorously call this area "Glitter Gulch." Several lodges are located in Kantishna, an abandoned mining village at the end of the Denali Park Road.

(top) The park's river valleys often make for good hiking opportunities.

(bottom) The interior of the park can be accessed by buses that run along the 92-mile Denali Park Road.

The Denali Park Road and its extensive shuttle bus system are signature features of the park. The road runs deep (92 miles) into the park's interior, ending at the old mining town of Kantishna. Shuttle buses run along the entire road and must be used beyond mile 14 (no private vehicles are allowed beyond that point). Riding them is a highlight for many park visitors; the buses not only meet the transportation needs of hikers and campers but also offer frequent wildlife sightings. Tickets for the green transit buses and brown tour buses can be purchased at the Denali Bus Depot and online; reservations are recommended.

Hiking in Denali is exhilarating, but it requires preparation. Unlike parks in the Lower 48, the trail-less character of most of this park, its sometimes harsh weather conditions, and its potentially dangerous wildlife demand consultation with staff at the park's Backcountry Desk inside the Denali Visitor Center. Overnight trips require a permit from this facility. Be sure to consult with rangers before undertaking a hike in the park's large trail-less portion. The hiking season generally runs from late May through early September.

The Last Word

We've been deliberate in including a great range of walking and hiking opportunities in this book. Denali is clearly at the wilderness end of the spectrum. Nearly all the park is a wilderness area, one of the largest and wildest in the United States. The objective of park managers is to provide hikers with a sense of discovery and self-reliance—a rare and exciting opportunity, but one that also comes with responsibilities. Begin the Denali experience by riding the Denali Park Road, walking the park's maintained trails, and day hiking in some of the river valleys accessible by the park's shuttle buses. If you wish, work with staff at the Backcountry Desk to prepare yourself for the range of backpacking experiences the park offers. Regardless of the type of walking you do in the park, you'll be richly rewarded and pleased that wild places like Denali are being preserved.

Dry Tortugas National Park

Florida | nps.gov/drto

This remote 100-square-mile park sits in the Gulf of Mexico 70 miles west of Key West, Florida. Nearly all the park is open water, though there are seven small islands—the westernmost and most isolated of the Florida Keys. The most important island is Garden Key, home of massive historic Fort Jefferson, built in the mid-1800s to protect strategic US anchorages and shipping lanes. The park protects this historic site as well as coral reefs, marine and bird life, the surrounding sea, and the sea turtles (*las Tortugas*) for which the area was named. The park is also known for legends of shipwrecks and sunken treasures. Primary park activities include historic tours, swimming, snorkeling, scuba diving, picnicking, fishing, and birding.

(above) The lighthouse on Loggerhead Key marks the harbor entrance.

(left) Historic Fort Jefferson is likely to be inundated by rising sea levels attributable to climate change.

Everglades National Park

Florida | nps.gov/ever

In her exceptional book *The Everglades: River of Grass*, Marjory Stoneman Douglas wrote: "There are no other Everglades in the world. They are, they have always been, one of the unique regions of the earth, remote, never wholly known. Nothing anywhere is like them." At more than 1.5 million acres, the park that Douglas did so much to help preserve is the third-largest national park in the continental United States, and most of the park is the grand wilderness named in her honor. Douglas was right: Everglades National Park is truly unique, so much so that it's also a World Heritage Site, an area considered to be globally important.

This national park is significant for at least three reasons. First, there's the natural history of the area, the vastness that's a blend of the tropical and the temperate, part Caribbean and part North American. This mix of environments has led to remarkable biological diversity. Second, this was the first national park established to honor biological diversity; prior to establishment of the Everglades in 1947, national parks were designed to protect scenic beauty, not necessarily ecological integrity. Third, despite establishment of the national park, modernity has conspired to threaten the Everglades through water diversion, agricultural development, urban growth, climate change, and other issues. The result has been what may be the grandest environmental restoration effort in American history. But is it enough to save the Everglades?

Occupying much of the southern tip of Florida, the park represents only about one-fifth of the original Everglades ecosystem, which continues north to the vast region of Florida that is drained by the Kissimmee River and Lake Okeechobee. The underlying geology of the park is primarily limestone, formed by a shallow marine environment that deposited calcium carbonate in the form of sand, seashells, and coral. This almost uniformly flat limestone is covered in freshwater much of the year and is the primary aquifer for this extensive region of Florida.

The park is surprisingly diverse, comprising several types of ecosystems. In addition to its extensive network of freshwater marshes that carry water south (slowly, about 100 feet per day), extensive

(above) Much of the Everglades is composed of saw-grass prairies that seem to extend forever.

(opposite) A great blue heron hunts in the Everglades' vast wetlands.

(above) More than 350 species of birds have been documented in the park.

(above right) The Anhinga Trail, along a system of boardwalks, is the most popular walk in the park.

marine and estuarine areas surround much of the park; large complexes of mangrove forests line much of the coast. These ecosystems provide habitat for a great variety of wildlife, an impressive 40 species of mammals, more than 50 species of reptiles, more than 350 species of birds, and nearly 300 species of salt- and freshwater fish. The park's glamour species include black bears, alligators, American crocodiles, manatees, the critically endangered Florida panther, four species of sea turtles, and a great variety of wading and song birds. Alligators are a freshwater species readily seen throughout the park; American crocodiles are marine animals with a more restricted range.

Humans occupied the Everglades region as early as 10,000 perhaps even 20,000 years ago, but most of these Native Americans lived primarily in coastal areas. The NPS estimates that there were as many as 20,000 indigenous people in the Everglades region when the Spanish encountered them in the late sixteenth century. These native people formed the Seminole nation in the early nineteenth century and were forcibly relocated to Indian Territories west of the Mississippi. A few hundred avoided resettlement by living in what is today Big Cypress National Preserve, just north of the Everglades. Some Seminoles and members of the related Miccosukee Tribe live in and around the modern-day park and are consulted in national park management.

Modern settlement of South Florida began in earnest in the nineteenth century, with initial efforts focusing on draining the land by diverting water into canals leading out to the sea. More

Shark Valley offers a long walk through vast wetlands with good opportunities to see alligators, birds, and turtles.

recently, an extensive system of water-control structures—canals, levees, gates, spillways, and pumping stations—has been created to move much of this water to South Florida's rapidly growing cities. Development has had the unfortunate consequence of depriving what is now the national park of the water that is vital to the survival of its specialized and water-dependent plants and animals and the complex interactions among them. Concern over the deteriorating condition of the Everglades emerged in the early twentieth century and escalated over the next few decades, led by citizen environmental groups. In 1930 Congress established Everglades National Park, but the park was not dedicated until 1947. Unfortunately, that has not stopped the diversion of water from the park, which has become an ecological crisis.

In response, Congress passed the Water Resources Development Act in 2000, authorizing $7.8 billion for a twenty-five-year Everglades restoration project, but much of the promised funding has not materialized. Ironically, this leaves the Everglades—the first national park to be established primarily for ecological preservation—one of the most threatened national parks in the nation, perhaps the world.

Other increasingly urgent threats to the park include climate change (in the form of more frequent and violent hurricanes and rising sea levels that may result in massive saltwater intrusion into the park's vast freshwater ecosystems) and introduction of exotic, nonnative plants and animals.

The park's gumbo-limbo trees are often called "tourist trees" by locals because their red and peeling bark is similar to the skin of visitors who spend too much time in the South Florida sun.

For example, release of unwanted pet Burmese pythons into the Everglades has resulted in an estimated population of tens of thousands of these aggressive animals.

Walking Everglades

Driving the park's roads is just an introduction to its rich biology and aesthetic beauty. Though the trail system isn't extensive, take the opportunity to experience and appreciate the park in the more intimate way that only walking can offer. If that's not intimate enough, you can always go "slough slogging." Read on . . .

Anhinga Trail

If there's a signature walk in the Everglades, it's got to be the Anhinga Trail. Like a number of the park's trails, it's short—less than 1 mile—and it's all on a paved berm and elevated boardwalk over the saw-grass marsh of Taylor Slough. The boardwalk keeps feet dry and also makes for a great extended viewing platform. Anhingas are large fish-eating birds common in much of the park; here they perch on the railings of the boardwalk and nest in adjacent trees from January through early summer, making themselves readily visible. Other notable birds in the area include double-crested cormorants, roseate spoonbills, black vultures, wood storks, herons, egrets, and moorhens. American alligators are also common in the area and are most easily seen in winter and spring, when fish tend to congregate in remaining wet areas. Look closely in the water for turtles and water snakes. Look as well for several kinds of epiphytes, or air plants—ferns, orchids, and bromeliads—that grow in the surrounding trees. This and other trails served by boardwalks are fully wheelchair accessible.

Pa-hay-okee Overlook Trail

Just off the park's main road and served by a short elevated trail, this area offers one of the starkest but most striking views in the park. The name of the overlook is derived from the Seminole language and means "grassy waters." Saw-grass prairies that seem to extend forever, just like the one you see before you, make up much of the Everglades region. These prairies are dynamic ecosystems—rivers, really—with water that may be only a few inches deep but miles wide; they flow at an almost imperceptible rate. Punctuated with hammocks of hardwood trees, the vast prairie to the north is the southern edge of the massive Shark River Slough, a complex of prairies that flow south and west through the park, carrying water from Lake Okeechobee and Big Cypress Swamp to the Gulf of Mexico. As this freshwater meets the Gulf, it creates a brackish water estuary that supports an expanse of mangroves that protect the shoreline from erosion and serve as a nursery for a host of marine organisms.

Look for several kinds of epiphytes, or air plants, in the park—ferns, orchids, and bromeliads that grow in trees.

Mahogany Hammock Trail

This is another of the park's short, elevated boardwalks just off the park's main road. A hammock is formed when the park's underlying limestone is slightly higher than the surrounding area, allowing soil to accumulate and ultimately offering habitat for trees. This hammock features beautiful West Indian mahogany and a diversity of other plants. Both the large prairie and clearly defined moat of deeper water help protect the hammock from periodic lightning-caused fires. Look carefully for warblers and other songbirds during spring and fall migrations, barred owls, a variety of snakes, ferns, bromeliads, and orchids. But watch out for poison ivy, which tends to drape from trees.

Shark Valley Trail

Shark Valley is located in the northern portion of the park, directly off Tamiami Trail (US 41), and is one of the main attractions of the park. The 15-mile paved elongated loop starts at the visitor center just beyond the park entrance. There are several options for seeing this area, including 2-hour tram tours narrated by park rangers and others; you can also rent a bike. If this is too much riding and not enough walking, you can walk along the route for as long as you wish. (Be careful not to walk too far—the sun is hot, and some visitors become dehydrated.) On a walk of just a mile or two, you're likely to see alligators, turtles, and lots of birds, some of them up close and personal!

Slough Slogging

The park offers a very unusual form of hiking called "slough slogging." As the name suggests, this involves walking through the park's marshes and cypress domes, sometimes up to your knees (or beyond). No high-tech equipment is needed, just long pants, socks, and a pair of (preferably old) running shoes. The NPS regularly conducts ranger-guided slough slogs, and this is the recommended way to learn how and where to do it.

Alligators are common in the park and are most often seen in winter and spring, when fish tend to congregate in the remaining wet areas.

Logistics

The first consideration for walking in Everglades National Park is the weather. There are only two seasons: wet and dry. The former lasts from May through November, the latter from December through April. Avoid the wet season—it's often rainy, hot, and humid. Periodic hurricanes also occur during that time. Perhaps worst of all, swarms of mosquitoes can make life miserable. Enough said?

The park has four visitor centers, the largest of which is the Ernest F. Coe, just inside the east park entrance. The only two areas in the park that support hiking are the east entrance (near the twin towns of Homestead and Florida City) and the north entrance (the Shark Valley area). Both areas are about an hour to an hour-and-a-half drive from Miami. Homestead/Florida City has a range of accommodations and other visitor services. The park includes two large campgrounds on the main park road—one near the Earnest F. Coe Visitor Center, the other at the end of the road at Flamingo.

The Last Word

While hiking is somewhat limited at Everglades National Park because there is relatively little upland area, several trails and short boardwalks offer great opportunities to see wildlife in their natural habitat. There are several other parks and preserves adjacent to or near the national park; all of them offer hiking trails. And don't forget about slough slogging!

Gates of the Arctic National Park and Preserve

Alaska | nps.gov/gaar

Nearly 8.5-million-acre Gates of the Arctic is the second-largest national park in the United States, protecting portions of the iconic Brooks Mountain Range in northern Alaska. Initially designated as a national monument in 1978, it was redesignated a national park and preserve under the provisions of the 1980 Alaska National Interest Lands Conservation Act. Entirely above the Arctic Circle, this northernmost US national park is a vast landscape that includes tall mountains, wild rivers, iconic wildlife, and an expansive wilderness. But it includes no roads or trails and is the least visited US national park. Travel on foot can be exhilarating but challenging due to rough terrain, river crossings, and grizzly bears. Floating the park's wild rivers is a common way to travel through the area.

(above) These stones were probably used by the original inhabitants of this area as either a cairn or a hunting blind.

(left) Two grizzly bears walk along the Kobuk River in an early-fall snow.

Gateway Arch National Park

Missouri | nps.gov/jeff

This historically important national park in St. Louis, Missouri, near the starting point of the Lewis and Clark Expedition, celebrates the area's role in the westward expansion of the nation in the early nineteenth century. Other important themes include the vital role of President Thomas Jefferson in opening the West, the debate over slavery that was raised in the trial of Dred Scott in the area's Old Courthouse, and the design and construction of the park's iconic arch. The park includes the Museum at the Gateway Arch. Originally established as the Jefferson National Expansion Memorial in 1935, the park was elevated to national park status in 2018. Most visitors tour the park's historic attractions and stroll the grounds of this 91-acre park located on the Mississippi River.

(above) The iconic Gateway Arch celebrates western expansion of the United States.

(right) Visitors are invited to stroll the grounds of Gateway Arch National Park.

Glacier Bay National Park and Preserve

Alaska | nps.gov/glba

Glacier Bay National Park and Preserve in southeast Alaska is a highlight of the state's famed Inside Passage and includes 3.3 million acres of mountains, forests, glaciers, and waterways. Much of the area was proclaimed a national monument in 1925 under the provisions of the 1906 Antiquities Act and was expanded and established as a national park and preserve in 1980 under the Alaska National Interest Lands Conservation Act. The park is also part of a binational UNESCO World Heritage Site. Most visitors see the park from the deck of a cruise ship and return home with fond memories of marine mammals and dramatic tidewater glaciers calving into the bay. The more adventurous way to see the park is by kayaking in Glacier Bay, rafting the Alsek River, and hiking the large trailless wilderness, but these all require considerable experience and expertise. Bartlett Cove, the only developed area in the park, offers a lodge and a few short trails.

(top) The mighty Alsek River flows through Glacier Bay and out to the sea.

(bottom) A tidewater glacier calves into Glacier Bay.

(left) Most visitors to Glacier Bay National Park and Preserve see the area from the deck of a cruise ship; here, the ship approaches Margerie Glacier.

Glacier National Park

Montana | nps.gov/glac

In the late 1800s conservationist George Bird Grinnell, cofounder of the Audubon Society, traveled to northern Montana to an area he would later christen the "Crown of the Continent." Here were expansive old-growth forests, the high peaks of the Continental Divide, an estimated 150 active glaciers, a series of turquoise lakes, and a diverse collection of native wildlife that included the iconic grizzly bear. Over the next two decades, he worked to protect this area as a national park, succeeding in 1910 when more than 1 million acres were designated as Glacier National Park, America's tenth national park. The park abuts Waterton Lakes National Park in Alberta, Canada, and in 1932 the parks joined to form the world's first International Peace Park. Glacier also received World Heritage Site status in 1995. Appointed the first director of the NPS in 1916, Stephen Mather believed that the best way to protect the national parks was to promote their accessibility, so he directed that a road be built to show off the park. The resulting 50-mile Going-to-the-Sun Road traverses the heart of the park, following the shores of Lake McDonald and Saint Mary Lake (the park's two largest) and up and over dramatic Logan Pass. This is one of the world's most scenic drives; the road also provides access to some of the park's most magnificent trails.

The geology of Glacier is complex. Most of the rocks are sedimentary, deposited in shallow seas over a very long period of time. However, this land is part of the great Rocky Mountains, which have been uplifted, folded, and faulted, and now the initial flat layers of stone have been substantially rearranged. The park's namesake glaciers have also been an obvious geologic force. The park was heavily affected by the continent's last ice age, and these effects include the remaining glaciers, the wide U-shaped valleys they carved, the lakes that formed in these wide valleys, the cirques (bowl-shaped areas near the tops of mountains where glaciers have plucked away portions of the mountain), tarns (bodies of water left by melting glaciers), moraines (rocks and other materials carried by glaciers and deposited on their edges and terminus), and arêtes (sharp-edged ridges where glaciers have eroded both sides of a mountain) that characterize many of the taller peaks. The park is a poster child for the effects of climate change; only 25 glaciers remain of the estimated 150 when the park was established in the early 1900s. Scientists predict that the last of the park's glaciers will disappear by 2030.

Nearly all the flora and fauna that existed in the park when it was established can still be found here. The park's varied elevations and aspects offer a wide variety of habitats, including dry plains,

(above) Virginia Falls is one of many striking waterfalls in Glacier National Park.

(opposite) The park's broad, U-shaped valleys are characteristic of the effects of glaciers on the landscape.

The park is a poster child for climate change: It's estimated that the last of the park's namesake glaciers will melt by 2030.

rivers and lakes, extensive subalpine forests, and alpine tundra. The result is more than 1,000 species of plants, including wildflowers that bloom from spring through summer. Distinctive species include bear grass and glacier lilies. Iconic wildlife include grizzly and black bears, mountain goats, bighorn sheep, moose, elk, mule and white-tailed deer, bobcats, coyotes, mountain lions, wolverines, and lynx. Nearly 300 species of birds have been recorded.

Though Crown of the Continent is the name bestowed on Glacier by conservationist George Bird Grinnell, the Blackfeet Indians called it "Backbone of the World." But before the Blackfeet, the region offered shelter and hunting grounds to many other Native American tribes, including Flathead, Kootenai, Shoshone, and Cheyenne. The Blackfeet sold 800,000 acres of land to the US government with the provision that they would retain subsistence rights, but these provisions were invalidated once the national park was established. Today the Blackfeet maintain a reservation on the eastern side of the park; the Flathead Indian Reservation is south and west of the park. The 1800s witnessed attempts at economic development of the area, including fur trapping and prospecting, but none were very successful until the Great Northern Railway completed track near the park in 1891 and ultimately built a series of hotels and chalets to attract and house visitors. Tourism has been the business of the park ever since.

Walking Glacier

Glacier is clearly one of the crown jewels of the National Park System, and its more than 700 miles of trails offer convincing evidence. The trails are as diverse as the park, accessing mountains, glaciers, lakes, forests, meadows, and wildlife. The trailheads found all along Going-to-the-Sun Road and the Many Glacier region provide especially rich hiking. The park also includes 110 miles of the Continental Divide National Scenic Trail. While the park has roads, trails, campgrounds, and other visitor facilities and services, the vast majority (93 percent) is wilderness, ensuring opportunities to hike, embrace nature, and find solitude.

Saint Mary and Virginia Falls Trail

Glacier is known for many things, including waterfalls, and this relatively short and easy trail to these two gems is a bargain. The trailhead is on the Going-to-the Sun Road at the east end of expansive Saint Mary Lake; it's 1.2 miles (one-way) to Saint Mary Falls and about a half mile farther to higher Virginia Falls. Both are impressive and popular. You'll notice that part of the trail runs through the remains of a recent wildfire. Try to see the stark beauty of this place and appreciate the fact that periodic wildfires are a natural part of this ecosystem, though a long history of forest fire prevention and the cascading effects of climate change are making these fires more intense.

Avalanche Lake Trail

This is another of Glacier's trails that offers a lot for a little; although the trail is 6.2 miles (round-trip), the walking is pretty easy and very pleasant. The trailhead is off the Going-to-the-Sun Road, just a few miles north of Lake McDonald on the west side of the park. This trailhead is also the trailhead for the Trail of the Cedars, a short (0.7-mile round-trip) fully accessible nature trail that passes through large and impressive groves of old-growth red cedar and western hemlock, more closely associated with the rainforests of the Pacific Northwest. Avalanche Creek and Sperry Glacier provide the necessary moisture to support this old-growth forest. You must walk a portion of the Trail of Cedars to reach the Avalanche Lake Trail; we suggest taking the east side of the Trail of Cedars loop, as it's more scenic. The Avalanche Lake Trail begins just after the narrow, fluted gorge created by the rushing water of Avalanche Creek. Avalanche Lake, the prize of this hike, is a couple of miles from the gorge and is rimmed on three sides by steep rock walls that rise hundreds of feet. A series of long and impressive cascades make their way down the face of these cliffs. Follow the trail along the west side of the lake until you reach its terminus. The creek and lake are named for the massive avalanches that have occurred here over the centuries. Like many of Glacier's more popular trails, trailhead parking doesn't begin to meet peak summer demand; get here early in the day.

(top) To reach lovely Avalanche Lake, hikers first walk through groves of centuries-old red cedar and western hemlock.

(bottom) The park's iconic bear grass and other wildflowers abound in the park; note Grinnell Glacier in the background.

(top) Bighorn sheep inhabit the park along with grizzly and black bears, mountain goats, moose, elk, mountain lions, mule and white-tailed deer, and bobcats.

(bottom) Glacier National Park joined with adjacent Waterton Lakes National Park (Canada) to form the first International Peace Park.

Grinnell Glacier Trail

Grinnell Glacier is one of many in the park that are shrinking before our eyes. Surely one of the most dramatic glaciers in the park, it's also one of the few that can be approached on a maintained trail. The trail leads out of the Many Glacier area and is a moderately strenuous trip of 11 miles (round-trip) with about 1,600 feet of elevation gain. The trail is varied over its course, first following the shores of Swiftcurrent Lake and Lake Josephine, then rising at times, leveling off in delightful alpine meadows, and offering striking views, including turquoise Grinnell Lake, a massive headwall, and several striking cascades. The last climb is up and over the large terminal moraine left by Grinnell Glacier and on to the shores of alluring Upper Grinnell Lake. Here you'll have close-up views of the main glacier with its characteristic fissures and ice caves, another small glacier (The Salamander) that used to be connected to Grinnell, and Gem Icefield, a former glacier that has been reduced by climate change. Don't be tempted to climb or walk on any glacier—they can be especially dangerous. We were fortunate to see bighorn sheep at Upper Grinnell Lake and a grizzly bear along the trail. It's possible to shorten this hike by a few miles by taking a tour boat across Swiftcurrent Lake and then on to the upper end of Lake Josephine (and return that way as well), but you'll have to check with the concessionaire about their schedules and pricing.

Highline Trail / Garden Wall

The Highline Trail is a long-distance, multiday route through the northern part of the park; the Garden Wall is the most iconic section of the trail and one of the most popular hikes in the park. Though this section is nearly 12 miles one way (you can arrange a shuttle so you don't have to hike the trail in both directions), it's mostly downhill (from east to west) on a well-maintained trail. Most hikers consider it a long day hike, though it could be a two-day backpack trip (requiring a permit). The trail begins in the geographic middle of the park at Logan Pass, where there is a large parking area and visitor center. Much of the trail was carved from the landform known as the Garden Wall, a giant arête that is the Continental Divide; prepare yourself for unparalleled views and a little bit of exposure to boot. (The NPS has installed a hand cable for security in the short ledge-like portion of the trail.) Other sections of the trail include high alpine meadows, showy wildflowers (including the park's iconic bear grass), krummholz (high-elevation forest severely stunned by cold temperatures and wind), and opportunities to see lots of wildlife, including mountain goats, bighorn sheep, marmots, pika, even the occasional grizzly.

At mile 7.6 you reach the Granite Park Chalet, one of a series of backcountry huts constructed by the Great Northern Railroad in the early days of the park; nearly all are now gone. At the chalet you leave the Highline Trail and walk generally west to meet The Loop, the grand switchback on the Going-to-the-Sun Road. This is the key to making this trail an 11.6-mile point-to-point hike rather than a 23.2-mile out-and-back. If you have access to two vehicles, leave one at the parking lot at The

Loop and drive the other one to Logan Pass (about 8 miles) to start your hike. Another option is to park your car at Logan Pass, hike to The Loop and snag a ride back to Logan Pass on the park's free shuttle bus. A third option is to leave your vehicle at The Loop, get a ride to Logan Pass on the shuttle bus, and start your hike. But be advised that the parking lots at both Logan Pass and The Loop can't accommodate peak demand, so you must park your car early (say, by 7 a.m.). Still another option is to park at Logan Pass, walk a few miles of the trail (which many people consider the most dramatic), and then return to Logan Pass. That's a lot of logistics to consider, but you'll be glad you hiked what is one of the grandest trails in the National Park System. (Of course you could always hike the full Highline Trail, about a three-day backpacking trip.)

Logistics

Glacier has an extensive infrastructure to support park visitors. Three visitor centers (at the main east and west park entrances and at Logan Pass) provide hikers with up-to-date, on-the-ground advice about trail conditions and other issues; ask questions and follow the advice of park staff. The park includes thirteen campgrounds and six hotels/lodges, including Glacier Park Lodge, Many Glacier Hotel, and Lake McDonald Lodge, all of them historic. The Great Northern Railway constructed a series of backcountry huts in the early days of the park, but only one, Granite Park Chalet, is still operating. (As of this writing, Sperry Chalet is being rebuilt after a recent wildfire.) While the park is open year-round, long winters and deep snow limit the primary visitor season to mid-June through mid-September. To help address traffic congestion and air pollution on the Going-to-the-Sun Road, a free shuttle bus plies the road during this period. (As of this date, the status of this shuttle bus system is uncertain.) American visitors wanting to travel to adjacent Waterton Lakes National Park by car, tour bus, boat, or on foot will need a passport, passport card, or enhanced driver's license (currently issued by only a few states and provinces). The presence of grizzly bears in the park requires special precautions to protect both hikers and bears; please see the park newspaper and visitor center displays for information on this and other issues.

The Last Word

Glacier is an achingly beautiful and ecologically significant national park that makes it a favorite of many national park–goers (including us). But it's a sad commentary that the park is changing before our very eyes—in a human time scale—due to advancing climate change. What an irony that the park is losing its namesake feature—its glaciers—projected to melt away within a few decades. This means we should all do what we can to address this issue, including reducing our carbon emissions. We should also hike the park in an effort to appreciate and bear witness to all that is good about this place, the Crown of the Continent and the Backbone of the World.

Ice-out at Upper Grinnell Lake typically doesn't occur until mid-July.

Grand Canyon National Park

Arizona | nps.gov/grca

Grand Canyon National Park is clearly one of the crown jewels of the National Park System. This immense canyon—277 serpentine miles long, as much as 18 miles wide, and more than a mile deep—is not only a national park but also a World Heritage Site, signifying its international importance. The canyon is an open book of geologic history that dates back nearly 2 billion years; it also includes a rich cultural history and a staggering suite of recreational opportunities. Well over 1.2 million acres in northern Arizona, the park is surrounded by other public lands and Indian reservations, making it seem even larger. Colorado River explorer Major John Wesley Powell wrote that the Grand Canyon is the "most sublime spectacle on earth," and President Theodore Roosevelt added that it is "the one great sight which every American should see." Indeed, calling it the "Grand" Canyon seems almost an understatement.

Of course the park's primary attraction is its geology. The striking upper portion of the canyon readily visible from the rims is a series of sandstone, limestone, and shale layers that were deposited millions of years ago, remnants of ancient seas, deserts, sand dunes, and swamps. Near the bottom of the canyon, in its inner gorge, lie the very oldest rocks, 1.8 billion years old. The canyon was created by a gradual uplifting of the vast Colorado Plateau and the erosive force of the Colorado River and its ancestral rivers, as well as water running off the rims of the canyon, wind, and the freeze-thaw cycle.

The mighty Colorado River drains much of the southwest quadrant of the United States and is a vital source of water in this arid land. It rises in the Rocky Mountains and flows 1,450 miles before emptying into the Gulf of California. *Colorado* is Spanish for "red river" and references the natural color of the river as a result of the sediment that's washed into it from the surrounding lands. However, the section of the river that flows through Grand Canyon is now often clear as a result of the Glen Canyon Dam, constructed just upstream in the 1960s. The dam slows the flow of the river, causing most of the sediment to be deposited at the bottom of the reservoir; when water is released through the dam, it comes from near the bottom of 600-foot-deep Lake Powell and is clear and cold. Consequently, the riparian habitat of the river, including many species of plants and animals, has been greatly altered. Recently, the dam has been operated in a way to more closely mimic the natural flow of the river.

(top) Hiking the vast Tonto Plateau offers well-deserved solitude.

(bottom) President Theodore Roosevelt said the Grand Canyon is "the one great sight which every American should see."

(opposite) The Bright Angel Trail is one of the most storied and iconic trails in all the US national parks.

The 14-mile Rim Trail offers ever-changing perspectives of the Grand Canyon.

The canyon represents a wide range of elevations, from the Colorado River at roughly 2,000 feet to the 7,000-foot South Rim and 8,000-foot North Rim. Consequently, flora and fauna are highly diverse. South Rim forests are primarily pinyon pine and Utah juniper, with some Gambel oak and ponderosa pine; the North Rim features Engelmann spruce, Douglas and white fir, ponderosa pine, and quaking aspen. The inner canyon is highly arid, showcasing plants such as sagebrush, creosote bush, scrub oak, and assorted cacti. Prominent mammals in the park include elk, mule deer, mountain lions, bighorn sheep, coyotes, and ringtails. Commonly seen birds include nuthatches, juncos, jays, chickadees, flickers, and ravens (amuse yourself by watching the ravens play in the air currents directly above the canyon rim). The endangered California condor has been reintroduced to this region and is often seen in the park.

Like many western national parks, Grand Canyon has a colorful history. This area of the Southwest has been home to a number of Native American tribes for 10,000 years. The first European visitors were the Spanish in the 1540s, but they found little of interest, only an overwhelming barrier to transportation. Later, prospectors explored the canyon for minerals, generally without great success. In 1869 John Wesley Powell, a one-armed Civil War veteran and scientist, and his small party were the first people known to have floated the Colorado River through Grand Canyon. This is a great American adventure story, since the river was rumored to have huge waterfalls and other hazards. Powell and his men endured significant danger and hardship on their long voyage, but they were successful in mapping this area and assessing the availability of water and the limits this would place on economic development of the region. In the late nineteenth and early twentieth centuries, the Santa Fe Railroad began developing the canyon for tourism, building a spur line to the South Rim and constructing the elegant El Tovar Hotel. Congress established Grand Canyon National Park in 1919.

Walking Grand Canyon

Grand Canyon offers a spectrum of hiking opportunities, both along the rims and down into the canyon. Some of these hikes can be challenging, even dangerous to uninformed visitors; however, proper preparation, including an informed choice of trails, can make these hikes safe and enjoyable. We recommend several trails that span the range of hiking opportunities.

Grand Canyon hikers enjoy walking through 1.8 billion years of geologic history.

Grand Canyon Rim Trail

The Grand Canyon Rim Trail is underappreciated. Most visitors to Grand Canyon's South Rim (where the majority of visitor facilities and services are located) walk out to a few overlooks of the canyon and take a brief stroll through Grand Canyon Village. Technically, they experience the Rim Trail, but they're missing a very special opportunity. Walking the 14-mile Rim Trail can be done in a day, but that's not what we suggest. Linger and soak in what you're seeing. Take two or more days to walk the Rim Trail and you'll be filled with a deeper appreciation of the wonder that's Grand Canyon. The Rim Trail lies directly on the South Rim of the canyon and extends from Yaki Point (the trailhead for the South Kaibab Trail) in the east to Hermit's Rest in the west. It's paved for much of its length and is gently graded, with some sections wheelchair accessible; the Rim Trail can offer remarkable peace and quiet, even moments of solitude. The park's extensive shuttle bus system serves the trail, allowing you to walk as long and as far as you want and then return to your origin by bus (or vice versa).

Bright Angel Trail

The Bright Angel Trail is one of the most storied trails in all the national parks and is one of the two primary trails into the canyon. The trail connects the South Rim to the Colorado River over 10 miles of dramatic scenery, 1 mile of descent, and 1.8 billion years of geologic history; it's a breathtaking hike by any definition. Given the natural and well-founded tendency to want to hike into the

At the bottom of the canyon is the "inner gorge"; here lie the oldest rocks, dated to more than 1.8 billion years.

canyon—and the rewards of the very different perspective it offers—we recommend walking the Bright Angel Trail, but only with the proviso that you're appropriately thoughtful about how far you wish to walk. Hiking to the river and back on the Bright Angel Trail is a substantial undertaking (this is a 20-mile hike that includes 5,000 feet of elevation loss and gain) and requires planning and preparation; the trailhead is located in Grand Canyon Village. The NPS strongly discourages visitors from attempting this hike in a single day. The canyon can be very hot—well over 100°F at the bottom—and drinking water is available at only a few places along the trail. The hike can be done more safely and enjoyably in two or more days with overnights at Indian Garden Campground, Bright Angel Campground, and/or Phantom Ranch (a rustic lodge and restaurant at the bottom of the canyon). We encourage you to consider hiking to other destinations along the trail and then returning to the trailhead on the South Rim; popular sites include Mile-and-a-Half Resthouse (3 miles round-trip), Indian Garden (9.6 miles round-trip), and Plateau Point (12 miles round-trip). All of these destinations will give you the genuine experience of being *in* the canyon.

South Kaibab Trail

The 7-mile South Kaibab Trail is the other primary route from the South Rim to the Colorado River and starts at Yaki Point, accessible by shuttle bus. *Kaibab* is Paiute, meaning "mountain lying down," their term for the Grand Canyon. Much of the trail follows a natural ridgeline in the canyon, resulting in spectacular panoramic views. At 14.5 miles to the river and back, this is a shorter route

than the Bright Angel Trail, but it's also steeper and offers no drinking water. The NPS strongly discourages visitors from attempting this hike in a single day. The hike can be done more safely and enjoyably in two or more days, but there are only two reasonably accessible accommodations, Bright Angel Campground and Phantom Ranch, both at the bottom of the canyon. As with the Bright Angel Trail, we encourage you to consider hiking to other destinations along the trail and then returning to the trailhead on the South Rim; popular sites include Cedar Point (3 miles round-trip) and the Tip Off (9 miles round-trip). Once again, both destinations will give you the genuine experience of being *in* the canyon, something the vast majority of Grand Canyon visitors don't have.

Grand Canyon is not only a national park but a World Heritage Site, a reflection of its global importance.

Colorado River via the South Kaibab and Bright Angel Trails

Okay, you've decided to hike to the Colorado River, starting and ending at the South Rim. If you've given this trek appropriate consideration and prepared yourself, congratulations: In our view, this is one of the world's great hikes. The classic route to the river and back is down the South Kaibab Trail (roughly 7 miles and relatively steep) and up the Bright Angel Trail (about 10 miles, with a gentler grade, a campground along the way, and occasional drinking water). Both trails are well maintained, and wayfinding is easy. Spending at least one night at the bottom of the canyon will make for a safer and more enjoyable adventure.

Grand Canyon Rim-to-Rim

Of all the fine hikes in the National Park System, this is one of the most classic: a more than 21-mile cross section of the canyon's nearly 1.8 billion years of geologic history, including crossing the Colorado River and hiking two of the canyon's most fabled trails. Since the North Rim is 1,000 feet higher than the South Rim, most hikers walk from north to south to save some elevation gain. The North Kaibab Trail drops off the 8,000-foot North Rim at Bright Angel Point and follows the natural fault line of Bright Angel Creek, an ancient Native American route through the canyon, taking just over 14 miles to reach the Colorado River. Cottonwood Campground is 6.8 miles from the North Kaibab Trailhead and offers an overnight option. As the trail approaches the Colorado River, you find Bright Angel Campground (7.2 miles from Cottonwood Campground) and Phantom Ranch,

Colorado River explorer John Wesley Powell wrote that the river is the "most sublime spectacle on earth"; today thousands raft the river and hike many of its otherworldly side canyons.

both located on a large delta formed where Bright Angel Creek flows into the Colorado River. You can cross the Colorado River on one of two bridges in this area; these are the only bridges along the nearly 300 miles of the river in the park. Once you've crossed the river, you can choose between the Bright Angel Trail and the South Kaibab Trail. Regardless of your choice, you can experience an overwhelming sense of satisfaction by completing one of the world's most iconic hikes. This hike includes the logistical challenge of getting to the North Rim to start your hike; see the park's website for commercial shuttle services, or inquire at the park's visitor centers by phone or e-mail. (See Part 3 of this book for how to contact the NPS by e-mail.)

Logistics

As always, visits to the national parks should start with a stop at one of the NPS visitor centers; the primary visitor center at Grand Canyon is near the entrance to Grand Canyon Village. Here, displays and rangers will help you plan your visit to the park, provide local weather and trail conditions, and advise you about hiking opportunities and other ways to enjoy and appreciate the park. You'll be warned that hikes into the canyon are often referred to as "mountain climbing in reverse"—you descend first and then must ascend the often steep trails. Don't underestimate this challenge. The South Rim of the park is open year-round, but winters can be cold and snowy and summers sometimes hot. The inner canyon can be well over 100°F in summer, and the NPS cautions against hiking below the rim then. Visit the park in the off-season, if possible—spring is especially nice when wildflowers are in bloom. The North Rim is closed in winter. The park includes a number of free shuttle bus routes; using these can expand your hiking options and relieve you of the problem of trying to find a parking spot.

Grand Canyon offers a great range of lodging options. On the South Rim you'll find the historic El Tovar Hotel and Bright Angel Lodge as well as several motels. The South Rim also has a large campground at Grand Canyon Village and another at Desert View, east of the village. A few miles south of Grand Canyon Village, just outside the park entrance, the gateway town of Tusayan offers campgrounds and a range of contemporary motels. On the North Rim is the historic Grand Canyon Lodge, built by the Union Pacific Railroad; there's also a campground.

The Last Word

As one of the icons of the National Park System, Grand Canyon demands the respect that only walking can offer. There are many ways to walk the park, including pleasant strolls along the rim and deep dives into the park's interior. Hiking the park can be challenging, especially the routes down to the river and back, but hiking offers a lifetime of rewards as you reflect on such epic journeys. However, you must be prepare yourself physically and plan your trip carefully.

Grand Teton National Park

Wyoming | nps.gov/grte

The Tetons are mountains as they should be, a postcard of the best of Western mountain scenery; many mountains in the West are higher, but none are more dramatic. These mountains rise 7,000 feet directly out of the surrounding plains, with no foothills to get in the way, and the ridgelines are craggy and caked with snow and even the occasional glacier. Grand Teton National Park includes the major peaks of the 40-mile-long Teton Range along with much of Jackson Hole, the valley that frames the scene and adds to the park's ecological integrity. The Snake River meanders through the plains and accents the view. This park of more than 300,000 acres lies only a few miles south of Yellowstone, with the John D. Rockefeller Jr. Memorial Parkway connecting the two. This complex of some of the very finest components of the National Park System is a treasure.

The Tetons are a relatively young range of mountains, formed 6 to 10 million years ago (and still rising!). However, the geology of the park is complex, combining many of the forces that have shaped much of the earth, including plate tectonics, volcanism, deposition, erosion, and glaciation. Geologists classify the Tetons as a fault-block mountain range; two enormous blocks of the Earth's crust shifted along a fault line, one tilting down and the other lifting up, with the former creating the valley of Jackson Hole and the latter the Teton Range. Glaciation formed many of the iconic characteristics of the park and the surrounding landscape, including its U-shaped valleys, moraines that have formed many of the park's lakes (Jackson is the largest at 15 miles long and 8 miles wide), and cirques found on many of the mountains. About a dozen small glaciers remain in the mountains, all of them formed within the last 700 years or so; all are melting relatively rapidly. The park's highest peak is Grand Teton at 13,776 feet, and there are another nine peaks above 12,000 feet. Ranging from 6 to 13 miles wide, Jackson Hole is a 55-mile-long elevated valley at the base of the mountains; it's relatively flat, although it includes a few isolated buttes and hills.

The park's elevation range is about 7,000 feet, giving rise to several types of habitats, including alpine forests and meadows, sagebrush flats, wetlands, and lakes/ponds/rivers. These habitats support a great diversity of plants, including forests of lodgepole pine, subalpine fir, Douglas fir, Engelmann spruce, limber pine, and whitebark pine, the latter an important source of seeds eaten by red squirrels and grizzly bears. Aspens and cottonwoods dot the lower elevations. A great diversity of flowering plants bloom from spring through summer. Iconic animals include black and grizzly bears, gray wolves, coyotes, river otters, mountain lions, moose, bison, pronghorn, bighorn sheep, and elk.

Grand Teton National Park includes the major peaks of the 40-mile-long Teton Range of the Rocky Mountains.

Thousands of elk migrate through the park in the spring and fall, moving between Yellowstone and the National Elk Refuge south of the Tetons. Birders have recorded more than 300 species in the park.

As in most western parks, Paleo-Indians used the region, in this case for as long as 11,000 years. Evidence suggests that they may have followed the migration of elk, spending summers in Jackson Hole and winters in lower valleys. Early European-American explorers in the first decade of the nineteenth century encountered Shoshone people. John Colter, a member of the Lewis and Clark Expedition, left the group on the expedition's return trip to trap furs in the Teton region, and he's thought to be the first non-native to see the Teton Range in 1807–08. French Canadian trappers christened the mountains *les trois tetons* ("the three breasts"), later shortened to Tetons. A federal government expedition to the Yellowstone region in the early 1870s sent a party to the Teton region, and homesteaders began to settle the area shortly after, though the growing season is exceptionally short. Agricultural use of the area eventually evolved to more successful ranching and tourism.

Interest in tourism and conservation of the area developed in the first few decades of the twentieth century, and Congress established Grand Teton National Park in 1929. However, it was a relatively small park (less than 100,000 acres), including only some of the mountains and lakes and none of the valley of Jackson Hole. Horace Albright, superintendent of Yellowstone National Park, met

(above left) Morning fog lifts over Phelps Lake in the park's Laurance S. Rockefeller Preserve.

(above) An early-morning view of Mount Moran is reflected in lovely String Lake.

(opposite) Rising directly from the surrounding plains, the Tetons are mountains as they should be.

(above) The three-quarter-mile trail around String Lake makes for a delightful morning walk.

(below) The iconic hike up Cascade Canyon follows beautiful Cascade Creek.

with John D. Rockefeller Jr. in Jackson Hole in the late 1920s, and the two hatched a plan to expand Grand Teton National Park in spite of local opposition. Rockefeller formed the Snake River Land Company and began buying ranches in the Jackson Hole area with the purpose of donating this land to the park. Local residents and politicians were not informed of the plan, and when it became public knowledge and local sentiment was not entirely supportive, the federal government refused to accept the land. In 1943 President Franklin Roosevelt created a new 221,000-acre Jackson Hole National Monument. After Rockefeller threatened to sell his accumulated 35,000 acres, the federal government finally accepted his donation. In 1950 the original national park, the national monument, and Rockefeller's land were combined to create the present-day Grand Teton National Park. The Rockefeller family donated its JY Ranch to the park in 2007; this area of the park is now called the Laurance S. Rockefeller Preserve and is a gem.

Walking Grand Teton

The park offers more than 230 miles of maintained trails that span the spectrum from short nature walks to epic multiday backpacking trips. Trails wander through the large valley of Jackson Hole, trace the shoreline of mountain lakes, and climb the park's canyons into the mountains. There are many good choices, but we recommend the following to get a good sense of the park's significance and diversity.

String Lake Trail

A chain of lakes grace the eastern foot the Tetons, and all offer exceptionally rewarding hikes. These lakes are often seen only by hikers because they're hidden from park roads by the terminal moraines that created them. String Lake is one of the smallest of these lakes and can easily be circumnavigated on a mostly level 3.4-mile loop trail. The trail starts on the east side of the lake; begin your hike early, taking full advantage of the morning sun and the startlingly clear reflections of the mountains on the lake's surface. Connecting trails lead to Jenny Lake to the south and Leigh Lake to the north if you want a longer hike.

Historic Districts

Of course it's the sublime beauty of the Grand Tetons and their surroundings that steals the show, but the park has an important cultural component as well (as do all national parks). Visitors are well-served by reserving adequate time to walk through the park's two historic districts and making a pilgrimage to the Murie Ranch. The Mormon Row Historic District honors the 1880s families who homesteaded the Grovont area; here are the remaining homes and proud barns (including the picturesque Moulton Barn) that marked this community. The Menor's Ferry Historic District focuses on the Snake River ferry developed and operated by 1894 homesteader William D. Menor. The

Much of the land in Jackson Hole was added to the national park in 1950.

site includes his whitewashed home, a general store, a blacksmith shop, and a few other buildings. The park also includes the Murie Ranch, home of prominent conservationists Olaus and Margaret "Mardy" Murie and Adolph and Louise Murie. The Muries hosted national meetings here that led to creation of the Wilderness Act in 1964.

Phelps Lake Loop Trail

As noted earlier in this chapter, the Rockefeller family was instrumental in creating Grand Teton, and the most recent gift was by Laurance S. Rockefeller, who donated the family's 3,100-acre retreat to the park. The area is formally called the Laurance S. Rockefeller Preserve but is commonly known as the "LSR." This unit of the park includes a network of trails that explore the area's sagebrush meadows, forests, wetlands, and lakes and creeks, including lovely Phelps Lake. The 7-mile walk around Phelps Lake is magical, especially in the early-morning light with its reflections of the Tetons. Reserve an hour or so to appreciate the area's wondrous Preserve Center.

Cascade Canyon Trail

The Tetons are marked by several distinctive canyons that penetrate the mountains from the east, and Cascade Canyon may be the most spectacular. The route to and through the canyon is marked by several attractions that make fine potential destinations and hikes of varying lengths. The hike

One of the "bear trees" in Laurance S. Rockefeller Preserve; scars on aspen trees are caused by bear claws.

begins near the Jenny Lake Visitor Center with two options: a delightful 2.4-mile walk along the shore of Jenny Lake to the mouth of Cascade Canyon or a short ferry ride across the lake. We opted for the latter and enjoyed the ride, saving our time and energy for the hike up the canyon. The first mile of the hike up Cascade Canyon offers two attractions, a short spur trail to Hidden Falls and Inspiration Point, an overlook of Jenny Lake and the park to the east. Then the trail begins in earnest, climbing noticeably for the first mile or so and continuing less steeply and with frequent views of Cascade Creek and the surrounding mountains. At mile 4.4 the trail splits; this marks a good turnaround point for many hikers, a memorable round-trip walk of 8.8 miles (assuming you take the ferry across Jenny Lake in both directions). However, an attractive option is to continue your hike by going northwest on the North Fork Cascade Canyon Trail up to 9,035-foot Lake Solitude. This will extend your round-trip hike to 14.2 miles and about 2,500 feet of elevation gain, but you'll be generously rewarded with a large cirque full of wildflowers and a dramatic lake with icebergs well into the summer. If you'd prefer a backpacking trip, designated campsites are available in the upper elevations of this route, but they require a permit.

Teton Crest Trail

One of the most intense ways of experiencing the park is the multiday Teton Crest Trail, featuring up-close and personal views of Grand, Middle, and South Teton Peaks; climbing through a series of high-mountain passes; walking the shores of Marion Lake, Lake Solitude, and Holly Lake; passing through subalpine meadows of wildflowers; and enjoying a well-earned measure of solitude. But this will require a three- to five-night backpacking trip (for which a permit is required). The trip generously begins with a ride up the Teton Village Tram to 10,450 feet, but be advised that there are still plenty of high passes left to climb as you make your way north among the crests of the mountains. You can complete your hike by exiting the mountains through Paintbrush Canyon for a one-way distance of about 35 miles, but this distance can be shortened by hiking down through any of the canyons that return to the valley floor. This backpacking trip is challenging, but it's one of the best hikes in the National Park System.

Logistics

Grand Teton offers a range of options for both camping and lodging. There are eight campgrounds in the park, with more than 1,000 campsites. You also can camp in the park's backcountry with a required permit. There are six options for lodging with a range of amenities and costs. Additional campgrounds and lodging are located outside the park, primarily in the town of Jackson and surrounding national forest lands. Four visitor centers are scattered around the park: Colter Bay, Jenny Lake, Laurance S. Rockefeller Preserve, and Craig Thomas Discovery. The park is open year-round,

but the hiking season is relatively short due to long, harsh winters and lots of snow; most hiking trails are usually accessible from mid-June through mid-October. The park includes the Jackson Hole Airport.

The Last Word

Grand Teton is a glorious park with world-class scenery and wildlife and an engaging human history. The park's trail system is large, varied, and dramatic enough to support many days of the finest hiking. Of course with Yellowstone just a few miles up the road, this region of the northern Rocky Mountains is a hiking mecca. Be sure to budget several days at Grand Teton to complement your time in Yellowstone.

Dramatic Lake Solitude rewards hikers at the head of Cascade Canyon.

Great Basin National Park

Nevada | nps.gov/grba

The name is suggestive of this national park that sits alone in the vast expanse of Nevada. This is the heart of the massive Basin and Range geographic province that characterizes much of the American West and Southwest, an area of generally north–south-oriented mountain chains divided by large, arid, sagebrush-covered valleys. America's great nineteenth-century geologist, Clarence Dutton, famously described the area as resembling "an army of giant caterpillars marching toward Mexico." The word "basin" suggests the unusual drainage pattern of much of this region: Rivers and streams do not drain into any ocean but disappear underground or pool in shallow lakes and marshes, where the water eventually evaporates. But the park's name can also be deceptive. First, most of the park is the "range" portion of the Basin and Range landscape. Second, the park is highly diverse, including a mountain of more than 13,000 feet, a glacier, beautiful alpine lakes, a magical system of caves, groves of ancient bristlecone pines, and more.

As is often the case, the geology of the park has a long and complicated history that's not fully understood. It includes periods of major faulting, uplift, and volcanism that have resulted in the present-day high-elevation Snake Mountain Range; thirteen peaks rise more than 11,000 feet. Most recently, the mountains were glaciated, forming the area's characteristic steep canyon walls, U-shaped valleys, cirques, and moraines found in the range's higher elevations. After the last ice age, some 10,000 years ago, these glaciers began to melt. This process has recently been exacerbated by climate change, and only the relatively small Wheeler Peak Glacier remains.

The park's geology has also left behind striking Lehman Caves. This cavern started forming hundreds of thousands of years ago when surface water absorbed carbon dioxide from the atmosphere and became slightly acidic. This solution then began to dissolve the area's underlying marble and limestone, creating today's large cavern. In a second stage of development, precipitation percolated down through the cavern, carrying dissolved limestone and depositing it to form the cave's elaborate decorations, including stalactites, stalagmites, columns, draperies, flowstone, popcorn, and soda straws. However, the cave is best known for its elaborate shields, large stone disks that are sometimes connected with stalactites and draperies; be sure to see a shield called The Parachute.

Plant and animal habitat varies greatly with the especially wide range of elevations in the park. The lower valley is hot and arid and sparsely covered in sagebrush and associated desert vegetation. This gives way to extensive forests of pinyon pine and juniper. Higher forests are composed

(top) Aspens punctuate the park's landscape at the 10,000-foot level.

(bottom) The park's great range of elevations supports many habitats, including tall mountains and lush alpine meadows.

(opposite) The park features thirteen peaks that rise more than 11,000 feet.

(top) Colorful wildflowers decorate the park even at the very highest elevations.

(bottom) Lehman Caves is known for its elaborate shields, large stone disks that are often connected with stalactites and draperies.

of Engelmann spruce and Douglas fir. Subalpine areas are covered with lush meadows and forests of limber pine, spruce, and aspen. Stands of ancient bristlecone pines are found between 9,500 and 11,000 feet; these are the oldest living things on the planet, some nearly an astonishing 5,000 years old. These trees grow very slowly in their harsh high-elevation environment, and their wood is especially dense and resistant to insects and disease. Their stunted and gnarled appearance is shaped by the high winds and low temperatures they endure. In the 1960s, before Great Basin National Park was established, a bristlecone pine was cut down by scientists and found to be nearly 5,000 years old. (Impressive, but it's also a good reason national parks are needed to protect these trees!) Many species of animals are found in the park, including mountain lions, mule deer, pronghorn, elk, and coyotes, and more than 200 species of birds, including California quail, sage grouse, and golden eagles.

Archaeological studies have found that prehistoric people lived near ancient Lake Bonneville about 10,000 years ago. Much later, Native Americans now known as the Fremont People occupied small villages in the area of the present-day park, hunting in the mountains and irrigating fields in lower elevations to grow corn, beans, and squash. There are several rock art sites from this period, though some have been vandalized (another good reason to protect such sites as national parks!). In the 1870s Absalom Lehman established a ranch in the vicinity of the park and raised food for local prospectors and miners. In 1885 he discovered what is now Lehman Caves and spent much of the rest of his life guiding visitors through the cavern. Stalactites, stalagmites, and other cave formations were so dense that he used a sledgehammer to establish a route through the cave (yet another good reason for national parks!). In the late 1870s George Wheeler, a member of a US military expedition, climbed what is now Wheeler Peak and bestowed his name on the 13,063-foot mountain, highest in the park. Ultimately, interest developed in protecting this area, and Lehman Caves National Monument was established in 1922. Creation of a larger park was opposed by local ranchers and miners, and the national park wasn't established until 1986 (the park includes Lehman Caves).

Walking Great Basin

Great Basin includes more than 60 miles of trails that lead to many of the area's scenic features, including the summit of Wheeler Peak, alpine lakes, Wheeler Peak Glacier, bristlecone pine forests, rivers and streams, and, of course, walks through Lehman Caves. Plan at least a few days to walk the best of the park's trail system.

Lehman Caves (Grand Palace Tour)

As with other national parks that include large caves, you can explore them on foot, but only on tours led by NPS rangers. Three tours are offered; we recommend the Grand Palace Tour, the most extensive, visiting all areas of the cave that are open to the public. (Much of the park's cave system is closed to protect the caves' fragile character.) This tour takes about 90 minutes and is offered several times a day; reservations are recommended.

Bristlecone Trail / Glacier Trail

These combined trails lead to two of the park's most interesting features, an impressive grove of bristlecone pines and the foot of the park's only glacier. The Bristlecone Trail starts at the end of Wheeler Peak Scenic Drive at nearly 10,000 feet and climbs moderately for 1.7 miles, rising about 600 feet. Here there's a short loop trail through one of the park's bristlecone groves that includes a series of interesting interpretive panels. These trees are truly iconic, even magical, some of them approaching 5,000 years old; stop to think about all the history these tress have witnessed! Even after they die, some trees remain standing another 2,000 years. From this loop trail you can return to the trailhead for a round-trip hike of 3.4 miles, or you can follow the main trail another half mile or so to reach the foot of Wheeler Glacier, the only glacier in the park and one of the southernmost glaciers in the United States. This is a small rock glacier where snow and ice fill the spaces among a field of boulders and cobbles. While it includes the characteristics that define all glaciers (e.g., it "flows" downhill), it lacks much of the scenic appeal of more conventional alpine glaciers. The round-trip distance of the trail that reaches the viewing area of the glacier is 4.6 miles, with a total elevation gain of 1,000 feet.

Wheeler Peak Summit Trail

This is what many visitors would consider the most iconic trail in the park—a challenging hike to the 13,063-foot summit of Wheeler Peak, the park's highest mountain. Begin the hike near the terminus of Wheeler Peak Scenic Drive and walk gently uphill through a series of lovely aspen groves and then some open meadows with great views of the ridgeline of the Snake Mountains. Eventually the trail climbs more seriously, rising above tree line and mounting the great northern ridgeline of Wheeler Peak. Follow this ridgeline all the way to the summit and take in the astounding views in all directions; the climb along the ridgeline is relentless and steep throughout most of its distance as it works its way through an extensive talus and scree slope with rough footing. You'll occasionally pass shallow rock windbreaks that have been constructed by hikers for shelter, as well as some platforms built by the Wheeler Survey party in the early 1880s; this survey contributed to more precise measurements of mountains in the area. The hike to the summit is 8.6 miles round-trip and gains about 3,000 feet; because of the steepness and roughness of the trail and its very high elevation, we found it challenging but rewarding.

The final pitch to the summit of Wheeler Peak is a steep climb over an extensive talus and scree field with snowfields that last through August.

(above) The park's bristlecone pines are the oldest living things, some approaching 5,000 years old.

(above right) The park is a prototype of the vast Basin and Range geographic province.

Logistics

Great Basin is a relatively small national park—less than 100,000 acres—and doesn't need a large tourist infrastructure. It has a scenic road that connects many of the parks primary features, including the major trailheads. There are two visitor centers, one just outside the park in the town of Baker and the Lehman Caves Visitor Center just inside the park (a small cafe and gift shop are adjacent). There are four campgrounds in the park but no other form of lodging; limited commercial facilities and lodging are available in Baker. The park is open year-round, but winters are generally cold and snowy; summers are warm and subject to afternoon thunderstorms. Late spring and early fall can be ideal, though snow may fall in any month. Lehman Caves is unaffected by outside weather and stays a constant 50°F.

The Last Word

To say that Great Basin is off the beaten track might be an understatement. Prepare yourself for long, straight, and lonely roads, but this is part of the fun. Great Basin receives about the same number of visits annually that Grand Canyon receives in a week, and you'll enjoy a national park like many used to be—limited facilities and services, lightly visited, and offering opportunities for solitude along the park's diverse trail system.

Great Sand Dunes National Park and Preserve

Colorado | nps.gov/grsa

Yes, Great Sand Dunes National Park and Preserve has impressive sand dunes, but there's so much more. First, the sand dunes are even more than impressive, they're massive: There are 30 square miles of them in Colorado's broad San Luis Valley between the picturesque Sangre de Cristo and San Juan mountain ranges, and they're the tallest dunes in North America, up to 750 feet high. You can climb among these dunes to your heart's content (although walking through soft sand can be tiring!). The dunefield is set against the often snow-covered 13,000-plus-foot Sangre de Cristo Mountains, making one of the most unusual landscapes in the National Park System. Second, the park includes much of the land that is responsible for creating and preserving the dunes—the high-elevation Sangre de Cristo Mountains and the surrounding grasslands, streams, and wetlands. Truly, the park is so much more diverse than its name suggests.

What about the "and Preserve" included in the park's name? This is common in Alaskan national parks and an important distinction, but Great Sand Dunes is the only park in the Lower 48 to use this terminology. The "Park" portion of the area includes all the dunes, but some of the land added to the park in the early 2000s was designated a preserve in order to allow some traditional uses such as hunting, generally not allowed in national parks.

The dunes are a relatively recent phenomenon, at least in geologic time, having been formed an estimated 440,000 years ago. But the conditions needed to create the dunes go considerably farther back in time. The Sangre de Cristo Mountains were created by tectonic forces that pushed this land to an elevation of more than 13,000 feet. The San Juan Mountains to the west were the result of a colossal volcanic eruption, perhaps the largest eruption in the history of the Earth. The 7,000-foot-high San Luis Valley between these mountain ranges is enormous, larger than the state of Connecticut. Both mountain ranges shed substantial amounts of snowmelt and runoff, along with associated terrestrial debris, onto the valley floor, creating a very large ancient lake; this lake ultimately pushed through its southern shoreline and drained into what is now the Rio Grande River. A mammoth sheet of sand left behind became the parent material of the present-day sand dunes; this sand sheet now covers much of the San Luis Valley.

The park's dune field is set against the 13,000-foot Sangre de Cristo Mountains, making an exceptionally dramatic view.

Prevailing winds out of the southwest drove much of this sand against a large natural pocket of the Sangre de Cristo Mountains defined by Mosca, Medano, and Music Passes, but periodic strong storms out of the northeast blew the sand back to the west, piling it on top of itself and forming the large, tall sand dunes we see today. This process played out over tens of thousands of years. While the form of the dunefield varies somewhat over time, the basic structure of the dunes is fairly stable as a result of the balance between the opposing winds. Streams that flow from the Sangre de Cristo Mountains—Medano and Sand Creeks—deposit more sand in the valley and continue to feed the formation of sand dunes (as well as being primary sources of water for the valley). A shallow layer of dry sand that can get extremely hot in summer covers the dunes, but they are damp and cool underneath.

The wide range in elevations of the park—from about 7,000 feet to more than 13,000 feet—results in very diverse flora and fauna. The NPS recognizes seven life zones in the park, each defined by elevation, climate, and aspect. Alpine tundra is found above tree line at about 11,000 feet and above. Small plants survive by growing close to the ground, sheltered from high winds. Look for bighorn sheep, marmots, and pika here. Subalpine forest is found between 9,500 and 11,500 feet, where spruces and firs are able to survive heavy winter snows, wet meadows offer lots of wildflowers, and animals include mule deer, elk, black bears, and beavers. Montane forests and pinyon-juniper woodlands are found between 8,000 and 9,500 feet and, in addition to those trees, feature ponderosa pines, Douglas fir, aspens, and cottonwoods, all of which provide habitat for black bears, Abert's squirrels, grouse, and turkeys. The park's vast dunefield is a life zone of its own, though little vegetation can survive this harsh habitat; only one mammal—Ord's kangaroo rat—lives here, though mountain lions, elk, and coyotes wander through. The extensive sand sheet that covers the valley and the associated grasslands compose another life zone that includes a variety of grasses and shrubs such as rabbitbrush, prickly pear cactus, and yuccas; elk, mule deer, pronghorn, and bison can often be seen here. The salt-encrusted plain, or sabkha, is an area of wetlands and crusty sand held together by alkaline minerals leached from the valley's high water table; migratory birds such as sandhill cranes and American white pelicans are found in these wetlands. Finally, streams and riparian areas, in particular along Medano and Sand Creeks, support oases of open water and cottonwoods, willows, and alder, which provide homes for North American beavers and American white pelicans. Rio Grande cutthroat trout live in Medano Creek.

People have used the San Luis Valley and surrounding area for at least 11,000 years. It's thought that early nomadic people hunted mammoths and prehistoric bison. In historic times, Ute, Apache, and Navajo tribes either lived here or claimed a strong attachment to the area. Utes called the dunes *Saa waap maa nache* ("sand that moves"), and the Apache called them *Sie-anyedi* ("it goes up and down"). Spanish explorer Don Diego de Vargas was the first known European to visit the valley.

(top) The trail to 10,000-foot Mosca Pass leads through lush cottonwoods and aspens.

(bottom) Lovely grasslands surround much of the park.

(opposite) The park includes 30 square miles of sand dunes in Colorado's broad San Luis Valley.

(above) The historic Medano-Zapata Ranch, owned by The Nature Conservancy, includes a herd of some 2,000 bison; the ranch is in the process of being transferred to the NPS.

(above right) Star Dune, the highest dune in the park, is 750 feet tall; this is a challenging hike in the soft sand.

Shortly after purchase of the Louisiana Territory, President Thomas Jefferson sent out several expeditions to explore this vast area, the most famous of which was the Lewis and Clark Expedition. But General Zebulon Pike (namesake of Pikes Peak) led two others. After exploring the massive dunefield he found in eastern Colorado, Pike wrote in his journal that the dunes appeared to be "exactly that of a sea in a storm (except as to color), not the least sign of vegetation existing thereon." Settlers entered the valley in the latter half of the nineteenth century, and there were minor gold and silver strikes at about the same time, continuing into the early twentieth century. Expanded gold mining and a proposal for a concrete manufacturing operation caused valley residents to call for action by the federal government to protect the dunes, and that spurred establishment of a national monument in 1932. Research documented the importance of the area's water resources, including streams and their high-mountain watersheds as well as the valley's underground aquifer, to the natural processes that created and maintain the dunefield. A cooperative effort among government agencies and private conservation groups arranged for purchase of critical private lands and transfer of some land from the USDA Forest Service to form a newly designated and expanded Great Sand Dunes National Park and Preserve in 2004; this new national park is now nearly 150,000 acres, soon to be increased by inclusion of neighboring lands owned by the nonprofit Nature Conservancy.

Walking Great Sand Dunes

This diverse park offers hiking that ranges from its signature and distinctive sand dunes to wetlands, grasslands, subalpine evergreen forests, and alpine tundra—there's something for nearly everyone.

The trail system isn't extensive, but it's highly varied. Do the hikes we describe below and come away from the park with an appreciation of its diversity and allure.

The Dunes

There are no maintained trails on the sand dunes, as this is a very dynamic landscape, but all 30 square miles of the dunefield are open to walking: Have an adventure and walk where and as far as you want. However, you'll soon find that walking up and down in soft sand is very tiring, so set your sights on a reasonable hike. Many hikers start from the parking lot just beyond the visitor center and walk to the 700-foot summit of High Dune, where there are fine views of the dunefield. It took us about 3 hours for this challenging round-trip walk that included some extra wandering over the ridgelines of the surrounding dunes. Star Dune, at 750 feet, is the highest and is about a mile and a half beyond High Dune, making for an average round-trip of about 5 hours. Note that zigzagging (traversing) up the sand slopes is less tiring than walking straight up the steep slope, and walking along the ridgetops of the dunes is easier than frequently ascending and descending them. Camping among the dunes is allowed and offers an unusual experience steeped in solitude, quiet, and exceptional night skies; a permit is required.

Dune Overlook Trail

As impressive as the park's dunefield is from ground level, its full geographic extent can be best appreciated from above. The trail to Dune Overlook offers this elevated perspective by means of a 2-mile (round-trip) out-and-back hike that begins from the Pinon Flats Campground. This pleasant walk through the foothills of the Sangre de Cristo Mountains rises about 500 feet to the viewing area.

Mosca Pass Trail

Mosca Pass is a nearly 10,000-foot pass in the Sangre de Cristo Mountains reached by an out-and-back 7-mile (round-trip) hike that begins near the park visitor center. The trail shows off much of the park's diverse habitat as it follows lush Mosca Creek and its associated cottonwoods and aspen groves and ultimately ascends into subalpine forests of spruce and fir and meadows filled with wildflowers. The trail follows an old Native American route, gaining about 1,500 feet of elevation as it passes into the preserve section of the park. Most of the trail is in the Sangre de Cristo Wilderness.

Medano-Zapata Ranch

The Nature Conservancy, a nonprofit conservation organization, currently owns the historic 100,000-plus-acre Medano-Zapata Ranch just west of the park (the ranch is inside the national park and preserve boundary). This land will ultimately be transferred to the NPS and will be a wonderful addition to the park; the ranch includes rare wetlands, historic homesteads, and a herd of

Surrounding lands that will soon be transferred to the park include historic homesteads.

If you take an extended walk among the dunes, keep track of your location by sighting landmarks among the surrounding mountains.

some 2,000 bison. At the present time, the ranch is private land, and permission is needed to access the area. However, we found the area has a 1-mile loop trail through groves of old-growth cottonwoods that simply required registration at the guest ranch maintained by the Conservancy. The Conservancy also offers specialized tours of the ranch; we went on a "bison tour" and were glad we did—it was remarkable. The tour was expensive, but we found it well worth the cost.

Logistics

The park's visitor center is located just beyond the entrance; Pinyon Flats Campground is in this area as well. A commercial campground, motel/cabins, and store are just outside the park, but they're a bit funky. The guest ranch maintained by The Nature Conservancy offers room and board but is expensive. Other commercial facilities and services can be found in surrounding towns, but they're at some distance from the park. The park is open year-round, but its high elevation is subject to cold temperatures and snow in winter; summer is the peak season, but spring and fall are delightful. In summer the surface of the sand dunes can be very hot at midday—hot enough to burn bare feet; wear close-toed shoes/boots and try to time walking on the dunes to morning and evening. If you take an extended walk in the dunefield, keep track of your location by sighting landmarks among the peaks of the Sangre de Cristos.

The Last Word

Great Sand Dunes is a relatively new national park with a striking and highly diverse landscape. Yet it receives relatively few visitors (compared to nearby Rocky Mountain National Park, for example). Take advantage of this while you can to enjoy the park's comparatively uncrowded trails.

Great Smoky Mountains National Park

North Carolina and Tennessee | nps.gov/grsm

Great Smoky Mountains National Park is a land of superlatives. As part of the great Appalachian Mountain Range, the Smokies are among the oldest mountains on Earth. Once as high as the present-day Alps and Rockies, natural forces have eroded, sculpted, and rounded them into the more gentle landscape we see today. The park is the most biodiverse of all the US national parks; more than 10,000 species have been documented, and scientists believe that as many as 100,000 species may live here. The global significance of this biological diversity is recognized in the park's designation as a World Heritage Site. The park is one of the largest natural reserves in the eastern United States and attracts nearly twice as many visits each year as any other national park.

The park's more than 500,000 acres lie along the spine of the Great Smoky Mountains, half in North Carolina and half in Tennessee. It includes dramatic mountain vistas, rocky streams, many impressive waterfalls, old-growth forests, a remarkable array of flowering plants, iconic wildlife, and remnants of early American settlements. The park's characteristic "smoke" is actually fog or mist derived from rain and evaporation from the area's vegetation. The park has more than 800 miles of trails, including 71 miles of the iconic Appalachian Trail; this is a hiker's park—take the time needed to see the park in the intimate way that only walking can provide.

The remarkable biodiversity of the Great Smokies is the park's defining characteristic; no place of equal size outside the tropics can compare. The reasons for this biodiversity start with the underlying geology of the area. The mountains were formed more than 200 million years ago when the North American and African tectonic plates collided. This area was far enough south to be spared the effects of recent ice ages; therefore the mountains have had a million years without major geologic change, giving them an especially long period for plants and animals to diversify. Other factors that contribute to the park's biodiversity include its wide range of elevations (from less than 1,000 feet to nearly 7,000 feet) and its abundant precipitation. The park's lower elevations average 55 inches of precipitation a year; upper elevations can receive up to 85 inches. The park includes more than 100 species of trees and 1,600 species of flowering plants; in both cases, this is more than any other US national park.

Prominent types of vegetation include old-growth forests, with many trees that predate European settlement. Among the park's extensive collection of flowering plants, masses of showy mountain laurel and rhododendrons draw visitors from around the world. The Smokies also feature

(top) Masses of showy laurel and rhododendron (shown here) draw visitors from around the world.

(bottom) Elk have recently been reintroduced in the park.

"balds," grassy, treeless areas below tree line on a number of ridgetops. The origin of balds is mysterious, and ecologists have posited that they may be due to fire, grazing, violent storms, or even of Native American origin. Nevertheless, they offer visitors stunning views of the surrounding landscape and are the destination of several of the park's most popular trails.

Of course this wide range of habitats means that many animals thrive in the park, including more than sixty species of mammals. Iconic examples include black bears, white-tailed deer, red and gray foxes, and elk. This is the largest protected bear habitat in the East, home to approximately 1,500 bears, and the NPS has recently reintroduced elk in the park. Open areas such as Cades Cove and Cataloochee offer especially good wildlife viewing opportunities. The park includes more than 200 species of birds, 39 species of reptiles, and 50 species of fish. A remarkable 30 species of salamanders reside in the park, perhaps more than any other place on Earth.

Like all national parks, Great Smoky Mountains is experiencing a variety of ecological challenges. The park suffers from air pollution, resulting in diminished visibility, although clean air legislation has brought about some recent improvements. Moreover, acid rain has impacted the park's high-elevation red spruce population. Forest decline from introduction of nonnative pests is especially evident, including the death of Fraser firs above 6,000 feet, caused by the balsam woolly adelgid; eastern hemlocks above 5,000 feet are dying from the hemlock woolly adelgid. Fortunately, the park's high-elevation old-growth hemlocks—sometimes called the "redwoods of the East" because they can live more than 500 years and grow to more than 150 feet high—have not been affected.

For centuries before there was a national park, the Cherokee people lived in this area in a sophisticated society that hunted and gathered in the forests. Spanish explorer Hernando de Soto found numerous Cherokee villages in 1540 while traveling through the southern Appalachian Mountains. However, under the Indian Removal Act of 1830, more than 15,000 Cherokee were marched out of their homelands for resettlement in Oklahoma to make way for gold mining and early American settlement. About 4,000 perished on this arduous six-month journey, the infamous Trail of Tears. Some Cherokee hid in the mountains, and their descendants still live in the region.

Frontier people began settling the area in the eighteenth and early nineteenth centuries, and the park's popular Cades Cove settlement is an excellent example of this rural, self-sufficient lifestyle. The community once had nearly 700 residents and included three churches, several log homes, barns, a gristmill, and a blacksmith shop. However, the Civil War severely disrupted life in this region. The early twentieth century saw clear-cutting of large areas of virgin forests, and this led to calls for preservation of the area. Early park supporter Horace Kephart publicly asked, "Shall the Smoky Mountains be made a national park or a desert?" The park was finally established in 1934, helped by a $5 million gift from John D. Rockefeller Jr. Since most of the land included in the park was privately owned, these properties had to be purchased, and many residents were eventually displaced.

(above) Ramsey Cascades is one of many waterfalls in the park.

(opposite) Remnants of historic life in the park are preserved at Cades Cove and other locations.

(above) The park's more than 800 miles of trails include 71 miles of the Appalachian Trail (marked with white blazes).

(center) The park's characteristic "smoke" is actually fog or mist derived from rain and evaporation from the area's vegetation.

(right) Great Smoky Mountains is the most biodiverse of all the national parks; more than 10,000 species have been documented, and scientists estimate the park might include as many 100,000 species.

Walking Great Smokies

How to choose among so many grand possibilities—more than 800 miles of trails that feature so many of the park's finest attributes? We've had the pleasure of hiking many of these trails and have selected several we think best represent the wide diversity of the park. Hike them and see if you agree.

Clingmans Dome Trail

This is a good place to start your outdoor activities in Great Smokies. It's probably the most popular walk in the park, reaching the top of its highest mountain at 6,643 feet (the third-highest mountain in the East). The summit is topped by a fanciful observation tower that offers the best views in the park. The walk is a 1.2-mile (round-trip) journey on a paved trail, but it's very steep (frequent benches ease the climb) before you reach the 375-foot-long ramp of the observation tower and the viewing platform. And there they are, row after row of lush mountain ridges, often muted by the area's characteristic "smoke." Unfortunately, you can't help noticing that many of the trees in the foreground are dead or dying. Several factors are conspiring to kill trees in the park, including acid rain, ozone, climate change, and the aforementioned balsam woolly adelgid (introduced from Europe). On the way down the trail, note signs for the Appalachian Trail, which runs right through this area, and consider bagging a few steps on the famous AT.

Laurel Falls Trail

It's hard to resist hiking to many of the park's waterfalls, and here's one for the whole family. Laurel Falls is sublime and is reached by a 1.3-mile (one-way) paved trail. Most of the walk to the falls is gently uphill (and the return trip gently downhill!). It's also one of the park's nature trails—be sure to obtain a copy of the interpretive brochure at the trailhead. This is a popular trail, and for good reason; you get a lot of reward for relatively little effort. Nearly everyone turns around at the falls and returns to the trailhead for a 2.6-mile round-trip, but there's an option to continue along the (now-unpaved) trail through an old-growth forest and on to Cove Mountain.

Charlies Bunion Trail

This hike begins and ends at Newfound Gap, the highest point on the park's memorable Newfound Gap Road. From the parking lot, step onto the iconic AT and enjoy a walk of 8 miles (round-trip) along this world-famous trail. There are several steep ascents, but the trail is generally well-maintained and is marked with the white blazes that characterize the AT throughout its roughly 2,200 miles. At mile 3 there's a short side trail to Icewater Spring Shelter, one of many shelters along the AT; visit it to get a sense of the life of an AT thru-hiker. At mile 4 a short path on the left leads to Charlies Bunion—a steep rock promontory with sweeping views. The side path forms a loop around the rocks and returns to the AT, where you should retrace your steps to Newfound Gap. By the way, the unusual name comes from an early park supporter who, in a 1920s hike to the area, said the promontory looked like the bunion on the foot of his hiking companion.

Ramsey Cascades Trail

In a park filled with waterfalls, Ramsay Cascades may be the most impressive, and it has the added advantage of a strikingly beautiful trail that leads to its base. This 8-mile out-and-back hike features showy spring wildflowers, groves of rhododendrons, and old-growth forests that feature giant yellow poplars (tulip trees). Much of the trail follows and crosses several "prongs," the local name for streams. The last quarter mile is a bit of a scramble that brings you to the base of the falls. The boulders that frame the falls make a great place for a well-deserved and scenic picnic lunch before retracing your steps to the trailhead. Resist climbing up and around the falls; this can be dangerous.

Mount LeConte (Alum Cave Trail)

Several trails lead to the summit of Mount LeConte. At 6,593 feet, it's only the park's third-highest mountain, but it's a favorite of many Great Smokies hikers. We chose the Alum Cave Trail because it features more open views and a number of natural attractions, including Alum Cave Bluffs, two varieties of rhododendrons, and Arch Rock. It's the shortest route to the summit (about 10 miles round-trip and 3,000 feet of elevation gain), but also the steepest. Just before you reach the summit, you pass romantic LeConte Lodge; built in the 1920s, it's a rustic resort of cabins and a restaurant, the only accommodations within the park. (The lodge offers snacks and pack lunches for day hikers.) A short scramble beyond the lodge brings you to High Top (the true summit) and Myrtle Point, which offers the finest views from the summit area. Since we had only one car, we hiked back down to the Alum Cave Trailhead, but look at a map for ways to hike Mount LeConte using a combination of trails to add variety to your hike (but you'll need a shuttle between trailheads).

The hike to Charlies Bunion culminates in expansive views of the Great Smoky Mountains.

The park's abundant precipitation gives rise to many streams, or "prongs" as they're locally called.

Quiet Walkways

The park contains an innovative series of Quiet Walkways that offer an appealing alternative to the often crowded trails such as those described above. These short trails have no purposeful destination; they simply wander through some of the lovely landscape that is the Great Smokies. Look for the small signs and parking areas along park roads, and sample a few of these walks that feature beauty along with a refreshing measure of solitude and natural quiet.

Logistics

The park is open year-round, but winter weather can be harsh, with snow and ice. Spring brings the peak wildflower bloom and is a wonderful season to visit; consider taking part in the Spring Wildflower Pilgrimage, held in the park in April and offering a series of guided hikes. Fall is also an excellent time to visit, with October a very popular month for fall foliage. The park's many attractions and its proximity to several major population centers means that the summer season can be especially crowded. The park's main access road, US 441 (Newfound Gap Road), crosses the park, is wonderfully scenic, and provides access to many trailheads. This and the road that serves the Cades Cove area, including several trailheads, are often heavily congested. (Use the strategies we describe in "Principle 5: Avoid the Crowds" in Part 3 of the book to deal with large numbers of visitors.) There are three major visitor centers in the park: Sugarlands near Gatlinburg, Tennessee; Oconaluftee near Cherokee, North Carolina; and a third on the Cades Cove loop road.

Rustic and colorful LeConte Lodge is the only hotel in the park; it's a backcountry facility requiring a demanding 5-mile hike to reach. The lodge serves hearty meals to hungry hikers, and the views are epic. More conventional hotels and motels are found in the two gateway towns of Gatlinburg and Cherokee. Gatlinburg and its neighbor Pigeon Forge offer many services but have a well-deserved reputation for being among the tackiest gateway towns to the national parks. Shame! There are ten campgrounds in the park, though none have RV hookups; there are many commercial campgrounds outside the park.

The Last Word

Great Smoky Mountains is an internationally significant refuge of biodiversity, as well as one of the most gently beautiful places in the National Park System. Its roads are lovely but often congested, adding to the appeal of its more than 800 miles of trails, including the AT; there are trails for all abilities and interests. Take to your feet to enjoy and appreciate the genuine Great Smoky Mountains.

Guadalupe Mountains National Park

Texas | nps.gov/gumo

Tucked into the sparsely populated southwest corner of Texas, hard on the New Mexico border, lie the remote Guadalupe Mountains, an improbable fossil reef left behind by an ancient sea. The area was then uplifted to form the heart of present-day Guadalupe Mountains National Park. At nearly 9,000 feet, these mountains are the highest in Texas and tower over the surrounding Chihuahuan Desert. Guadalupe Peak and the dominating cliff called El Capitan have been landmarks for travelers through this region for centuries, probably much longer. The dramatic landscape encompassed by this relatively sparsely visited national park offers beauty, history, and isolation.

Geologists come from many parts of the world to see and study these unusual mountains. Their origin is traced back to what geologists call the Permian period, approximately 250 to 300 million years ago. At this time the supercontinent of Pangea was still intact, and much of the land that's now Texas and New Mexico was near the equator. Pangea was surrounded by an enormous tropical ocean, but an inlet covered parts of northern Mexico and southern Texas. Sea life including sponges, algae, urchins, and clams, precipitated from the ocean and eventually formed a 400-mile-long horseshoe-shaped reef of fossils of these organisms—today's Capitan Reef. The inlet to the sea was eventually constricted and the lake evaporated, leaving behind the fossil reef that was ultimately covered in sediments from nearby mountains. About 25 million years ago, significant geologic faulting occurred in this area that uplifted portions of the reef as much as 2 miles, creating the Guadalupe Mountains. Subsequent erosion exposed the ancient reef.

The park has three primary ecosystems: desert, canyons, and alpine highlands (sometimes called sky islands). The vast Chihuahuan Desert extends out from the base of the Guadalupe Mountains, and much of it is included in the park. This area averages less than 20 inches of rain a year and is especially hot in summer. However, many well-adapted plants and animals live here. Desert plants include cacti, agaves, yuccas, and chollas; common animals include lizards, snakes, coyotes, javelinas, and mule deer. The mountains contain a series of dramatic canyons, the best known of which is McKittrick Canyon, a popular center of hiking activity. Uplands that receive precipitation in the form of rain and snow feed springs and streams that have helped carve these canyons. Characteristic trees include maple, ash, oak, Texas madrone, Texas walnut, ponderosa and pinyon pines, and juniper. Wildlife includes jackrabbits, coyotes, porcupines, foxes, ringtails, mule deer, elk, and mountain lions. The park's alpine highlands are remnants of 15,000 years ago, when the climate was cooler and

Nearly 85 miles of diverse trails cross the park's desert, canyon, and mountains.

wetter. Fragments of the forests that still occupy the higher regions of the mountains in such places as The Bowl are popular for hiking. The forest includes ponderosa and white pines, Douglas fir, and aspen. A small population of elk (reintroduced after being hunted to extirpation in the early 1900s), mule deer, black bears, and mountain lions can be found in this habitat. The park rewards birders with nearly 300 species that either reside in the park or migrate through; noteworthy species include roadrunners, turkey vultures, golden eagles, red-tailed hawks, multiple species of hummingbirds, canyon wrens, Scott's orioles, peregrine falcons, and multiple species of owls.

Human habitation of the park has been traced back 10,000 years or more; the first people were hunter-gatherers who left behind projectile points, baskets, pottery, and rock art. In historical times, Mescalero Apache lived in this region. Spanish explorers in the sixteenth century traveled through the area and introduced horses to the Apache, who used them to great advantage in hunting, travel, and war. In 1858 Pinery Station was constructed as part of the Butterfield Overland Mail, one of the first transcontinental mail routes in the country. The Apache rebelled at this and other invasions of their homeland and carried on a decades-long war with homesteaders, miners, and eventually the US Cavalry. The Apache used the mountains for refuge, but by 1880 they had been driven onto reservations.

The park incorporated many existing ranches, including the Frijole Ranch. The ranch house was constructed in 1876 and served as a community center and post office; it is now a park museum. Many of the historic ranches in scenic McKittrick Canyon were purchased in 1921 by Wallace Pratt, an oil and gas geologist; nearly 6,000 acres of this land was later donated to the NPS and formed the core of the national park established by Congress 1972.

Walking Guadalupe

The park contains more than 80 miles of diverse trails that traverse desert, canyon, and mountains and vary widely in length and challenge. Several trails may be linked for a backpacking adventure. You might share some of the park's trails with horses, but enjoy this classic Western tradition; please yield the right-of-way and stand quietly off the trail, as some horses spook easily. The park features especially good fall foliage—typically the last two weeks of October and first two weeks of November—McKittrick Canyon and Devil's Hall are magical then.

McKittrick Canyon Trail

This may be the most popular hike in the park, and for good reason. The canyon has a perennial stream, which means you walk through an area that's lush compared to the surrounding desert. Tree species include several hardwoods, such as bigtooth maple, oaks, velvet ash, Knowlton's hop horn-beam, little-leaf walnut, and Texas madrone, all of which light up in the fall with shades of yellow,

(top) At nearly 9,000 feet, Guadalupe Peak is the highest in the park and all of Texas; it's reached by an 8.4-mile round-trip trail that rises 3,000 feet.

(bottom) The Frijole Ranch House was constructed in 1876 and served as a community center and post office; it's now a park museum.

(opposite) The Guadalupe Mountains are an improbable fossil reef left behind by an ancient sea.

(above) The hike to Devil's Hall ends where the steep canyon walls close in to about 15 feet.

(above right) The hike through McKittrick Canyon is the most popular in the park, especially in the fall.

orange, and red; the contrast with the surrounding rocks and desert vegetation is stunning. This is often called the best hike in Texas, and it was certainly one of our favorites. This out-and-back trail of 6.8 miles (round-trip) to The Grotto (a good turnaround point) is easy to moderate; most of the hike closely follows the stream. Along the way you'll pass the remains of stone-roofed Pratt Cabin (the vacation home of Wallace Pratt, who donated land to help establish the park) and Hunter Line Cabin (a temporary residence for ranch hands). The hike can be extended another 2 miles to The Notch, but this will require a climb of 2,600 feet. You can also turn this into an unforgettable back-packing trip to Pine Springs, a two- to three-day hike.

Devil's Hall Trail

Despite the name, this is an especially delightful hike. (The name is derived from the historic tendency to give unattractive names to places that have unusual geology.) The trail briefly follows the route to Guadalupe Peak but then diverts and drops into Pine Springs Canyon and follows the wash upstream. Like McKittrick Canyon, you enjoy a mix of desert vegetation with lots of hardwoods sprinkled in, offering a showy display of color in the fall. As the wash becomes more deeply incised, you must scramble up, over, and around a series of boulders that have been washed into the canyon by flash floods. As you near the head of the canyon, you ascend the Hiker's Staircase, a series of natural ledges that climb a steep (but short) slope. Shortly after this you reach the culmination of the hike—the dramatic narrows called Devil's Hall, where the steep canyon walls close in to about 15 feet. The NPS recommends that you turn around at the end of the narrows, making a moderate hike of 4.2 miles (round-trip), though the scrambling required makes hiking slower than what otherwise might be expected.

Guadalupe Peak Trail

Another popular hike is the climb to the highest peak in the park (and in all of Texas). This 8.4-mile (round-trip) hike rises 3,000 feet to reach the mountain peak at 8,751 feet. The journey up the mountain starts among the cacti and yuccas of the Chihuahuan Desert, rises through pine forests in the upper elevations, and finally scrambles up the exposed bald of the summit. Views from the top are humbling and can extend 100 miles or more. The summit frequently has strong and gusty winds (gusting to at least 40 miles per hour on our hike); such winds can result in thermal loss, leading to hypothermia, so take warm clothes. If you'd like to take more time on the mountain, there's a small sheltered backcountry campground a mile below the summit. The hike to Guadalupe Peak is moderately strenuous.

Logistics

The park is remote, offering lots of opportunities for solitude; however, this also means that relatively few visitor facilities and services are available. The park has no lodging but contains two campgrounds, Pine Springs and Dog Canyon; a portion of the parking lot that serves Pine Springs has been turned into RV campsites (no hookups). Pine Springs Visitor Center is a good source of park information. Gasoline, groceries, accommodations, and restaurants are located more than an hour from the park. The park is open year-round, but winter can be cold and windy with some snow; summers are hot. Spring is often windy, leaving fall as the ideal season to visit. Fall foliage creates an especially busy period here, although not on the same scale as some of the better-known national parks.

The Last Word

Guadalupe is off the beaten track, with relatively low visitation, but its geology is fascinating and the landscape sublime. Take the time to know this park by hiking the highest mountain in Texas, through canyons that many people believe are the most beautiful in the state, and in the stark but stunning Chihuahuan Desert. Appreciate the unusual solitude this park provides.

(top) The Hiker's Staircase is a series of natural ledges that climb a steep drop-off on the trail to Devil's Hall.

(bottom) The massive cliff called El Capitan has been a landmark for travelers through this area for centuries, probably longer.

Haleakalā National Park

Hawaii | nps.gov/hale

Haleakalā National Park is on the eastern end of Maui, one of the eight major islands that make up the island-chain state of Hawaii. The park is divided into two detached and very diverse areas—the massive Haleakalā Volcano and its steep slopes, a stark but beautiful place; and the coastal area of Kīpahulu with its rain forests, streams and waterfalls, and the Seven Sacred Pools. The park has substantial elements of both nature and culture. The former includes the remarkable geology of the volcano; a diverse collection of native plants and animals, most of them found naturally nowhere else on Earth; and terrestrial and marine environments. The latter is the distinctive language and culture of the Native Hawaiians or *Kānaka Maoli*, which is deeply ingrained in contemporary Maui and the national park. The park is committed to preserving the area's natural and cultural resources.

Like all Hawaiian volcanoes, Haleakalā is the result of a very long geologic process that includes plate tectonics and "hot spots" in the Earth's crust. This 10,000-foot volcano is part of the massive Pacific Plate that's moving northwest at an estimated rate of about four inches a year. A portion of the plate sits where superheated magma from deep inside the Earth wells up through the Earth's crust, depositing many layers of lava that harden and build on one another to form an impossibly large mass in the form of a volcano. Looking at today's impressive volcano vastly underestimates its true size. Even though it's more than 10,000 feet above sea level, it extends another 18,000 feet to the sea floor, making it more than 28,000 feet high in total, the third tallest mountain on Earth. It's estimated that the volcano once extended up to 15,000 feet above sea level but has substantially eroded over geologic time.

An important artifact of the volcano's erosion is the large dramatic valley that exists at the summit of Haleakalā. This valley is commonly called a crater, but that's not technically correct; the great depression at the top of the volcano is really a V-shaped valley more than 3,000 feet deep and 3.5 miles wide caused by erosion. The valley is partially filled with lava flows, forests, and more than a dozen cinder cones, and the array of colors and forms makes it especially striking. Is Haleakalā an active volcano? Most geologists agree that it is, but that it presents only a moderate threat to humans. The last eruption was about 400 years ago, and there are no current manifestations of an imminent event (e.g., small earthquakes, changing landforms), though volcanic eruptions are difficult to predict. Haleakalā is considered dormant rather than extinct.

After Haleakalā emerged from the sea, it was barren and lifeless. The nearest landmasses were more than 2,000 miles away, making biological colonization a very long process. It's estimated that

(top) The coast of the park's Kīpahulu District is dramatic, but swimming can be dangerous.

(bottom) Hikers make their way down into massive Haleakalā Crater; climbing out of the crater is considerably harder than walking down into it.

(opposite) There's a stark beauty to Haleakalā Crater; several park trails begin at or near the summit.

(above) The park provides vital habitat for the endangered silversword; hotter temperatures and less rain caused by climate change add to the difficulty of preserving this plant.

(below) The endangered nēnē, Hawaii's state bird, finds important protected habitat in the park.

before the arrival of humans about 1,500 years ago, new species arrived on the island only every 10,000 to 100,000 years. This process included birds that migrated over the island or were blown off course, seeds and insects that were blown onto the island or may have fallen from passing birds, and other plants and animals that may have floated to the island on ocean debris. These plants and animals adapted to this new environment and eventually evolved into new species and subspecies. For example, more than forty species of Hawaiian honeycreepers (birds) evolved from an original species that arrived on the island millions of years ago.

Because so many species evolved in the isolation of the island, more than 90 percent of the island's naturally occurring native plant and animal life is endemic (found naturally nowhere else on Earth). Introduction of exotic species by humans over the past several hundred years is now threatening native species. Haleakalā protects more endangered species than any other unit of the National Park System. The nēnē, or Hawaiian goose, Hawaii's state bird, was extirpated from several of the state's islands; scientists have reintroduced them, but they remain threatened. The distinctive silversword plant is another high-profile species found in the park's higher elevations; it also is threatened. The park's wide variation in elevations—sea level to more than 10,000 feet—offers a great variety of habitats, from humid subtropical lowlands to subalpine deserts. Marine species include whales, turtles, dolphins, and seabirds.

Anthropologists believe that the first humans traveled to the Hawaiian Islands more than 1,500 years ago. Probably from Polynesia, they sailed and paddled double-hulled canoes loaded with supplies to support colonization of the islands an impressive 2,500 miles; their ability to navigate by the stars was exceptional. People from Tahiti arrived sometime later. The rich language and culture of the original Hawaiians flourished until European contact in the late 1700s. Native language and culture continue to play an important part in the lives of many contemporary residents and are manifested in many sites in the national park. For example, *Haleakalā* means "house of the sun" and refers to the legend in which the sun was convinced to move across the sky more slowly to increase the amount of daylight each day. *Kuleana* is a strong force in Hawaiian culture and refers to the responsibility to care for all things physical and spiritual; the importance of protecting Haleakalā reflects this belief. The park was established in 1916, the same year the NPS was created. The original name was Hawai'i National Park, and the park included Hawai'i Volcanoes on the Island of Hawaii. Upon completion of the road to the summit of Haleakalā Volcano in 1935, young men of the Civilian Conservation Corps constructed trails and cabins. In 1962 Haleakalā became a separate national park; land was added starting in 1976 to create the park's Kīpahulu coastal section.

Walking Haleakalā

The park includes nearly 40 miles of trails, 30 of them in the summit area and the balance in Kīpahulu. Trails range from easy to strenuous and feature views and hikes into the volcanic crater/valley, native plants and animals, a 400-foot waterfall, sacred pools, many cultural sites, and an ocean beach. Note that much of the park is designated wilderness, offering an especially intimate way to experience the park. Due to the fragile character of much of the park, hikers must stay on maintained trails to limit their potential impacts.

Leleiwi Overlook Trail

Less than half a mile (round-trip), this trail leads to an observation point near the summit of Haleakalā Volcano and offers stunning panoramic views. The walk to the observation point leads through unusual native plant and animal species, including some that are endemic to this area. Be careful crossing the park road to the trailhead and back.

Keonehe'ehe'e (Sliding Sands Trail) / Halemau'u Trail

This is probably the most iconic walk in the park, starting at the 9,800-foot summit visitor center and making a dramatic descent into the Haleakalā Crater basin—19 square miles of stark wilderness. The trail leads through the crater's colorful cinder desert and includes interesting cinder cones, silverswords, and other attractions. This can be a challenging hike because you are at altitude and the footing is loose (consider the trail's name), but there are variations that can determine its length and difficulty. And remember, hikers can turn around at any point and return to the trailhead. Some visitors walk just a quarter mile to the trail's first overlook. If you walk farther, a possible turnaround point is Kapalaoa Cabin, 5.6 miles from the trailhead, where you can return to the trailhead or spend the night, though you'll need a reservation. The end of the Sliding Sands Trail (about 9 miles from the trailhead) is at Palikū, where there is a cabin and campsite. Hikers who return to the Sliding Sands Trailhead from Palikū the next day need to be advised that this is a climb of well over 3,000 feet on the soft footing of the trail's cinders.

Another version of this hike descends into the crater/valley via the Sliding Sands Trail and then returns to the rim of the crater via the Halemau'u Trail, which adds an appealing element of diversity to the hike and requires less elevation gain. Using the shortest distance option of the crater's trail network, this is a popular 11-mile hike that can be done in a very long day or as an overnight hike, camping or staying in one of the park's popular backcountry cabins or campsites. However, there's a logistical hurdle to this route: Hikers must return to the Sliding Sands Trailhead, 7 miles up the road, to retrieve their vehicle. The park has created a hiker pickup parking area near the Halemau'u Trailhead where hikers can leave their car and ask other visitors for a ride to the Sliding Sands Trailhead.

Kūloa Point Loop Trail

A short trail in the Kīpahulu section of the park leads to a series of attractions, including a Hawaiian cultural demonstration area, Kūloa Point (the mouth of 'Ohe'o Gulch), archaeological sites, and

The beauty of the Seven Sacred Pools in the park's Kīpahulu Unit makes them a popular destination.

Waimoku Falls is a popular hiking destination.

dazzling ocean views. The NPS does not recommend swimming in the Seven Sacred Pools because of potential flooding and rock falls. The pools are sometimes closed to swimming; consult with rangers at the Kīpahulu Visitor Center for local conditions. This easy hike is only half a mile (round-trip).

Pīpīwai Trail

This 3.7-mile trail in the Kīpahulu section may be the best hike in the park and perhaps in all of Maui. Just half a mile along the trail, visitors reach the impressive 184-foot waterfall at Makahiku. But the best it yet to come. The trail continues through bamboo and guava forests, using some sections of boardwalk and footbridges, to the base of 400-foot Waimoku Falls, one of the park's prime attractions. The trail gains about 800 feet of elevation; it can be muddy and slippery in sections, making the hike at least modestly challenging.

Logistics

There are two units of the national park, Haleakalā Volcano and Kīpahulu; you must drive out of the park to get from one unit to the other. Be aware that the road to the summit of Haleakalā Volcano is about 40 miles and very steep over much of its course, and the road to Kīpahulu (the Hana Highway) is narrow and winding. There are four campgrounds in the park, two accessible by road (Kīpahulu and Hosmer Grove) and two in the backcountry (Palikū and Holua). There are also three backcountry cabins. There are no hotels or other lodgings in the park, but the communities around the park offer places for visitors to stay. There are no food or other substantive commercial facilities or services in the park. You can obtain on-site, up-to-date information about the park and its trails at three visitor centers, two in the Haleakalā Volcano area and one at Kīpahulu.

The park is open year-round. Many residents suggest that fall and early winter are the best times to visit; temperatures at lower elevations are cooler, and there are fewer visitors. Hiking in the park is unforgettable, but you must be prepared. Temperatures at the summit of the volcano can vary wildly, even dropping below freezing at times. Proper rain gear is often necessary on the volcano and the coast. Hiking trails can be steep and include loose cinders and rocks; climbing out of the volcano's crater/valley can take twice as long as the descent.

The Last Word

There's a great deal to enjoy at Haleakalā: the size, power and beauty of the volcano, the stunning waterfalls and ocean views, the rich diversity of its unusual plants and animals, and the highly developed culture of the Hawaiian people. Walk an assortment of the park's trails to more fully appreciate these and other dimensions of the park. But remember the Hawaiian concept of *kuleana*—the obligation to respect this place and behave in ways that will contribute to its conservation.

Hawai'i Volcanoes National Park

Hawaii | nps.gov/havo

Visitors to Hawai'i Volcanoes National Park have front-row seats to one of the most dynamic landscapes on Earth. Of course all the Hawaiian islands are of volcanic origin, but the Island of Hawaii, generally called the "Big Island," is the only one of the eight major islands that's still volcanically active. In fact, it has two of the world's most active volcanoes. Immense Mauna Loa rises nearly 14,000 feet above the surrounding ocean. Measured from its base on the ocean floor, some 18,000 feet below sea level, it's the Earth's largest mountain, much higher and more massive than Mount Everest. Its bulk is estimated at an astonishing 19,000 cubic miles. Mauna Loa last erupted in 1984. Kīlauea is much shorter—only a little more than 4,000 feet above sea level—but is especially active, erupting more or less continuously since 1983, including the highly destructive lava flows in 2018. This is the world's longest-lived historical volcanic eruption, and scientists believe it could continue for much longer.

Hawaii sits in the Pacific Ocean directly on top of a place in the Earth's crust where lava pushes up under the mantle of the planet, powering active volcanoes; Hawai'i Volcanoes is at ground zero. The park was established in 1916, and scientists have been studying these volcanoes for many years, learning much about the creation of these special islands and the very birth of the planet. The park is so important to scientists and the public that it was designated a World Heritage Site in 1987.

The Hawaiian Islands were created by undersea volcanic activity, a process that began some 70 million years ago and continues today on the Island of Hawaii. Magma and other materials emitted from these volcanoes hardened and grew over time, eventually breaking through the sea to create a chain of islands. It's truly astonishing that you can often witness this process firsthand in the park as lava flows reach the ocean and solidify into new land. Hawaii is the youngest island in the archipelago and is still very volcanically active, as manifested nearly everywhere in the park. Another island is now forming to the southeast of Hawaii as a result of an undersea volcano; however, it's not expected to break the surface of the ocean for another 200,000 years or so.

Volcanoes emit two types of lava, both found in abundance at Hawai'i Volcanoes. 'A'ā lava flows are composed of a layer of brittle fragments or cinders called "clinkers," very rough and challenging to walk on, and tough on shoes. Extremely hot liquid lava (more than 2,000°F) creates pahoehoe lava flows; they are characterized by ropey, corrugated surfaces and cracks caused by contraction during cooling. It can also be rough, but is generally easier to walk on than 'a'ā. Other materials emitted

Lava from Kīlauea Volcano flows into the sea, creating new land.

from the park's volcanoes include gasses and ash. Since all these materials can be very dangerous to humans, you must follow park regulations to help ensure your safety.

The range of elevations in the park—from sea level to nearly 14,000 feet—may be the greatest in the National Park System, giving rise to many types of environments, including lava deserts, rain forests, coastal beaches, and an alpine mountain summit. After the Hawaiian Islands emerged from the sea, they were eventually colonized by many forms of life. This was a long process; the islands are among the most isolated places on Earth—more than 2,000 miles from any continent or other significant landmass. The islands were initially populated by plants and animals through the processes of "wind, water, and wings": Seabirds such as noddies, albatross, and plovers flew directly to the islands as soon as they were habitable for resting and nesting. Other birds were blown to the islands by wind and storms. Some of these birds carried seeds clinging to their wings and in their digestive tracts. Seeds, insects, spiders, snails, and other forms of life were carried to the islands on floating ocean debris. All of these plants and animals adapted to this new environment, evolving in the process and creating new species and subspecies. This colonization took place over more than 30 million years; as a result, a remarkable 90 percent of the islands' native plant and animal life is endemic, meaning it naturally occurs nowhere else on Earth. Unfortunately, humans have more recently introduced other forms of life, and these newer species threaten much of the islands' natural diversity. Even the state bird, the nēnē, or Hawaiian goose, is now threatened. In addition to terrestrial species, the warm, shallow waters that surround the island support humpback whales, sea turtles, and other marine animals.

It's believed that the first humans on the islands traveled there around 1100. These people were probably from the present-day Marquesas in Polynesia, with later arrival by Tahitians (Society Islands), who sailed and paddled double-hulled canoes a remarkable 2,500 miles. The boats were loaded with supplies such as pigs, dogs, and chickens, as well as plants such as taro, sweet potatoes, coconuts, sugarcane, bananas, and medicinal plants to support colonization of the islands. Many native Hawaiians consider Kīlauea a sacred place, the body of Pele, the Hawaiian goddess of volcanoes and fire and creator of the Hawaiian Islands. Captain James Cook landed on the island several times in the late eighteenth century and was eventually killed by the inhabitants. Tourism emerged as one of the island's primary economic activities in the middle of the nineteenth century, giving rise to a movement to create a national park on the islands of Hawaii and Maui. The park was established in 1916, becoming the eleventh US national park, and the first to be formed on a US territory.

Walking Hawai'i Volcanoes

Hawai'i Volcanoes is laced with more than 150 miles of trails that include black sand beaches, arid deserts, rain forests, and the volcanoes themselves. What better way to see and appreciate these

(above) Pahoehoe lava is formed by extremely hot liquid lava and is characterized by a ropey, corrugated surface.

(below) Park trails include the area's extensive rain forests.

(opposite) The Island of Hawaii (the Big Island) sits on a "hot spot" on the Pacific Ocean floor, powering Kīlauea Volcano.

(above) The nēnē, Hawaii's state bird, is one of many endemic species in the park—plants and animals that evolved on the isolated Hawaiian Islands and are found naturally nowhere else on earth.

(below) Ancient Hawaiians left thousands of petroglyphs in the park; be sure to walk the Pu'u Loa Petroglyphs Trail.

places than to walk through them? More than half the park is designated wilderness, affording intimate opportunities to experience these remarkable natural and cultural resources. However, you must accept the realities of the changes that occur in the park, sometimes on a daily basis, that can close some park roads, observation areas, and trails; you must also respect the potential dangers inherent in this experience by heeding all warnings issued by park managers. It's strongly advised that you check the park's website and speak with rangers for up-to-date information. *Mahalo.*

Crater Rim Trail

As the name suggests, this trail encircles Kīlauea's large summit caldera, offering many dramatic views of its volcanic features and the surrounding landscape. See and hear gasses and steam as they arise from the floor of the caldera and its 400-foot cliffs, and appreciate the lush rain forests that line much of the Rim Trail. The trail offers stunning views from many perspectives as it circles the large crater, and Crater Rim Drive offers many access points to the trail. This is a long loop trail (over 11 miles) but is relatively flat; most hikers select sections of the trail to walk. *Note:* Parts of the trail may be closed due to volcanic activity, including emission of dangerous gasses; check current conditions before you head out.

Kīlauea Iki Trail

After circling portions of Kīlauea's summit caldera, it's time to take this unusual opportunity to walk into this major volcanic crater and across the floor of a solidified, but still steaming, lava lake. Along the floor of the volcano, see steam vents and cinder and spatter cones and pass the Pu'u Pua'i cinder cone, source of Hawaii's highest lava fountain—an impressive 1,900 feet—recorded in 1959. This 2.4-mile out-and-back walk leads through a rain forest before descending 400 feet into the crater.

Pu'u Loa Petroglyphs Trail

Native Hawaiian culture is often depicted in petroglyphs—images carved in stone—and more than 20,000 of these interesting images are found along the Pu'u Loa Trail, just off the Chain of Craters Road as it approaches the Pacific Ocean. The trail is a boardwalk constructed over a vast, 500-year-old lava field and offers excellent views of many of the petroglyphs found here. Native Hawaiian elders placed the *piko* (umbilical cord) of their children at this site in hopes they would have a long and prosperous life. This 1.4-mile out-and-back trail is generally easy. Please stay on the boardwalk and off the lava and petroglyphs; also, refrain from making rubbings of petroglyphs, which can damage them.

Nāpau Trail

A few miles down the park's impressive Chain of Craters Road is the Mauna Ulu Trailhead, providing access to the Nāpau Trail, a route that passes many interesting volcanic features, especially the Mauna Ulu crater, Pu'u Huluhulu cinder cone, and Pu'u 'Ō'ō volcanic cone. Mauna Ulu erupted

from 1969 to 1974, and its name translates as "growing mountain," a reference to the height it attained. The summit of the Puʻu Huluhulu cinder cone is easily reached on a short side trail and offers wonderful views all the way to the sea. Puʻu ʻŌʻō erupted from 1983 to 2018, and its especially large lava flows covered miles of the park's landscape, burying the Coastal Highway in more than 100 feet of lava and pouring into the sea to create new land. Today you can hike the Nāpau Trail for 7 miles to Puʻu ʻŌʻō, where there is a designated campsite (which requires a permit). Puʻu Huluhulu is only 2.5 miles (round-trip) from the trailhead; however, the trail is mostly over flows of both ʻaʻā and pahoehoe lava, and the going is slow. We found this an excellent destination.

Logistics

The park is open year-round, but fall is normally the driest period, offering the most favorable hiking conditions. Due to the extreme range in elevation, the climate varies quite a bit from place to place. For example, beaches are normally warm and breezy, the summit of Kīlauea can be wet and cold, and elevations over 10,000 feet can drop below freezing, with occasional snow. The Kīlauea Visitor Center is a great source of park information. There are two campgrounds in the park, Kulanaokuaiki and Nāmakanipaio, and three backcountry cabins; the only hotel in the park is the historic Volcano House. All other commercial facilities and services are located outside the park. When hiking trails through lava fields, *ahu* (stacked rocks) mark the way.

The Last Word

Walking through the dramatic and dynamic landscape that is Hawaiʻi Volcanoes is a privilege; see firsthand some of the foundational geologic processes that have shaped the landscape here and in many other regions of the world. This is a rarity: geology on a human time scale. Take the opportunity to see it at ground level.

(top) Steam rises from the craters of Kīlauea Volcano.

(bottom) Visitors must accept the dynamic character of the park landscape; the NPS has to occasionally close some park roads, observation areas, and trails.

Hot Springs National Park

Arkansas | nps.gov/hosp

The natural hot springs in and around what is now the town of Hot Springs, Arkansas, were used by Native Americans for 8,000 years before the springs were "discovered" and appropriated by European Americans. Because the sulfur-laden springs were thought to have curative powers for rheumatism and other ailments, the area was set aside as a federal reservation in 1832, a precursor to the concept of national parks. The area developed into a resort known as "The American Spa." "Bathhouse Row" contains a grand collection of bathhouses, the largest in the United States, outstanding examples of Gilded Age architecture. National park status was bestowed on the area in 1921, and Fordyce Bathhouse serves as the park's visitor center. There is a network of short trails in and around the town as well as a few longer hiking trails in the park's surrounding lands. Visitors are encouraged to walk these paths and trails as part of park's program of promoting good health.

(top) Hot springs were considered a medicinal treatment for many ailments.

(right) Large bathhouses served visitors who traveled to Hot Springs, Arkansas, to "take the waters"; these buildings have been restored and are open to the public.

Indiana Dunes National Park

Indiana | nps.gov/indu

Indiana Dunes National Park is one of our newest national parks in both time and space. The park has been a part of the National Park System since the 1960s, when it was established as Indiana Dunes National Lakeshore, but it was elevated to national park status in 2019. It sits in the middle of an industrialized metropolitan area, bounded on the west by the city of Gary, Indiana, and on the east by Michigan City, Indiana; Chicago is just 50 miles down the road. Many people probably associate this area with the steel mills and other industries that have long occupied this region, but thanks to the foresight and persistence of many area residents, the park now protects a remarkable collection of natural and cultural resources. Indiana Dunes is a patchwork of 15,000 acres of land along the Lake Michigan shoreline that features astounding biodiversity, as well as recreational opportunities that include eight beaches and 50 miles of trails. The park is also a grand collection of partnership organizations, including 2,000-acre Indiana Dunes State Park. Like many national parks, the name of the park reflects one of its most obvious and interesting resources—its extensive and massive sand dunes—but the park is much more than this.

Referencing their size and power, the five interconnected Great Lakes are often called North America's "Inland Sea." Together they hold 21 percent of Earth's freshwater. Lake Michigan is the third largest of the lakes by surface area, second in terms of volume (a staggering 1,180 cubic miles of water!), and is nearly 1,000 feet deep. The Great Lakes were formed primarily by glacial action beginning about 1.2 million years ago and ending some 10,000 years ago. The massive glacial complex, up to 2.5 miles thick, eroded existing mountains and bedrock into rubble and sand and deeply excavated the area; the terminal moraines of the glaciers dammed the waters that flowed south out of them to create the lakes. Water level in Lake Michigan has varied dramatically over this long period, creating a range of shorelines, and winds have whipped the sands into the park's large namesake dunes that approach 200 feet high. (The highest of the Indiana dunes, Hoosier Slide, no longer exists. It was mined for sand before the park was established and carried away in boxcars as the raw material for Ball mason jars and other glass products; how sad!) Older sand mounds, formed when water levels were higher and now located farther from the lake, are currently covered in trees and shrubs, making it difficult to recognize them as they originally were; newer dunes are located closer to the present-day lake and are substantially less vegetated. The dunes are known for their "singing sands," the mysterious sounds that emanate when the dunes slump due to wind or visitors walking near the crest.

The winds off Lake Michigan create artful patterns on the park's extensive sand dunes.

Even though the park is relatively small, it's surprisingly diverse, as manifested in its many habitats: beaches, dunes, ponds between dunes, marshes, oak savannas, prairies, rivers, and bogs. In fact, the park is one of the ten most biologically diverse among the more than 400 units of the National Park System. This diversity is a function of its range of habitats as well as the remnant species of its glacial origins and present-day arid conditions in portions of the park; here, arctic plants such as bearberry grow in close proximity to desert plants such as prickly pear cactus. Notable animal species include white-tailed deer, red foxes, and opossums, along with more than 350 species of birds, including cranes, hawks, and warblers. The park includes several natural areas: Cowles Bog, Glenwood Dunes, Great Marsh, Heron Rockery, Miller Woods, Mnoké Prairie, Mount Baldy, Pinhook Bog, Tolleston Dunes, and West Beach.

Archaeological evidence suggests that the Indiana Dunes area was used for seasonal hunting grounds by Native Americans for about 10,000 years, ending around 800 CE. Several small earthen ceremonial mounds characteristic of the early indigenous inhabitants of the Midwest have been found. European settlement began in the early to middle nineteenth century, eventually driving out the Native Americans. In 1899 University of Chicago professor Henry Chandler Cowles published an explication of the area's unusually diverse flora, and this led to a movement to protect the dunes and the surrounding land. Just weeks after establishment of the NPS in 1916, Director Stephen Mather held hearings in Chicago addressing creation of a "Sand Dunes National Park," but it was successfully opposed by proponents of industry. Indiana Dunes State Park was established in 1926, but this was a relatively small area. In the 1950s the battle over Indiana Dunes was joined by forces that advanced economic development in the form of a "Port of Indiana" (to allow for shipping between the Great Lakes and the Atlantic Ocean) and more steel mills and power plants versus those who supported a national park. Dorothy Richardson Buell, president of the Save the Dunes Council, led a nationwide campaign for the park; opponents referred to her and her female colleagues as a "tea club" of "harmless birdwatchers." Illinois Senator Paul Douglas led the charge for the park in Congress, becoming known at the "third senator from Indiana." Indiana Dunes National Lakeshore was established in 1966, enlarged several times, and recently elevated to national park status.

Walking Indiana Dunes

The park contains more than 50 miles of trails supplemented by additional trails in the state park that sits near the center of Indiana Dunes. These trails introduce visitors to many of the diverse habitats encompassed by the park, some of the most important cultural/historic attractions, and prime recreation sites ranging from heavily-used beaches to more remote and secluded areas. We recommend the following.

(top) Walkers can appreciate a rare black oak savanna.

(bottom) Wetlands are often found amid the sand dunes.

(opposite) Indiana Dunes preserves precious natural areas adjacent to industrial development.

(top) Stairs and boardwalks help protect fragile sand dunes.

(bottom) The park offers a stark contrast between the Chicago skyline and the natural preserve of Indiana Dunes.

Dune Succession Trail

This is one of three complementary trails that begin at the West Beach complex. The trail is a loop of about a mile and includes an extensive system of boardwalks with 250 steps, all designed to protect the dunes from human footsteps. As the name of the trail suggests, it emphasizes the process of sand dune succession—the changes in sand dunes and the plants that grow there—from the deposition of sand from the bottom of the lake to the climax vegetation of deciduous woodland. Start your walk from the beach and you'll follow this succession from the earliest stages to "grandparent" dunes covered in mature oak and hickory forest. You also get great views of Lake Michigan and the seemingly improbable Chicago skyline. Consider adding the other two loops—the West Beach Trail and the Long Lake Trail—for a hike of about 3.5 miles.

Chellberg Farm / Bailly Homestead

This pleasant complex of trails reminds visitors of the rich historical and cultural components of the park. Joseph Bailly was a French-Canadian fur trader and entrepreneur who built his family home here in the 1820s. The homestead includes an imposing main house, several rustic log structures, and a family cemetery and was a gathering place for both Native and European Americans. The property is now a National Historic Landmark. The nearby Chellberg Farm is typical of Swedish farmsteads in the late nineteenth and early twentieth centuries. The Chellberg family emigrated to northwestern Indiana in 1863, a four-month journey from Sweden, and became part of a growing Swedish community in the area. Anders and Johanna Chellberg developed a successful farm that they and their descendants ran until 1972, when the farm was sold to the NPS for inclusion in the park. An easy and interesting 1.3-mile loop trail connects the Bailly and Chellberg properties; a longer walk can be had by continuing on the Little Calumet River Trail.

Miller Woods Trail

The trail through this ecologically significant area starts at the Paul H. Douglas Center for Environmental Education on the west side of the park. Walking the trail reminds visitors of the cutting-edge ecological research of Professor Henry Cowles, who studied the geology and biology of the area in the late 1890s and how he synthesized his extensive field work at Indiana Dunes to support the theory of plant succession. This 3.2-mile out-and-back trail traverses the park's east–west sand ridges known as swell and swale; a rare black oak savanna community occupies the swells, and wetlands are found in the swales. The oak savannas are fire-dependent, requiring periodic fires to enrich the soil with organic matter and control the spread of invasive species. The NPS uses prescribed burns and selective cutting to mimic the natural role of fire. This lovely, biologically rich trail leads to an extended beach along the lake.

Mount Baldy Trail

At 126 feet high, Mount Baldy is one of the park's highest and most interesting sand dunes. Because of the prevailing and often strong northwest winds, it's migrating inland at about 4 feet per year (an astounding rate for a geologic process!). Note this movement of the dune, as it's in the process of covering the trailhead parking lot and nearby inland forest. In sand dune terminology, this is a "starving" dune, beach erosion removing more sand each year than is replaced by the sand that washes ashore from the bottom of the lake. The abnormally high erosion is caused by a seawall that was built to protect Michigan City Harbor. To try to compensate, the US Army Corps of Engineers began "feeding" the beach in 1974, trucking and piping in large "meals" of sand (no, we're not making this up). Be sure to ask the park rangers about this process. Visitors can only climb this dune on ranger-led hikes to protect the safety of hikers as well as the ecological integrity of the dune. The trail is an out-and-back hike of about a mile and requires a scramble up a steep slope of loose sand. The hike is especially informative, and the views from the top are outstanding. Note the marram grass that is colonizing and stabilizing the top of the dune, making for a dynamic landscape. NPS literature suggests that if this process is allowed to continue, Mount Baldy might not be so bald in the future.

Logistics

Located in northwest Indiana, the park is readily accessible by automobile to the residents of the Chicago metropolitan area, but unlike most national parks, it can also be reached by train. The South Shore Train that runs between Chicago and South Bend makes four stops near park access points. The park is small by national park standards; nevertheless, it can be a bit complicated to navigate because of the intermixture of public and private lands. A stop at the park's visitor center can help with this. The park is open year-round, though winters can be cold, windy, and snowy; visitors can travel the park's trails on snowshoes or skies. Beaches are often busy in summer, and parking lots can fill early. The national park has one campground, Dunewood; it's RV friendly but has no electrical hookups. Indiana Dunes State Park also has a campground with RV hookups. There are no other lodgings in the park, but a range of accommodations and other commercial visitor facilities and services are available in surrounding towns.

The Last Word

Join the celebration of this new national park, part of a movement to bring parks to the people, protect vital natural and cultural resources in the midst of a large metropolitan area, and create vibrant partnerships between the NPS and community groups. This may be a model for more national parks in the twenty-first century. Walk the park's trails and bear witness to the value of Indiana Dunes—its unusual biodiversity, its distinctive history and culture, and the recreation opportunities it offers.

(top) Bailly's Trading Post gives visitors a sense of life on the early American frontier.

(bottom) An elevated boardwalk keeps hikers dry and protects fragile wetlands.

Isle Royale National Park

Michigan | nps.gov/isro

Want to get away from it all? Without having to travel to Alaska? Isle Royale National Park—an archipelago in the deep, legendary waters of Lake Superior—may be the answer. Of course you really have to *want* to go there, because the park is accessible by ferry or seaplane only. The main island is large, 45 miles long and nearly 10 miles wide, but the park also includes almost 450 other islands and the waters of Lake Superior out to a distance of 4.5 miles from the shoreline of all these islands. The main island is more than 99 percent wilderness and is laced with trails, making this a hiking and backpacking park. You'll share the island with its iconic wildlife and witness the decades-long dance between the park's two most famous species, wolves and moose. But you won't have to share it with many other hikers; annual visitation to the park is comparable to that of the most remote Alaskan national parks.

Isle Royale and its home on Lake Superior are the product of massive volcanization, geologic faulting, and glaciation. Repeated flows of lava into what is now Lake Superior hardened into layers of basalt that later faulted and were turned on end; the ends of these tilted blocks of basalt form the islands of today's Isle Royale. Later, great periods of glaciation gouged and polished the area, and meltwater filled Lake Superior, the largest freshwater lake in the world (by surface area; third largest by volume). Formation of the lake has isolated the present-day park from the mainland for the last 10,000 years.

Isle Royale has a range of landforms including ridges, valleys, lakes, shoreline, and wetlands; this diversity supports a wide collection of vegetation, some of it remnants from the forests of the last ice age and some of more recent southern origin. The area is heavily forested with coniferous trees such as white and jack pines, black and white spruce, balsam fir, and northern white cedar, and deciduous trees such as aspen, red oak, paper birch, mountain ash, and several species of maples. Because the island has been isolated from the mainland for so long, it supports only a fraction of the animal species found on the surrounding mainland. The park's iconic wolves and moose are the leading characters in the drama of this predator-prey relationship, which has been under a microscope since the early 1950s. There is some uncertainty about how and when moose arrived on the island, but it's thought they arrived early in the twentieth century, either having been transported by humans or swimming to the island on their own. Wolves arrived in the late 1940s by walking across the frozen surface of the lake during an especially cold winter. The island home of these predator and prey

(opposite) Isle Royale National Park is isolated by virtue of its location in Lake Superior, the largest freshwater lake (by surface area) in the world.

(above) Views from colorfully named Lookout Louise extend to the northern portion of the island and on to Canada.

(above right) The famous Greenstone Ridge Trail follows the ridgeline of the park for more than 40 miles from the east end of the island to the west.

species offers an usual opportunity to study their relationship in the relatively closed system of an island (little or no migration on or off); a research program started in 1958 is believed to be the longest-running wildlife study in the world. Other notable park animals include beavers, red foxes, red squirrels, loons, pileated woodpeckers, ospreys, and more than forty species of fish.

The human history of Isle Royale has been traced back as far as 4,500 years. Hundreds of shallow pits are found on the island, places where Native Americans mined the island's copper deposits, using the rare metal for tools and trading. European Americans prospected for minerals in the mid-nineteenth century, but mining didn't prove economically viable. Commercial interests in the island's timber developed in the 1920s. Fortunately, Albert Stoll, a writer for the *Detroit News*, led a long campaign to protect the island as a national park, and the park finally came into being in 1940.

Walking Isle Royale
The wilderness character of Isle Royale and its 165-mile network of trails combine to make this an ideal hiking park. Its diverse trail system leads along ridgetops, traces the island's shoreline, and brings hikers to many of its lakes, wetlands, and scenic viewpoints. There are opportunities for

Historic lighthouses dot the shoreline of Isle Royale and surrounding islands.

extended backpacking trips as well as a number of fine day hikes that lead from the island's two ferry landings, Windigo and Rock Harbor.

Stoll Trail

The long campaign of Albert Stoll to preserve Isle Royale as a national park is noted above, and it's only fitting that a trail be named in his honor. The Stoll Trail is an easy 4.2-mile (round-trip) walk from Rock Harbor that alternates between the inland forest and the rocky coastline. After a short stroll, you'll encounter the remains of a few small copper pits or mines that were used by native people more than 4,000 years ago. These pits are just a few of the more than 1,500 that have been found on the island. Artifacts made from this copper include fishhooks, beads, awls, and projectile points. Farther along the trail you'll find a monument honoring Albert Stoll; it was nicely decorated with a large moose antler the last time we saw it. The trail's end is marked by a walk on the dramatic rocks of Scoville Point, the end of land. If the weather is good, linger here to watch seabirds, the interplay of the land and water, and boats coming and going to Rock Harbor. Return to Rock Harbor the way you came, or take the Tobin Harbor Trail, a pleasant walk on the shoreline of Tobin Harbor, for a little variety.

(above) Wooden puncheons cross the island's many wetlands, keeping hikers dry and fragile plants protected.

(below) The forest floor is carpeted in a lush mix of ground covers.

Lookout Louise Trail

By happy necessity, this is both a boat trip and a hike, as the trailhead is accessible only by water. Reach the start of the trail at Hidden Lake by renting a canoe at the seaplane dock on Tobin Harbor and paddling about a mile or by taking a longer cruise on the MV *Sandy* from Rock Harbor; both options include nice views of Isle Royale from the water. The trail winds its way past Hidden Lake (a great place to spot moose) and then up and more up about a mile to reach the top of the ridge. From here it's only a tenth of a mile to reach the best viewing area in the park, where you'll see much of the northern and western portions of the park and the landscape of Canada's Thunder Bay area to the north. Watch your step—you're standing at the edge of a cliff. Local lore suggests that the name of the trail was derived from an admonishment to a young girl to be careful; if so, the trail might more appropriately be "Lookout, Louise!" Near its end, the trail crosses the Greenstone Ridge Trail; consider walking a portion of this famous trail as part of your hike, but you'll need to be prepared (see the description of this trail below).

Greenstone Ridge Trail

This is clearly the park's glamour hike—a long-distance trail that runs the length of the island and is considered one of the premier long-distance trails in the National Park System. To hikers in the know, it's simply "the Greenstone," the longest trail on the biggest island in the largest lake in the world. The trail is long (42.7 miles), but it's not difficult; it travels mostly along the island's ridgeline, with relatively little variation in elevation. A series of small campgrounds is scattered along the length of the trail, all just a short hike off-trail. The trail takes its name from the state's green gemstone found along the trail. The Greenstone offers a lovely spruce-fir forest sprinkled with aspens and maples; lakes and wetlands; wildlife that includes beavers, moose, and wolves; and striking views of the island, the surrounding lake and islands, and north to Canada. Extensive patches of thimbleberry reward hikers in July and August. Markers of the wilderness character of this trail include the howl of wolves, the cry of loons, the carpet of stars that grace the night sky, and lots of solitude. If backpacking isn't in your hiking repertoire, consider walking the first section of the trail on the east side of the island from Lookout Louise to Mount Franklin; it may be the most beautiful section of the trail. Start by hiking to Lookout Louise (described above), walking west on the Greenstone to the Mount Franklin Trail (4.8 miles), and returning to Rock Harbor for a hike of about 10 miles.

Logistics

Isle Royale is one of the few national parks that's not open year-round. Because of its remote location, difficult access, and severe winter weather, the park is closed from November to mid-April. The primary visitor season is June through mid-September, though mosquitoes and blackflies can be problematic in June and July. A system of ferries serves the island, departing from Houghton and Copper Harbor, Michigan, and Grand Portage, Minnesota. Seaplane service is offered from Hancock, Michigan, and Grand Marais, Minnesota. See the park's website for ferry and seaplane schedules. Ferries land at Windigo (at the southwest end of the island) and Rock Harbor (at the northeast end of the island), the island's only two developed areas. The *Voyageur II* ferry provides drop-offs and pickups at several other locations on the island, including McCargoe Cove, Belle Isle, Daisy Farm, Chippewa Harbor, and Malone Bay. Windigo includes a small marina, a camp store, and two rustic cabins. Rock Harbor includes a marina, lodge rooms, housekeeping cabins, restaurants, and a camp store. The park contains thirty-six small campgrounds, most of them in the wilderness portion of the park; there are also campsites on a few of the smaller outlying islands. A commercial water taxi operated by the Rock Harbor Lodge travels around the eastern half of the island and can be used to ferry hikers to and from trailheads. Because the park is remote, visitors must be prepared to be relatively self-sufficient. Hikers are asked to clean their boots and other equipment before arriving at the park to minimize the possibility of introducing invasive species.

The Last Word
If you're looking for an adventure, consider the wilderness of Isle Royale. Here you'll find some of the truest markers of a wild landscape, including the howl of wolves, the cry of loons, the Milky Way splashed across the sky, and the ancient drama of predators and prey. At Isle Royale you can enjoy quiet times for reflection and appreciation of nature whenever you choose.

(top) Many of the park's trails follow the island's rugged and scenic shoreline.

(bottom) The park includes lots of iconic wildlife, including wolves, moose, loons, and beavers (note lodge).

Joshua Tree National Park

California | nps.gov/jotr

Located in the vast deserts of southeastern California, Joshua Tree National Park is large, encompassing nearly 800,000 acres—larger even than its more famous neighbor to the north, Yosemite National Park. Joshua Tree includes portions of two deserts, the low-elevation Colorado Desert (part of the much larger Sonoran Desert) and the higher elevation Mojave Desert. The namesake feature of the park is the Joshua tree that's found in great forests, primarily in the Mojave Desert portion of the park. These dramatic treelike plants (technically yuccas) grow up to 40 feet high, many with upswept branches that reminded Mormon pioneers of the upstretched arms of the biblical figure Joshua leading them to the promised land. Other park attractions include striking granite rock formations, several oases of native fan palms, six mountain ranges, exemplary desert vegetation and wildlife, and a rich human history.

The park's granite rocks—giant domes, pinnacles, and massive piles of boulders—had their origin as magma that rose eons ago from deep within the earth. As the granite cooled and crystallized, it was split by cracks and joints. The granite continued to rise and was eroded by groundwater, smoothing and rounding the angular blocks. Soil erosion further exposed these rocks, and they were left scattered across the landscape in the dramatic and pleasing forms in which we find them today.

The park's five oases were formed when cracks in the underlying bedrock allowed groundwater to rise to the surface. These oases support clusters of fan palm trees, the only palms indigenous to California, along with cottonwood and mesquite trees. The surface water of the oases helps meet the needs of many of the park's diverse wildlife, including desert bighorn sheep, mountain lions, coyotes, seven species of rattlesnakes, jackrabbits, kit foxes, desert tortoises (a threatened species that spends much of its life underground), nineteen species of lizards, and ground squirrels. Many of these species are nocturnal, allowing them to tolerate the often extreme desert heat. In addition, the area supports many native birds as well as migrants; the park's birding checklist includes more than 250 entries.

Surprisingly, considering its desert location, the park is known for its showy flowering plants, including Joshua trees and several species of cacti. Many of the flowering plants are annuals that grow from seed, but only when environmental conditions are favorable; winter rains are especially important. The park's deserts bloom every spring, but occasionally attain "superbloom" status when conditions are just right; this phenomenon of nature was a highlight of one of our recent visits. Check at the one of the park's visitor centers about the wildflower status.

(above) Joshua trees, dramatic treelike yucca plants, grow up to 40 feet tall; note the flowers.

(opposite) The park's namesake Joshua trees are found in great forests in the Mojave Desert segment of the park.

(top) Lost Palms Oasis is the largest of the park's five oases; all are formed by water welling up through cracks in the underlying bedrock.

(bottom) The Lost Horse Mine produced more than 10,000 ounces of gold and 16,000 ounces of silver between 1894 and 1931.

The park's diverse natural history has attracted people for as long as 10,000 years. The earliest indigenous people were of the Pinto Culture, nomadic groups that lived as hunters and gatherers, subsisting on pinyon nuts, mesquite beans, acorns, cactus fruits, and local wildlife. Other groups of Native Americans followed, including the Serrano, Chemehuevi, and Cahuilla, who occupied the area at the time of European arrival in the eighteenth century. Little physical evidence is left of this prehistoric period except spear points, petroglyphs, and bedrock mortars formed for grinding seeds.

The late nineteenth and early twentieth centuries saw a flurry of human activity focused primarily on mining and ranching. Gold and other precious metals were found in many regions of the park, and the remains of several of the largest mines are featured on some of the park's hiking trails. Homesteading and ranching proved especially challenging due to the area's inherently arid conditions. The most successful of these ventures, the Desert Queen Ranch, developed by the colorful Bill Keys, is open to park visitors on a ranger-guided tour.

In the 1930s Minerva Hamilton Hoyt recognized the ecological values of the California deserts and the damage caused by economic exploitation and the growing number of automobiles. She and others formed the Desert Conservation League and successfully lobbied President Franklin Roosevelt to establish Joshua Tree National Monument in 1936. Growing recognition of the natural values of California's vast desert landscapes resulted in passage of the seminal California Desert Protection Act in 1994 that elevated Joshua Tree to national park status, created the nearby Mojave National Preserve, added protection to Death Valley National Park, and provided for Native American uses of these lands.

Walking Joshua Tree

Joshua Tree has dozens of hiking trails as well as virtually unlimited hiking in the park's more than 500,000 acres of wilderness. We suggest the following trails to experience and appreciate the natural and cultural diversity of the park.

Hidden Valley Nature Trail

Hidden Valley is a center of visitor activity in the northern, Mohave Desert section of the park. Yet many visitors don't take advantage of the 1.25-mile loop trail that is its heart. The trail traces the inside perimeter of the impressive ring of cliffs and boulders that inspired the name of this place. History suggests that cattle rustlers once hid their stolen horses and cattle here. Don't expect to be alone here, but embrace the diverse ways visitors are enjoying the park. Look up periodically to find rock climbers—novice and experienced—testing their abilities in this world-class climbing arena. We sat and watched several groups of climbers, but reaffirmed our decision to stick to the trails! The well-marked trail is easy, though some minor scrambling is required.

Barker Dam Nature Trail

Like all forms of development in Joshua Tree, Bill Keys' Desert Queen Ranch needed water. Early ranchers built small dams in washes to catch and store water, but Keys ultimately enlarged one of these water tanks by building what is now known as Barker Dam. The dam still stores water and is the destination of the 1.1-mile lollipop Barker Dam Nature Trail; the water tank supports a variety of bird life. The trail is an attraction in and of itself, richly signed with information about the natural and cultural history of the area. Look for an alcove with Native American pictographs. (Sadly, the panels have been vandalized.)

Ryan Mountain Trail

Ryan Mountain is a nearly 5,500-foot peak in the northwestern portion of the park. The trail to its summit is 3 miles (round-trip), ascending more than 1,000 feet; the trail features artfully executed rock steps to assist hikers where needed. Views from the summit may be the best in the park, featuring the Wonderland of Rocks and the huge Pinto Basin in the southern portion of the park. The trailhead includes a group of massive boulders, and you'll want to visit Indian Cave adjacent to the trailhead; here you'll find a natural rock lean-to marked by centuries of campfires. Consider hiking this trail in the morning to take advantage of the shade; you might be as lucky as we were and see bighorn sheep.

Lost Horse Mine Trail

Mining is difficult work, even more so in Joshua Tree with its hot summers, scarce water, and limited supplies of wood. Nevertheless, there used to be about 300 mines, though few produced much gold or other precious metals. An exception was the Lost Horse Mine, which produced more than 10,000 ounces of gold and 16,000 ounces of silver between 1894 and 1931. The mine's colorful history involves cattle rustling. Remnants of the mine reveal a relatively high level of development, including a steam-powered ten-stamp mill to crush the gold-bearing rocks (each stamp weighed 850 pounds) and the remains of a 3.5-mile pipeline to deliver water to the mine. Today hikers reach the mine using a nearly 8-mile loop. The mine is only 2 miles along the loop (in the clockwise direction), and this 4-mile out-and-back trek makes a delightful hike for those wanting a shorter option. The walk involves a moderate climb through the high-desert landscape of juniper, yucca, and scattered Joshua trees. After touring the mine, take a few minutes to scramble up to the ridge behind the mine for great views of this historic site and the surrounding landscape—we were glad we did. It's possible to continue around the full loop, but this part of the trail is not maintained, and wayfinding can be challenging.

(top) Barker Dam was built by colorful character Bill Keys as a water supply for his Desert Queen Ranch.

(bottom) When environmental conditions are right, including abundant winter rain, the park erupts into a "superbloom" of wildflowers.

(top) The hike up Ryan Mountain offers great views into the park's enormous wilderness.

(bottom) The park's iconic granite rocks—giant domes, pinnacles, and massive piles of boulders—had their origin as magma that rose eons ago from deep within the earth.

Lost Palms Oasis Trail

Lost Palms is the largest and we think the most dramatic of the park's five palm oases, and the nearly 8-mile (round-trip) hike to reach the oasis is one of the best in the park. The hike starts at lush Cottonwood Springs near the southern park entrance. Here you'll find a cluster of palms, a scattering of cottonwood trees, and ancient bedrock mortar holes. From this point on, the roller-coaster trail climbs a series of ridges and then drops into basins and washes, some quite narrow. The trail passes through vegetation characteristic of the Colorado Desert, including cholla, yucca, and ocotillo. We enjoyed watching hummingbirds feeding on the flowers. The landscape becomes rockier as you approach Lost Palms, a large concentration of these native trees that thrive in the natural springs. The contrast between this stately, lush copse of trees and the surrounding desert landscape is arresting. The last bit of the trail down to the palms is steep and can be challenging—we recommend using hiking poles. Look for bighorn sheep in the cliffs above the oasis.

Logistics

Three main entrances and associated visitor centers serve the park: Oasis in the north, Joshua Tree in the northwest, and Cottonwood in the south. Towns near each of these entrances—Twentynine Palms, Joshua Tree, and Indio, respectively—offer a range of visitor services, including accommodations. The park operates nine campgrounds, and more commercial campgrounds are located outside the park. The park is open year-round, but spring and fall are the primary visitor seasons; winter can be cold and summer very hot. Its proximity to the Los Angeles metropolitan area means the park is heavily visited, especially in spring and fall, and much of that use occurs on weekends and holidays.

The Last Word

Folklore suggests that deserts are sterile, hostile landscapes that lack aesthetic appeal. Hike in Joshua Tree and discover that desert parks like Joshua Tree offer deep insights into a rich and diverse natural world and colorful human history. Like Joshua trees themselves, you may raise your arms to the sky and celebrate your decision to hike this park.

Katmai National Park and Preserve

Alaska | nps.gov/katm

Katmai National Park and Preserve, located on the Pacific Ocean side of the remote Alaskan Peninsula, was established as a national monument in 1918 and elevated to national park status in 1980 under provisions of the Alaska National Interest Lands Conservation Act. The original objective of the park was to protect the lands surrounding the huge volcanic eruption of Novarupta, which formed what is known as the large Valley of Ten Thousand Smokes. The park includes nearly twenty volcanoes, many of which have been active since 1900. More recently, the park is known for its population of brown (grizzly) bears, which feed on abundant sockeye salmon at Brooks Camp and for the long prehistoric human habitation of the area. The park includes only 5 miles of maintained trails, but its extensive wilderness offers many opportunities for adventure and solitude, although hiking and backpacking here can be challenging.

(above) Grizzly bears feed on spawning salmon at famous Brooks Camp.

(left) East Mageik Lake is located in a basin once occupied by a glacier.

Kenai Fjords National Park

Alaska | nps.gov/kefj

This large and impressive landmass sits hard on the mighty Gulf of Alaska and features a signature system of large fingerlike fjords—narrow inlets with steep sides or cliffs created by a glacier, reminiscent of those found in Norway. But the park is even more than this, containing the largest icefield in the United States (an impressive 700 square miles), nearly forty glaciers (several of which flow directly into the sea), a staggering 545 miles of wild coastline, towering peaks that rise right out of the sea, and a collection of terrestrial and aquatic wildlife that only Alaska can offer. Yet the park is not well-known, and visitation is relatively low. Now is the time to take advantage of this opportunity!

Kenai Fjords National Park is located in south-central Alaska, making it more accessible than most Alaskan national parks; it's just a 2.5-hour scenic drive from Anchorage. At about 700,000 acres, the park is small by Alaska standards, though it's larger than most parks in the Lower 48.

The park was established in 1980 as part of the bureaucratic-sounding Alaska National Interest Lands Conservation Act (ANILCA); this blockbuster law settled the decades-long national debate over the fate of most of the land in Alaska. Nearly all of Alaska was owned by the federal government, but no one believed that this should be the future. Competing interests included the State of Alaska, Alaska Natives, private interests, and conservation organizations. ANILCA assigned nearly 44-million acres to a set of new national parks (more than doubling the size of the National Park System); one of these new parks was Kenai Fjords.

The natural history of Kenai Fjords goes back to the last ice age and well beyond. Two forces have helped shape this sometimes stark but exquisite wilderness land and seascape: dynamic plate tectonics and glacial and related forces. Half the land area of the park is covered by ice. The park's vast Harding Icefield is thought to be a vestige of an even more massive ice sheet that covered much of Alaska in the Pleistocene epoch. The glaciers that flow downhill from the icefield have carved deep valleys into the land; some of these have become the dramatic fjords we see in the park today.

The park's glaciers are retreating, and the newly uncovered land (mostly rock) is being colonized by lichens and mosses, with a few hardy plants such as fireweed and yellow dryas. The plants ultimately break down the rock, forming soil; this soil allows other plants to become established, including Sitka alder and willows. Larger trees eventually grow where conditions allow, including cottonwoods, hemlocks, and Sitka spruce, with an understory of shrubs, ferns, and other low-growing

(above) Steep slopes characterize the large, fingerlike fjords, reminiscent of those found in Norway.

(opposite) Exit Glacier provides an opportunity to see and appreciate the power of glaciers.

(above) An 8-mile (round-trip) hike ascends to the vast Harding Icefield, at 700 square miles, the largest in the United States

(above right) The park supports many marine mammals, including orcas, several species of whales, porpoises, dolphins, seals, sea lions, and sea otters.

plants. The tree line in the park generally doesn't exceed 1,000 feet because of the harsh environment, typical of Alaskan parks.

Kenai Fjords supports a great diversity of animals that wow most visitors. On land this includes black and brown (grizzly) bears, wolves, coyotes, lynx, moose, mountain goats, wolverines, and river otters. Marine mammals include orcas (technically dolphins, but also called killer whales), several species of whales, porpoises, dolphins, seals, sea lions, and playful, crowd-pleasing sea otters. The diversity and number of bird life are also outstanding, including charismatic clown-faced puffins, bald eagles, peregrine falcons, murres, cormorants, kittiwakes, ducks, and oystercatchers. Interestingly, many seabirds use their wings for swimming rather than flying, and many of these birds nest in large colonies on steep cliffs and outer islands. Bring binoculars and a camera—you're sure to see a lot of wildlife.

Three recent events have affected the natural environment of the park. First, as noted above, the park's glaciers are retreating; most scientists attribute this at least partially to human-caused climate change. Second, a very large earthquake shook this area in 1964, causing some of the land to drop as much as 7 feet. Notice the "ghost forests" along portions of the former coastline; inundated with salt water during the quake, many of these trees died. Third, the grounding of the *Exxon Valdez* oil tanker in Prince William Sound in 1989 contaminated about 20 miles of the Kenai Fjords coastline, although the oil didn't reach the fjords themselves.

The park has a rich cultural history though information is spotty. Early thinking suggested that the area had little or no permanent indigenous settlements, only transient use by indigenous peoples, but more recent investigation may suggest otherwise. A recent NPS study documented several village sites dating from 1200 CE. Since the coast-line has been subsiding for a very long period, and sea levels have risen as well, preferred coastal settlement sites would have been inundated some time ago. Several small gold mining attempts were made in historic times. At the time of the park's establishment, the area had few permanent inhabitants.

Many of the park's glaciers flow directly into the sea; they're called tidewater glaciers.

Walking Kenai Fjords

Given the truly wild character of Kenai Fjords, only a few hikes are generally accessible. But they are all extraordinary and offer hikers an up-front sense of this remarkable area. We've enjoyed the following walks in the park and highly recommend them.

Glacier View Loop Trail

Exit Glacier received its name in 1968 because it was the exit route used by the first party to cross the Harding Icefield; it's one of the few glaciers in Alaska that visitors can easily see up close. The trailhead for the Glacier View Loop Trail is near the terminus of Exit Glacier Road, just a few miles' drive from the park visitor center in the gateway town of Seward. This 8-mile road is a living lesson of changing climate patterns and their effect on the park's glaciers; signs are posted at the locations of the foot of the glacier over the past few decades, and the rate at which the glacier is shrinking is dramatic. At the end of the road, you'll find parking and a small nature center; immediately beyond the center is the Glacier View Loop Trail that offers striking views of the glacier. Water drains from under the glacier over a large outwash plain; most visitors take the time to walk the short trail and appreciate the drama of this spectacle and to view the active character of nature up close and personal. Be careful to follow all signs posted by the NPS. Rangers conduct regular guided walks of this area.

Harding Icefield Trail

The Harding Icefield Trail also leaves from the parking area at Exit Glacier. This is a much longer and more challenging hike, but it's filled with rewarding drama. Mileages vary among the descriptions of this trail, but it's about 8 miles out and back. The elevation gain also varies among trail descriptions, but the consensus is that it's between 3,000 and 4,000 feet. These numbers validate that the trail is quite steep in places. The trail quickly climbs out of the cottonwoods and alders

Meltwater from Exit Glacier (lower right) flows onto its outwash plain.

and offers jaw-dropping views of Exit Glacier as it snakes down the canyon from the Harding Icefield above. It's not surprising to see some of the park's most iconic wildlife, including black and sometimes even brown bears. At the top of the trail, you find the massive icefield in full view—it's absolutely stunning, with nothing but white snow and ice as far as the eye can see (and much, much farther!). Mountain peaks sometimes protrude through the ice, which is up to a mile thick. Such peaks are called nunataks, the upper elevations of mountains that haven't been subjected to glaciation. It's feasible to camp in the vicinity of the trail, though you should ask at the visitor center or check the park's website for up-to-date rules and advice. Be aware that it's dangerous to walk on the icefield and the glacier, and be very wary of bears, especially brown bears—give them lots of room. Ask at the visitor center if there are any ranger-guided hikes on the icefield; this would be an especially appealing way to appreciate this part of the park.

Other Hikes

Beyond the Exit Glacier area, Kenai Fjords is a grand wilderness. An amusing manifestation of this is that the park's highest mountain isn't even named! Even though there are no maintained trails beyond the Exit Glacier area, there are other hiking opportunities. The park has three public-use cabins for park visitors, and there are some excellent off-trail hiking opportunities associated with them. We stayed three days at Holgate Cabin, where we enjoyed front-row views of the Holgate Glacier as it calved into the sea. Each day we walked along the shore and back into the bush where it was not too dense. This remains one of our most memorable wilderness hiking adventures. Check the park's website for procedures on reserving these cabins. Another option is to arrange an off-trail hike with a local guide service; the NPS can provide a list of authorized guides.

Logistics

Kenai Fjords is very accessible for an Alaskan national park (many of them require hiring a bush plane). Seward, the park's colorful and tourist-friendly gateway town, connects to Anchorage by road (the Seward Highway/AK 9) and by the Alaska Railroad. Seward is also the point of embarkation/debarkation for some cruise ships that ply the popular Inside Passage route; consider adding a few days at the beginning or end of a cruise to explore the park. Summer (primarily June through August) is the only practical time to visit the park. A visit in the fall might work well, but it might also snow. Actually, visitors should come to the park prepared for cold and precipitation in the form of rain and/or snow no matter the month. There are no lodgings in the park, but there are several motels in Seward. The park's visitor center is located in the small boat harbor in Seward, and the NPS manages a small campground near Exit Glacier. Three public use cabins are located in the wilderness portion of the park; backcountry camping is available by permit.

The Last Word

Kenai Fjords, a large park with world-class land- and seascapes and iconic wildlife, is one of the few Alaskan national parks that is relatively easily accessible. Yet visitation remains relatively low by national park standards. There are several hiking opportunities on maintained trails and a vast wilderness that's waiting to be explored on foot.

Holgate Cabin offers visitors the opportunity to spend several nights deep in the park's vast wilderness.

Kobuk Valley National Park

Alaska | nps.gov/kova

Kobuk Valley National Park was designated a national park as part of the important Alaska National Interest Lands Conservation Act in 1980. It encompasses nearly 2 million acres above the Arctic Circle and is known for its extensive sand dunes, biannual migration of up to half a million caribou, the Kobuk River, and its vast wilderness. For 9,000 years, the area's indigenous people harvested caribou at Onion Portage on the Kobuk River, a tradition that continues today. No roads lead into the park, so visitors must access the area by chartered air taxi from the surrounding small villages of Nome, Bettles, and Kotzebue; these flights are weather dependent. Since the park has no maintained trails, hiking is limited to those who wish to explore the area on its own terms. The park is one of the least visited in the National Park System.

(top) Several hundred thousand caribou cross Kobuk Valley on their fall migration.

(bottom) The sun-bleached skull of a male caribou rests among the park's fall colors.

(right) Kobuk Valley National Park and Preserve includes striking sand dunes.

Lake Clark National Park and Preserve

Alaska | nps.gov/lacl

This park of 4 million acres is about 100 miles southwest of Anchorage, but it seems much farther as it can only be reached by small plane or boat. It was proclaimed a national monument in 1978 and achieved national park status in 1980. The park includes an especially wide variety of landscapes, including its namesake lake as well as other lakes and streams, coastal rain forests, high mountains, alpine tundra, glaciers, and two major volcanoes. Because of its wide variety of habitats, many major Alaskan terrestrial and marine wildlife species inhabit the park, and the area supports a rich salmon fishery. There are several small settlements in the park that are the ancestral homelands of native Alaskans. There's a small network of maintained trails in the Port Alsworth area, but hiking in the vast majority of the park requires advanced route-finding skills and associated outdoor expertise.

NPS/ Evan Booher

(top) Lucky visitors may see multiple grizzly bears at one time at Chinitna Bay.

(bottom) The Tlikakila River flows through the park below dramatic mountain peaks.

(left) Summer fades to fall in early September at Lake Clark National Park and Preserve.

Lassen Volcanic National Park

California | nps.gov/lavo

Lassen Volcanic National Park isn't as well-known as most of California's other national parks, and maybe that's just as well. Tucked into northeastern California, this is an early national park that celebrates one of Earth's most powerful forces: volcanism. And there's a lot to celebrate. There are four types of volcanoes, and Lassen is one of the few places in the world that has all four: plug dome, shield, cinder cone, and strato/composite. At more than 10,000 feet, Lassen Peak is one of the largest plug dome volcanos in the world; this type of volcano forms when lava is too thick to flow very far and a blast of steam ultimately shatters the area. From 1914 to 1917 a series of eruptions shook the area and spewed a 20-foot-high wall of lava, mud, and ash that melted snow and demolished surrounding forests. Shortly after, another eruption emitted a cloud of ash and steam 30,000 feet into the atmosphere, the ash falling up to 200 miles to the east. Though there have been no large eruptions since this period, Lassen is still an active volcano, as the park's boiling mud pots, fumaroles, and hot springs clearly illustrate. The power of Lassen is driven by plate tectonics; the Gorda Plate off the northern California coast is riding under the even larger North American Plate, creating friction and heat. Much of the park's snowmelt seeps underground, where it's heated by molten rock; the resulting steam helps fuel the force of the volcano.

Many factors contribute to the park's biological diversity. Elevations range from about 5,000 feet to more than 10,000 feet; the Cascade Mountains to the north and the Sierra Nevada to the south converge at the park; and wet Pacific storms drop lots of snow in the park, juxtaposed with the arid Great Basin to the east. Lower elevations of the park are covered in forests (including red fir, whitebark pine, aspen, and cottonwood) and meadows (with colorful wildflowers in spring and summer), while vegetation is sparse in upper elevations. Prominent wildlife includes black bears, mule deer, mountain lions, coyotes, martens, bobcats, red foxes, beavers, marmots, and pika, but most wildlife is found in the park's extensive wilderness.

As in most national parks, Native Americans were in the area long before it was visited by European explorers. Local tribes included the Atsugewi, Yana, Yahi, and Maidu. Lassen Peak was used as a landmark for settlers as they made their way to the fertile lands of the Sacramento Valley in the nineteenth century, and the volcano was named for Peter Lassen, a Danish blacksmith who settled in the area in the 1830s. In 1907 President Theodore Roosevelt established two national monuments in the Lassen area, Lassen Peak and Cinder Cone, primarily to spare the areas from timber harvesting.

(above) Lovely Cold Boiling Lake is one of the park's extensive thermal features.

(opposite) Though Lassen Peak appears to be sleeping peacefully, it's still an active volcano, as the park's boiling mud pots, fumaroles, and hot springs clearly illustrate.

(top) Manzanita Lake offers a nice reflection of Lassen Peak.

(bottom) The trail to the summit of Lassen Peak offers views of several extinct volcanoes.

In 1916 these monuments and surrounding lands became the present-day park. In 1972 Congress designated nearly 74 percent of the park as wilderness.

Walking Lassen

Lassen is a relatively small national park, just over 100,000 acres, but it includes a well-developed trail system of more than 150 miles. Trails lead to Lassen Peak, its high-elevation lakes, through deep forests, and to the park's many volcanic features; its trail system includes 17 miles of the Pacific Crest National Scenic Trail. Spend a few relaxing days exploring and appreciating the park on foot; the following trails will give you a good sense of the park's beauty and diversity.

Manzanita Lake Trail

Let's start with an easy one-and-a-half-mile stroll around Manzanita Lake, probably the most popular area in the park. Formation of this lake was especially eventful and involved a massive landslide released from nearby Chaos Crags, damming Manzanita Creek in the late 1600s, and mudslides into the lake generated by Lassen Peak's 1915 eruptions. It's fun to see the many ways visitors enjoy this lovely lake, boating (nonmotorized only), swimming, picnicking, fishing, birding, etc. If the water is calm, note the striking reflection of Lassen Peak on the surface of the water, best in afternoon and evening. The loop trail passes close to the park's museum and visitor center; take this opportunity to see the displays and exhibits, watch the park's interesting video, and ask rangers any questions you may have. Note the distinctive and pleasing architecture of this building and the adjacent building that holds the park's original seismograph.

Cinder Cone Trail

This one's fun. Yes, it's a little out of the way, but you won't ever forget it. Tucked in the relatively isolated northeast corner of the park, at the end of a 6-mile gravel road, lies Butte Lake, a small campground, and a very large cinder cone whose eruptions just a few hundred years ago created a landscape of volcanic wonders. This is all accessible via a short trail and a brief (but challenging!) climb up to the top of the 700-foot high cinder cone and maybe even down into the throat of this volcano. The hike begins with an approximately 2-mile walk through an enchanted forest of mature Jeffrey and ponderosa pines. Marvel at the number of pinecones that lie at the base of these trees and how squirrels have stripped many of the cones to their core. For most of this route, you'll be walking on the Nobles Emigrant Trail, the route used by thousands of immigrants to reach California's Sacramento Valley. Many of the long-lived trees that compose this forest were mature when these immigrant parties trudged among them. Adding even more drama, a massive lava flow known as the Fantastic Lava Beds, borders the trail. A series of waypoints along this section of the trail are described and explained in an interesting trail brochure available at the trailhead and the visitor

center. At the end of this part of the trail, the cinder cone comes into full view with its stark beauty juxtaposed against the gracefully curving trail that ascends it. This close-up view might serve as the terminus of a rewarding 4-mile (round-trip) hike, but consider making the climb. The soft cinder surface of the trail makes for slow going and fast breathing, but the views are to die for (not literally!). Easy does it to the summit of the cinder cone, where a pair of trails circle the rim and a trail even descends about 100 feet to the bottom of the crater. This is an otherworldly place with views to Lassen Peak and other volcanoes, the large lava field that stretches to Butte Lake and Snag Lake, and the colorful Painted Dunes. Return to the trailhead for a round-trip walk of about 5 miles and a backpack of memories.

Bumpass Hell Trail

Yes, there's a story behind the name of this large geothermal basin that includes steaming fumaroles, belching mud pots, and boiling hot springs. As the story goes, pioneer/hunter/cowboy/prospector Kendall Vanhook Bumpass stumbled across this place in 1865, breaking through the thin crust and severely burning his leg. He later led a local newspaper reporter to the site and broke through the crust again, ultimately leading to amputation of the leg. Bumpass famously called the place "hell," and the name stuck. But if you follow the advice of the NPS and remain on the trails and boardwalks they've provided, you'll find this a fascinating and enjoyable hike. From the parking lot along the park's main scenic road, walk about a mile and a half to reach the basin, where water is superheated by volcanic forces as much as 3 miles beneath the surface, resulting in the thermal features of the area, the most impressive in the park. Along the way, enjoy outstanding views of Lassen Peak, Lake Helen, and Brokeoff Mountain. The thermal basin includes interesting and informative signs about the area. You can then retrace your steps to the trailhead for a round-trip hike of 3 miles or continue another 2 miles to beautiful Cold Boiling Lake, where cold springs bubble up through the lake's surface. This makes for an out-and-back hike of 7 miles, or a point-to-point hike of about 4 and a half miles if you arrange a shuttle from the other end of the trail at pleasant Kings Creek Picnic Area.

Lassen Peak Trail

Summiting 10,457-foot Lassen Peak—the park's namesake—is the glamour hike, and dozens of your new best friends will join you for this very doable and satisfying trek, about 5 miles (round-trip), with an elevation gain of about 2,000 feet. The trail is a long series

(above) The climb up starkly beautiful Cinder Cone is one of the best adventures in the park.

(below) The trail to Bumpass Hell traverses the park's finest thermal features; be sure to stick to the trails and boardwalks.

of especially well-maintained switchbacks, making walking only moderately difficult over most of the route. A series of interpretive signs along the trail offer good reasons for a brief rest stop. The increasingly sweeping views also demand regular stops for photos. Hemlocks are found at the lower elevations but yield to a krumholtz of stunted whitebark pines higher up. At about 9,000 feet you reach the alpine zone, where only low-lying vegetation can survive the severe wind and weather. Near the true summit of the mountain you reach a large flat area on the rim of the volcano where you can see the remains of the park's other volcanoes and other high mountains outside the park, including Mount Shasta and the snow-covered peaks of the northern Sierras. As we reached this flat area, we were greeted with cheers from the other climbers—a first for us! The true summit of the mountain can be reached by crossing a small snowfield and scrambling up the rocks. Reverse your course to the trailhead, greeting other climbers with encouraging words.

Logistics

The park includes a system of eight campgrounds, the largest and most developed located at Manzanita Lake. The only lodging in the park is Drakesbad Guest Ranch, a former homestead that has been offering dude ranch visits since the early 1900s. You'll find other lodging and visitor facilities and services outside the park. Kohm Yah-mah-nee Visitor Center is located at the park's southwest entrance; Loomis Museum is near Manzanita Lake. The park is open year-round but receives as much as 40 feet of snow each winter. The main park road usually opens sometime between mid-May and mid-July, making June through September the primary hiking season.

The Last Word

Most national park–goers rush to and from the better-known national parks in the Cascade Mountains and Sierra Nevada of California, Oregon, and Washington, sparing Lassen much of the crowding you'll experience elsewhere. Most visitors find space available in the park's campgrounds and little traffic congestion, and many of the park's trails offer unusual opportunities for solitude. Enjoy walking in Lassen before it's more fully discovered!

Mammoth Cave National Park

Kentucky | nps.gov/maca

Mammoth Cave National Park lies in central Kentucky, and it more than lives up to its ambitious name. This is the largest known cave system in the world—by a longshot! With more than 400 miles of passageways, the cave system is longer than the world's second- and third-longest caves combined. Geologists think there may be as many as 600 additional miles of cave yet to be discovered. Of course, this says nothing of the park's 53,000 acres of above-ground terrain featuring rivers, forests, bluffs, sinkholes, and ridgetops. The size and diversity of the cave and its environs have earned it designation as a World Heritage Site.

Key ingredients of cave formation include limestone and groundwater, and both of these are found in abundance at Mammoth Cave. Approximately 325 million years ago, a vast inland sea covered much of the central United States; over millions of years, calcium carbonate deposits from marine life as well as precipitating calcite from seawater fell to the seafloor, creating a thick limestone layer that was exposed as the lake eventually disappeared. As rainwater infiltrated the soil, it absorbed carbon dioxide to form a weak carbonic acid. This slightly acidic groundwater dissolved the soft limestone to form underground streams that, in turn, carved long networks of subsurface passageways. In the case of Mammoth Cave, an ancient river deposited a layer of relatively impervious sandstone over much of the limestone. Consequently, a large portion of Mammoth Cave is dry and isn't as highly decorated with common cave formations such as stalagmites and stalactites. However, vertical cracks in the sandstone allow water to seep into parts of the cave to form elaborate draperies, stalactites, rimstone dams, and other features.

Extensive forests cover much of the park's aboveground portion and include beech, yellow poplar, sugar maple, white and black oaks, three species of hickory, hemlock, yellow birch, magnolia, and holly. The Green River and its major tributary, the Nolin River, provide water and riparian habitat that help support a diverse array of wildlife. Mammals include deer, bobcats, coyotes, and foxes. Waterfowl and other birds include wood ducks, kingfishers, and great blue herons. Mammoth Cave supports several species of bats, as well as one species each of cave salamander, eyeless cave fish, and cave shrimp.

Evidence suggests that Native Americans explored and used Mammoth Cave at least 4,000 years ago. Archaeologists' findings include cane torches used for illumination and other artifacts, as well as a number of mummified bodies. The use of the gypsum gathered in the cave by these people

A staircase leads down into the cave's natural entrance.

(left) Nearly 80 miles of trails traverse the park's varied aboveground terrain. This trail leads through an extensive hardwood forest.

(opposite) Mammoth Cave celebrates the longest known cave system in the world.

is unknown. Local legend suggests the cave was "rediscovered" by John Houchins around the turn of the nineteenth century. Reportedly, he shot and wounded a black bear that he then followed into the cave. After that, the cave's history includes its use as a church, a tuberculosis sanitarium, and a source of saltpeter (to make gunpowder) in the War of 1812; ultimately, tourism became the cave's primary function. In 1838 Stephen Bishop, a slave belonging to the property's owner, started leading tours, and he's credited with systematically exploring the cave and mapping many of its passages. A movement to establish the cave as a national park began in the early twentieth century. However, unlike national parks on the vast public lands of the western United States, all the land here was privately owned and had to be purchased, much of it by means of eminent domain. Nearly 600 farms were acquired, creating much animosity among local residents, a source of bitterness even today. Watch for evidence of these homesteads, including level home sites, stone and brick chimneys, small cemeteries, and "wolf trees" (large trees that offered valuable shade to farm homes). Congress established Mammoth Cave National Park in 1941 on more than 45,000 acres of land; the park has since grown to more than 50,000 acres. This surface land is vital to protecting the internal "plumbing" of the vast Mammoth Cave system.

The Green River, the longest river in Kentucky, divides the park into north and south sections. The former supports an extensive backcountry; the latter features the park's cave system.

Walking Mammoth Cave

The park can be walked above and below ground, and both should be pursued. Below ground, find long passageways that have been shaped by flowing water, some with decorative cave formations. Above ground, nearly 80 miles of trails traverse the park's varied terrain, including native forests, hollows, and streams that highlight much of the park's interesting natural and cultural history. The Green River divides the surface lands of the park into north and south sections, with the southern section supporting most of the developed portion of the park and the northern section offering a more expansive backcountry.

Mammoth Cave (Grand Avenue Cave Tour)

All visitors should take at least one of the excellent cave tours offered by NPS rangers. Most of these tours require a ticket, and there's a small associated fee. It's wise to reserve tickets—see the park's website for an up-to-date description of how to do this. There are more than a dozen tours to choose from. We recommend the Grand Avenue Tour, one of the longest in both distance and time—about 4 miles and 4 hours—and a little challenging in places (e.g., nearly 400 feet of elevation gain). This tour includes several of the shorter tours, making it an efficient way to see much of the diversity of the many miles of underground passages. Other good options include the Violet City Lantern Tour (conducted exclusively by lantern to simulate early exploration of the cave) and the Wild Cave Tour, a very demanding 6-hour spelunking experience.

River Styx Spring Trail / Green River Bluffs Trail / Heritage Trail

The southern section of the park offers an appealing network of short and moderate trails that show off many features of the park's landscape. Our favorites are the three trails noted here, and they can easily be combined. For example, the River Styx Spring Trail is a little more than a mile (round-trip) and offers pleasant walking through a mature forest featuring giant beech, sycamore, and maple trees. The trail leads past the historic natural entrance to the cave and then down to the banks of the Green River. A short spur offers a close-up view of River Styx Spring where it

The River Styx emerges from the cave and flows into the Green River.

emerges from the cave and flows into the river. The natural cane reeds you see in the forest were gathered by Native Americans and used to light their way into the cave thousands of years ago. You can retrace your steps to the trailhead or, better yet, pick up the Green River Bluffs Trail that leads a little over 1 mile through highlands along the Green River and through a peaceful hardwood forest with numerous limestone outcrops. The trail includes some gentle uphill walking and affords nice views of the Green River; the trail ends at the Headquarters Picnic Area, which is adjacent to the visitor center parking lot. Finally, consider walking the half-mile loop of the Heritage Trail. Enjoy the quiet forest and note the small level area that is evidence of an old homesite. The highlight of the trail is the Old Guide's Cemetery, where slave and early cave explorer and guide Stephen Bishop is buried.

Cedar Sink Trail

Though this trail is in the southern section of the park, it sits on the west side, away from the developed area. Sinkholes are vital components of Mammoth Cave, places where the underground erosion of the cave has collapsed the surface area, creating great depressions. Here, water runs into and/or out of the cave. The Cedar Sink Trail, a 1.6-mile lollipop route, includes several of the park's largest and most impressive sinkholes. It's also a magical place for spring and early-summer wildflowers.

Cedar Sink is one of many sinkholes dotting the park's landscape.

The trail is well maintained and is generally easy walking, though it ventures down into (and out of) two large sinkholes with the help of several sets of steel staircases. Here you can see for yourself how the surface water flows into and out of the cave. Most of the trail passes through mature, lush-seeming forest, alive with birdcalls. We saw no one else on the trail.

Sal Hollow Trail / Buffalo Creek Trail / Turnhole Bend Trail

These two trails in the northern section of the park offer a less-developed and quieter network of trails. The Sal Hollow and Buffalo Creek Trails (sorry, there are no bison in the park) are both accessed by the Maple Spring Trailhead but lead in different directions. The former is 8.1 miles (one way) and the latter is 4.4 miles (one-way); both have a lot to offer, including a long but easy and pleasant stroll. A portion of these trails can be hiked in tandem by connecting them with a short section of the Turnhole Bend Trail for a 5.5-mile loop; that's what we did. The loop includes classic upland forest with big trees, abandoned farms, small sinkholes, old gravel roads, and lots of spring wildflowers. We saw no one else on this hike. Want more? Several backcountry campsites can be used to turn these trails into a grand backpacking adventure.

Logistics

The park is open year-round; spring can be wet, summers hot and humid, and winters cold. However, the park's caves stay a constant 54°F. The park includes a visitor center, three campgrounds, a rustic lodge and cabins with food service, a gift shop, and a camp store and post office. Backcountry camping is available at designated sites and along floodplains, although a permit is required. Reservations for cave tours are advisable; check the park website for up-to-date information.

The Last Word

This is a diverse park featuring a world-renowned cave system, and like all caves, the below- and above-ground portions are vital to their existence and maintenance. Mammoth Cave offers the unusual opportunity to walk both. Choose one or more of the ranger-led tours inside the cave, but also save time to hike the interesting and diverse surface landscape.

(above left) A long set of steps descends into Cedar Sink, one of the largest sinkholes in the park.

(above) A few portions of the cave are highly decorated with speleothems, common cave formations.

Mesa Verde National Park

Colorado | nps.gov/meve

For 800 years Native Americans, now known as Ancestral Puebloans, lived atop the mesas of southwest Colorado. For most of that time, they lived in simple pit houses and pueblos, farming and hunting in the surrounding area. Then they dramatically changed their way of life, building new homes—cliff dwellings—in the natural alcoves just under the rims of the mesas. Most of these cliff dwellings were small, with fewer than ten rooms, but some were huge, multistoried, and complex, with as many as 150 rooms. Why did these people adopt this new lifestyle? Why, a hundred years later, did they abandon these structures and migrate to what is now Arizona and New Mexico near the end of the thirteenth century? (Some migrated to Texas after the Pueblo Revolt of 1680.) Regardless, they left behind a treasure trove of artifacts that offer fascinating insights into their life and culture, and much of this is preserved in Mesa Verde National Park.

Established in 1906, Mesa Verde was the first national park created to preserve and celebrate cultural rather than natural resources. It marked the beginning of what is now a very substantial component of the National Park System that preserves and interprets human civilization and society, including the interaction between people and their environment. Scientists have found nearly 5,000 archaeological sites in the park, including about 600 cliff dwellings, and the importance of the park is manifested in its designation as America's first World Heritage Site.

Even though the natural environment is not the original focus of the park, it's still interesting and strongly related to Ancestral Puebloan culture. *Mesa Verde* is Spanish for "green table," offering a clue to the area's mesa-top environment. But there's not just one mesa—generally defined as a high, flat plateau—but several that are divided by steep canyons. Composed mostly of sedimentary rock—sandstones and shale—that was deposited by ancient seas and wetlands, Mesa Verde is part of the massive Colorado Plateau, which was substantially uplifted by tectonic forces; subsequent stream flows carved the plateau into several distinct mesas. The land slopes slightly to the south, and this has contributed to formation of the large natural alcoves that house many of the larger cliff dwellings (groundwater flows south and erodes these alcoves). The park's largest cliff dwellings are found on Chapin Mesa and Wetherill Mesa. Elevations in the park generally range from 6,000 to 8,500 feet. Sagebrush dominates lower elevations, and pinyon-juniper forest (the "pigmy forest" of the Southwest) covers much of the rest of the park. Natural wildfires in recent years—and throughout history—have heavily burned large areas of this forest. Higher elevations support Gambel oaks

(above) Some of the park's trails are "crafted" to provide relatively easy access.

(opposite) With more than one hundred rooms, Cliff Palace is the largest cliff dwelling in the park.

(above) Mesa Verde includes several mesas that are cut by deep canyons.

(above right) The park's vegetation is a symphony of colors in the fall.

and occasional Douglas firs. Observant visitors may see mule deer and coyotes; bobcats, mountain lions, and bears may be present but are rarely seen.

The natural environment played an important role in Ancestral Puebloan culture. Soil provided for agricultural development; seep springs offered water for drinking; forests supplied wood for building and cooking fires; and native plants and wildlife were vital sources of food and medicine. Natural alcoves provided for the culture's characteristic, highly-developed cliff dwellings. But there may be another important way in which the natural environment had a direct effect on the Ancestral Puebloan culture. One of the theories about why these people migrated from Mesa Verde is that high population growth, a prolonged drought, and growing resource scarcity (trees, animals, fertile soil) may have forced them to move. Further study of the relationship between these Native Americans and their environment may offer vital lessons for contemporary society.

Evidence suggests that the Mesa Verde area was visited by nomadic Paleo-Indians as long as 10,000 years ago. However, the Ancestral Puebloan presence and culture featured in the park did not emerge until the first century CE, probably about the year 750, with the increased practice of more sedentary and communal lifestyles. Pit houses gave way to increasingly large mesa-top pueblos, often in small to large village complexes, and the inhabitants adopted increasingly sophisticated agricultural practices, including dry-land crops of corn, beans, and squash, building small reservoirs to capture rainwater and snow melt, and domesticating turkeys.

Adoption of cliff dwellings in the last century of Ancestral Puebloan tenure at Mesa Verde featured blocks of sandstone plastered with adobe mortar, often multiple kivas—believed to have spiritual significance—and sometimes towers, although their purpose is unknown. Artful white pottery with pleasing black designs was fashioned into pots, bowls, cups, pitchers, and other objects.

It's likely that some trappers and prospectors were shown the remains of the cliff dwellings and associated artifacts in the late nineteenth century by the Ute people who then occupied the Mesa Verde area as part of their reservation. Photographer William Henry Jackson visited the area in 1874, and his photographs were widely viewed. The Wetherills, local ranchers, explored the mesas and helped guide Frederick Chapin, a writer and photographer, through the area in 1889 and 1890. Chapin's 1892 book, *The Land of the Cliff-Dwellers*, focused more attention on the area. Gustaf Nordenskiöld, a Swedish scientist, conducted the first systematic survey of the area, publishing his book *The Cliff Dwellers of the Mesa Verde* in 1893. However, he removed many important artifacts and shipped them to Sweden; these artifacts now reside in a Scandinavian museum.

Loss of cultural artifacts and the damage done searching for them raised concern about maintaining the integrity of the area. After visiting Mesa Verde in the early 1880s, journalist Virginia McClurg worked to protect the area, including forming the Colorado Cliff Dwellers Association; her colleague, Lucy Peabody, lobbied Congress for protection of the area. In an expression of concern over looting and vandalism of Native American artifacts throughout the Southwest, Congress passed an important law in 1906, generally called the Antiquities Act, that allows the president to create national monuments by executive order, providing protection of historic, cultural, and scientific resources. This law has been used many times to create protected areas (usually called "national monuments") until Congress establishes them as national parks, and this process continues today. Just a few weeks after passing the Antiquities Act, Congress established Mesa Verde National Park.

Walking Mesa Verde

Nearly all visitors to Mesa Verde do some walking, as visiting the larger cliff dwellings can only be done on foot, sometimes with challenges such as uneven terrain and ladders. Most of the park is closed to hiking due to the fragility of the area's archaeological sites. Nevertheless, there are several walks that offer important insights into the area's history and prehistory as well as grand views of the park's scenic mesas, canyons, and surrounding lands.

Cliff Dwellings (Cliff Palace / Balcony House / Spruce Tree House / Long House)

These are the grandest and most iconic cliff dwellings in the park, and all demand a walk of a mile or two. Three of them—Cliff House, Balcony House, and Long House—require a ticket for entrance and include a ranger-guided walk. The tours last 1 or 2 hours, and all require navigating some steep

(top) Visiting some of the park's cliff dwellings is adventurous, requiring climbing and descending ladders and crawling through small openings.

(bottom) The Petroglyph Point Trail leads to a large panel of stylized symbols recorded by the ancient Ancestral Puebloans.

The tower in this cliff dwelling may have been used as a lookout.

and uneven surfaces, using ladders, even crawling through a narrow tunnel in one case. But this is all part of the adventure, suggesting the ways in which the residents of these magnificent dwellings entered, exited, and moved around them. Balcony House and Long House have a deserved reputation for being the most challenging. The cost of tickets is nominal, but buy them in person up to two days before the tour to help ensure availability; tickets are sold at the park's wonderful visitor center as you enter the park. Take time to see the exhibits and marvel at the displays of ancient artifacts left behind by the Ancestral Puebloans as they migrated south at the end of the thirteenth century. Check the park's website for up-to-date information about ticket sales. Spruce Tree House is also impressive, and you don't need a ticket; NPS rangers are stationed at the site to answer questions and watch over this precious cultural resource. We think all visitors who are able should take the walking tour of as many of these cliff dwellings as possible.

Petroglyph Point Trail

Aside from the walking tours noted above, our favorite hike at Mesa Verde is the Petroglyph Point Trail. The 2.4-mile loop begins and ends near the Chapin Mesa Archeological Museum. As the name suggests, the trail leads to the park's most impressive rock art panel, featuring the stylized symbols—dozens of them over a 12-foot-wide area—recorded by the Ancestral Puebloan people. Contemporary Hopi believe some of the symbols tell the story of the emergence of their ancestral people from the earth, their subsequent history, and perhaps their future. These images were chipped into the rock and are highlighted by the contrast between the dark "desert varnish" (a dark coating on exposed rock surfaces found in many arid locations) on the surface of the rock and the lighter color of the sandstone underneath. Reaching this impressive rock art panel requires an adventurous hike up and down what is sometimes a highly crafted trail of steep, narrow steps with occasional foot- and handholds—all located under the edge of the mesa. However, the return section of the hike is along the top of the relatively flat mesa and offers wonderful views of the Mesa Verde landscape where the Ancestral Puebloan people hunted and gathered, grew crops, and carried on their day-to-day lives.

Soda Canyon Overlook Trail

This short (about 1.2 miles) lollipop trail off the Cliff Palace Loop Road gently undulates through a classic pinyon-juniper forest as it makes its way to a series of three overlooks, two of which are the only places you can see Balcony House other than on the ranger-guided tour. Binoculars will be helpful, and the views are best in the morning, when the sun lights up the cliff dwelling. The third overlook is of large and impressive Soda Canyon and the prototypical landscape of Mesa Verde. Look for the natural alcoves just under the edges of the canyons, the types of alcoves where iconic cliff dwellings were constructed. Soda Canyon is named for the white calcium carbonate deposits below the rim of the canyon; this is the mineral that remains from seeps and springs vital to the native people.

Badger House Community Trail

Most Mesa Verde visitors confine themselves to the Chapin Mesa area, and for good reason—this is where so many of the park's most iconic cliff dwellings are found. But the park also has a quieter side that is just as impressive but a little more peaceful: Wetherill Mesa. Maybe it's the narrow, winding road to the mesa that filters out many visitors. But here are additional impressive cliff dwellings (e.g., Long House, the second largest in the park) along with a more complete story of the history of the Ancient Puebloan people as told along the 2.5-mile Badger House Community Trail. This relatively flat trail along the mesa top passes four important dwelling sites—collectively known as the Badger House Community—that trace 600 years of prehistory.

Special Backcountry Hikes

The NPS often offers a series of "special hikes" guided by rangers or other experts. These are wonderful opportunities to see sites that are not open on a regular basis or to tour some of the cliff dwellings at unusual times, such as sunrise. These tours are posted on the park's website and must be reserved.

Logistics

Making your way around Mesa Verde requires driving some long, narrow roads that lead into the park and on to large Chapin and Wetherill Mesas. Shortly after you enter the park, find the relatively new and impressive Visitor and Research Center. There is a large campground (Morefield) in the park that includes some RV sites and electrical hookups, along with Far View Lodge. Additional visitor facilities and services are available outside the park, primarily in Cortez and Mancos. The park is open year-round, but winter can be cold and snowy, and many of the major cliff dwellings and other attractions are closed. Summer can be hot; spring and fall are ideal times to visit and hike.

The Last Word

Mesa Verde is one of the most important parks in the National Park System, both for what it preserves and for the precedent it set in preserving many of the nation's most important cultural sites. People from all over the world come to this World Heritage Site to see for themselves the compelling evidence of an ancient and grand civilization. Today the park plays an especially important role to contemporary descendants of the Ancestral Puebloan people, illuminating their complex history and society. Though much of the park must remain closed to visitation because of the area's inherent fragility, there are several hiking opportunities that will deepen your appreciation of this place and those who once dwelled here.

All of the park's larger cliff dwellings have multiple kivas, believed to have spiritual significance.

Mount Rainier National Park

Washington | nps.gov/mora

For 100 miles in all directions, grand 14,410-foot Mount Rainier dominates the landscape, towering above the other peaks of the Cascade Mountains. The mountain is a volcano and looks like it, displaying the classic conic shape. But this is no extinct volcano; steam from deep within its core continues to escape from the summit. Conservationist John Muir, widely considered the father of the national parks, enthused: "Of all the fire mountains which like beacons, once blazed along the Pacific Coast, Mount Rainier is the noblest." The park is a study of two of the dominant geologic forces—volcanic mountain building and glacial erosion—working in opposition over deep time. The result is a magnificent landscape that features mountains, glaciers, wild rivers, ancient forests, rich wildlife habitat, and what may be the most glorious display of mountain wildflowers in the National Park System. And all of this is on the doorstep of the Seattle metropolitan area.

Though not especially large by national park standards, at 236,000 acres Mount Rainier is exceptionally diverse, comprising five distinct regions. The Paradise section draws most visitors for good reason; here are the world-famous subalpine meadows that bloom so exuberantly—more than one hundred species—as soon as the winter snows retreat. Longmire is also popular for its meadows and expansive views and sunsets. Ohanapecosh features old-growth forests (including the Grove of Patriarchs), wildlife, and waterfalls. High-elevation Sunrise offers hikes to glaciers, meadows, and lakes. Carbon River includes temperate rain forests, a glacial river, and deep Mowich Lake. A grand wilderness that covers 97 percent of the park overlays this diverse landscape.

Mount Rainier, a relatively young volcano that is probably no more than 500,000 years old, rules over its namesake park. Evidence suggests that it has erupted thousands of times and that accumulated lava and ash account for the present-day mountain. The height of the mountain has varied over the eons, rising with volcanic depositions and falling with violent, explosive eruptions and associated landslides. It is one of several well-known volcanoes in the Cascade Mountains, including Lassen Peak and Mount St. Helens, which famously erupted in 1980. The upper elevations of Mount Rainier are cloaked in ice and snow and include twenty-six named glaciers that have carved the park's classic U-shaped valleys and feed the area's mountain streams. The park's remarkable range of elevations—from 1,600 feet to more than 14,000 feet—provide an especially diverse variety of plants and animals. Dominant trees include impressive forests of Douglas fir,

(opposite) Fire and ice: the volcano that is Mount Rainier is covered in glaciers.

(above) The park is a study of the dominant geological forces—volcanic mountain building and erosion—working in opposition over deep time.

(center) The 93-mile Wonderland Trail, a classic American long-distance trail, circumnavigates Mount Rainier.

(above right) A single log bridge adds a sense of adventure on the hike to beautiful Comet Falls.

western red cedar, and western hemlock. Mountain lions, black bears, mountain goats, elk, and deer are some of the park's iconic mammals; interesting birds include northern spotted owls and marbled murrelets.

Artifacts and oral histories suggest that Native Americans from both sides of the Cascades used the land that's now the park for hunting, gathering, and spiritual purposes for more than 9,000 years. For some, the mountain is called *Tahoma*, meaning "the Big Mountain where the waters begin"; their descendants maintain a close connection with the mountain. The area was homesteaded and prospected in the late 1800s, but in 1893 the federal government established the Pacific Forest Reserve, an early national forest, managed primarily to ensure a long-term supply of timber and other forest products. However, a powerful lobbying effort on the part of the National Geographic Society (wanting to study volcanism and glaciation), the Northern Pacific Railroad (wanting to attract passengers to the area), the Sierra Club (wanting to preserve the area), and others convinced Congress to establish a national park in 1899, making Mount Rainier the country's fifth national park. This was an unusual instance of lands in a national forest being transferred to a national park. Over the next few decades, a road was developed for access to the Paradise area, and several large buildings (including the Paradise Inn and the park's administrative offices) were constructed in the distinctive grand and rustic "parkitecture" style.

Walking Mount Rainier

Climbing Mount Rainier is a prize for many mountaineers; this is a technical climb that attracts 10,000 people annually. But for the majority of us, this is a hiker's park, enabled by a network of 260 glorious miles of maintained trails. These trails lead to glaciers, old-growth forests, mountain streams and lakes, meadows full of wildflowers, and more. Walk them and experience the richness and diversity of Mount Rainier.

Grove of the Patriarchs Trail

Extensive rain and snow at Mount Rainier and the area's early establishment and protection as a national park have contributed to the groves of old-growth forests found throughout the park. One of the finest is the Grove of the Patriarchs, located near the Stevens Canyon entrance at the southeast corner of the park. This an easy 1.5-mile lollipop trail that crosses the Ohanapecosh River on a delightful suspension bridge and then loops through the grove that has established itself on a large island. You'll stroll among ancient and giant hemlocks, cedars, and Douglas firs, some a staggering 1,000 or more years old. A series of interpretive panels explain the life history of these trees and the place where they continue to live in peace. Notice what scientists now call "natural quiet," the sounds of nature without any disturbance by human-caused noise; try to be as silent as possible in the grove to help preserve and appreciate this increasingly scarce park resource. The boardwalk through grove helps protect the trees from soil compaction that would otherwise result from many visitors walking through the grove.

Comet Falls Trail / Van Trump Park Trail

This trail leads to two very different destinations, with lots of other rewards along the way. You'll find the trailhead just a few miles inside the Nisqually entrance station. The trail climbs moderately throughout its length, with occasional steeper pitches, passing through an attractive old-growth forest and generally along roaring Van Trump Creek (named for the first person to climb Mount Rainier). Soon you cross the stream on a bridge where you get impressive and close-up views of the creek as it passes through a narrow gorge. At about 2.5 miles you cross the stream on a log bridge (just one log!) and find Comet Falls around the bend; a drop of 320 feet makes this one of the highest waterfalls in the park and some say the prettiest. If you continue along the trail for another mile, you'll reach Van Trump Park, an open area with spectacular wildflowers, and nearby Mildred Point, where you can see four Cascade volcanic mountains: Rainier, St. Helens, Adams, and Hood. The

The Nisqually Glacier is retreating at an increasing rate in response to the park's changing environment.

Twin 1,000-year-old Douglas fir trees are a highlight of the Grove of the Patriarchs Trail.

round-trip distance for this hike is about 7 miles, with more than 2,000 feet of elevation gain. Animals that inhabit this area include marmots, pikas, and mountain goats.

Skyline Loop Trail

The Paradise area is the most popular place in the park, and everyone must (and does!) walk here, from a short stroll outside the large and handsome visitor center to a longer hike such as the one described here. We recommend the Skyline Trail, a 6-mile loop that shows you so much of the diversity and beauty of this aptly named paradise: perhaps the best wildflowers in the National Park System (and that's saying something), sublime waterfalls, in-your-face views of Mount Rainier (when it's "out"), and a taste of genuine mountain hiking. The flowers are everywhere in the lower portions of the trail, each bend in the trail offering seemingly prettier displays. The walking is slow here because you must stop to take so many pictures. Lovely Myrtle Falls is found just half a mile along the trail (walking counterclockwise). But eventually the trail climbs, moderately most of the time but sometimes more steeply (the trail gains 1,700 of elevation), ultimately reaching Panorama Point, where you and many other hikers will stop for water, snacks, and the jaw-dropping views of the mountain with its many active glaciers. We heard several small avalanches on our hike and enjoyed watching a group of would-be mountaineers learning proper use of ice axes and other snow- and ice-climbing techniques. Follow the trail downhill to reach the visitor center and close the loop.

Spray Park Trail

Some people familiar with Spray Park will tell you that it used to be kind of a secret place, in the less accessible and more remote northwestern quadrant of the park, but now it's been "discovered," maybe even spoiled. Don't listen to these cranks. Though more hikers are finding their way here, it's still a show-stopping trail with great views and even greater wildflowers. Find your way along a gravel road to the Mowich park entrance and lovely Mowich Lake. The 6- to 7-mile out-and-back hike (depending on how many meadows of flowers you decide to see) starts and ends here. The hike includes a walk in the woods, a few steps on the Wonderland Trail (see below), a spur trail to Spray Falls, a steep set of switchbacks, a stupendous view of Mount Rainier, and a series of subalpine meadows with flowers that rival any in the park. Be especially careful not to damage any of these very fragile wilderness meadows.

Wonderland Trail

No, we don't really expect you to walk the whole Wonderland Trail when *we* haven't, though we've enjoyed walking portions of it. But it titillated our senses and maybe it will yours too. This classic American long-distance trail circumnavigates Mount Rainier on 93 miles of trail. (This mileage gives you some insight into how big the mountain is.) It's steep as it navigates up and down over the

many ridges that radiate off the mountain and requires many river crossings. This is a grand back-packing trip for which you need a permit, and permits are allocated each year by lottery. Or you can walk sections of the trail as day hikes, as we've done. Think about it. Isn't it nice to know that such places and opportunities still exist?

Logistics

Despite the wilderness character of Mount Rainier, it's less than a hundred miles from the Seattle-Tacoma area. The park is open year-round, though roads and trails are generally inaccessible from late October through late May due to very heavy snow accumulation. (The park received well over 1,000 inches of snow at Paradise in the winter of 1971–72.) The Paradise area is generally open in winter for skiing, sledding, and other snow play. The park offers three developed campgrounds and dispersed camping throughout the designated wilderness, although a permit is required for the latter. There are two historic lodges with lots of character in the park, the Paradise Inn and the National Park Inn, both in the park's historic district. The NPS maintains eight visitor and information centers scattered around the park.

The Skyline Loop Trail offers wildflowers, sublime waterfalls, in-your-face views of Mount Rainier, and a taste of genuine mountain hiking.

The Last Word

Iconic Mount Rainier sits proudly on the skyline, a remarkable gift of wilderness so close to a major metropolitan area. It beckons many of the fortunate people who live in this region and many others from around the country and the world. Mount Rainier has only a short summer and fall season and can be crowded; escape the crowds by exploring the park's 260 miles of trails.

National Park of American Samoa

American Samoa | npsa

This unusual US national park is scattered across three islands of American Samoa, a US territory in the heart of the South Pacific Ocean, an area beyond most national park visitors' travel plans. The park preserves coral reefs, tropical rain forests, fruit bats, and elements of the Samoan culture. Much of the park is composed of coral reefs and ocean and features sea turtles, humpback whales, and many species of fish. The park was established in 1988, but the NPS could not purchase land for the park because of the inhabitants' traditional communal land system. Instead, land is leased from the Samoan village councils, and the park is jointly managed by the NPS and the government of American Samoa. Popular recreation activities include swimming and snorkeling. The park has a limited trail system that will take visitors through tropical rain forests, up steep mountains, and along beaches.

(top) The Matai cultural system allows the family patriarch to serve as the spokesman in the village council of chiefs.

(bottom) Damselfish can be seen in the waters around the park.

(left) The beach at Ofu is only one of many in the park.

North Cascades National Park

Washington | nps.gov/noca

North Cascades National Park is a spectacular wilderness of more than half a million acres that protects some of the most majestic mountains in the nation and includes seemingly endless views of glacially sculpted peaks and valleys. Often called "the American Alps," the park needs no such comparison; it stands (literally) on its own merits. As its name suggests, there are countless miles of mountain streams and cascades, many derived from the area's extensive system of glaciers, the largest concentration of glaciers in the United States south of Alaska.

However, reality can sometimes be complicated, and so it is with North Cascades. The park is bisected by Ross Lake National Recreation Area, another unit of the National Park System. The park is bounded on the south by Lake Chelan National Recreation Area, also a unit of the National Park System. National recreation areas usually include more development than national parks, and that's the case here. In fact, Ross Lake includes three dams and associated reservoirs that are used for power production, and Lake Chelan harbors a small village. All these areas—the national park and the two national recreation areas—are managed together by the NPS to form the bureaucratic-sounding North Cascades National Park Service Complex. This chapter focuses primarily on the national park.

The North Cascades are a unique geologic province where the Coast and Cascade Mountains overlap, thus linking a continuous mountain chain that runs from California to northern British Columbia and Alaska. The geologic history of the North Cascades is complicated, but the core of the park is composed of hard crystalline rocks characterized by especially steep slopes and deep valleys; several peaks exceed 9,000 feet. The west side of the park receives large amounts of rain and snow from storms off the Pacific Ocean, while the east side is relatively dry. There are more than 500 lakes and ponds and hundreds of streams, many of which come directly from the meltwater of the park's more than 300 glaciers. These glaciers are receding rapidly, and it's estimated that more than 50 percent of the park's ice cover has been lost over the past one hundred years. Some streams and lakes have a green or turquoise color from finely ground rock particles called glacial flour; Ross Lake, Diablo Lake, and Thunder Creek are classic examples.

The large range of elevations (nearly 9,000 feet) and high precipitation (as much as 180 inches a year) in much of the park result in exceptionally diverse flora and fauna. Extensive lower elevation old-growth forests include stands of western hemlock, western red cedar (some more than 1,000

(above) The park, its associated national recreation areas, surrounding national forests, and adjacent Canadian provincial parks immediately to the north offer an unusual and exciting opportunity to manage a 3-million-acre area at a large landscape level.

(opposite) The trail along Sahale Arm makes its way toward its namesake glacier in North Cascades National Park; note the hanging glaciers on the surrounding mountains.

(above) The park's classic U-shaped valleys are a clear sign of its history of glaciation.

(above right) Wildflowers fill the park's many subalpine meadows.

years old), and Douglas fir. At higher elevations there are large expanses of meadows that include grasses, wildflowers, and shrubs; the park has an especially large subalpine zone due to heavy winter snow cover. An alpine zone above 7,000 feet has relatively little vegetation. A great assortment of animals take advantage of these habitats, including black bears, coyotes, bobcats, lynx, cougars, mountain goats, bighorn sheep, deer, marmots, and pikas. A few grizzly bears remain in the park, although habitat could probably support a much larger number. (Expansion of the grizzly population is controversial.) Wolves are finding their way back into the park. More than 200 species of birds have been observed in the park, including golden and bald eagles, northern spotted owls, and peregrine falcons. All five species of Pacific salmon exist here: pink, chinook (king), sockeye, coho, and chum.

The park, its associated national recreation areas, surrounding national forests, and adjacent Canadian provincial parks immediately to the north offer an unusual and exciting opportunity to manage a 3-million-acre area at a large landscape level, where natural processes such as animal migration patterns, predator-prey relationships, and wildfires are allowed to continue their natural role. North Cascades can be the heart of this exciting opportunity.

North Cascades is bordered by Ross Lake National Recreation Area and its three reservoirs; the turquoise color of the water is caused by the sun's rays reflecting off the "glacial flour."

The area that includes North Cascades was used by Native Americans for nearly 10,000 years. Archaeologists have unearthed many sites that include cutting tools made from local chert, a type of rock. When white explorers traveled through this area, an estimated 1,000 Skagit Indians lived there. During the nineteenth century, fur trapping, mining, and timbering were attempted in the region, but none proved profitable in the long run. Government expeditions in search of routes through the mountains that would support railroads or other forms of mechanized travel were unsuccessful. In the 1920s several dams were built in the Skagit River Valley to generate electricity for the rapidly expanding metropolitan area of Seattle, but these are located in the Ross Lake National Recreation Area, not the present-day park. Environmentalists worked for decades to establish a national park in the area, but the USDA Forest Service owned and managed the land. Congress finally established the park in 1968, and the NPS assumed management responsibility.

Walking North Cascades

Lace your hiking boots up tightly as you take to the trails of North Cascades; hiking lore suggests that this area constitutes the steepest mountain chain in the continental United States, and we're not about to disagree. Ninety-nine percent of the park forms the Steven T. Mather Wilderness,

(above) The park's extensive groves of old-growth forests at lower elevations include large specimens of western hemlock, western red cedar, and Douglas fir.

(below) Hikers to Sahale Arm pass lovely Doubtful Lake. Note the cascade on the left, one of hundreds in the park that contribute to the park's name.

honoring the first director of the NPS; only the very finest areas in the National Park System carry the Mather brand. To reach most of the park's trails, you have to start at trailheads in the two national recreation areas or surrounding national forests and Canadian provincial parks, and this can make for long, challenging hikes. Notably, the park includes portions of the Pacific Crest National Scenic Trail and the Pacific Northwest National Scenic Trail.

Happy Creek Forest Walk / Happy Creek Falls Trail

Consider these trails a pleasant introduction and warm-up to hiking in North Cascades. This pair of trails is located off WA 20, the iconic North Cascades Highway that bisects the park, and are part of Ross Lake National Recreation Area. The trails highlight a prototypical ancient forest watershed formed and drained by aptly named Happy Creek, which bubbles and dances its way through the area. The forest is well stocked with "grandfather trees"—Douglas fir, western hemlock, and western red cedar—many of which are centuries old and have grown to more than 6 feet in diameter. The resulting forest canopy is largely closed, offering cool shade on warm summer days and helping ensure that the creek has high levels of oxygen, supporting aquatic life. Much of the forest's rocks and decaying trees are covered in thick moss and lichens. Two trails explore this forest. The first is Happy Creek Forest Walk, a one-third-mile elevated boardwalk that's fully accessible. This pleasant loop trail introduces walkers to the natural and cultural history of this special place. The second is adjoining Happy Creek Falls Trail, a 2.6-mile (round-trip) out-and-back trail that climbs through the forest to a scenic waterfall that's really a cascade (a series of steep drops), an example of the common and beautiful water features that lend their name to the park. This trail is characteristic of North Cascades: sometimes steep and rough, but always dramatic.

Cascade Pass Trail / Sahale Arm Trail

This is the real North Cascades—a long and challenging hike to a high mountain pass with the possibility of going on to a glacier. This is one of the best hikes in the National Park System and well worth the effort. It's one of the very few trails that begin in the park and doesn't require walking through one of the surrounding national recreation areas or national forests to reach park lands. Accessing the trailhead requires driving 24-mile Cascade River Road; most of it's paved, but the last section is gravel and can be pretty bumpy, though quite doable in a passenger vehicle. The large parking lot at the end of the road offers splendid views across the canyon to Johannesburg Mountain, cloaked in glaciers. From the trailhead the route gently switchbacks up through the forest of spruce, fir, and hemlock. After about 2.5 miles the trail emerges from the forest and onto an open land of flower-filled meadows and large talus slopes, reaching Cascade Pass at 3.7 miles. The open pass with its spectacular views, including the long and graceful Stehekin River valley, marks an appropriate and satisfying turnaround point for many hikers.

However, a big adventure awaits more energetic hikers as the trail continues to climb at a moderate pace, past lovely Doubtful Lake far below you, and then mounts Sahale Arm, a long, dramatic ridge. Wildflowers abound, including expanses of heather, lupine, and paintbrush—all the favorite foods of the many marmots that inhabit the area. At the end of the ridge, the route morphs into a steep and challenging climb over moraines pushed up by the Sahale Glacier above. The route leads to the very toe of Sahale Glacier and a stunning viewscape of the sea of peaks that surround this area, even as far as Mount Baker to the west and Mount Rainier to the south. Note the campsites at the toe of the glacier, ringed by low walls of rock to protect campers from the wind. This is a round-trip hike of approximately 12 miles (from the Cascade River Road parking lot) and gains about 4,000 feet of elevation. This trail can be done as a long day hike or a multiday backpacking trip (which requires a permit); we've done it both ways. On our most recent hike, we had to stop and remove a fallen tree from Cascade River Road, a symbol of this hike's eventful character.

A series of campsites at the toe of Sahale Glacier are available to backpackers.

Logistics

The park is open year-round, but winters are long, cold, and especially snowy. The visitor season starts in spring in the lower elevations and midsummer in upper elevations and lasts through September. The park has few visitor facilities or services of its own, though visitor centers and campgrounds that serve the park are located in the two national recreation areas that surround it. North Cascades Visitor Center in Newhalem is on WA 20 (North Cascades Highway) in Ross Lake National Recreation Area; Golden West Visitor Center is in the village of Stehekin in Lake Chelan National Recreation Area. (Note: Stehekin is accessible only by foot, boat, or airplane.) Several campgrounds and other commercial visitor facilities and services are available in these areas as well, including campgrounds in surrounding national forests. A permit is required to camp in the vast wilderness portion of the park. Because wilderness hiking in this remote park requires special attention to safety, it's wise to consult with staff at visitor centers about trail conditions.

The Last Word

It's wonderful to have large wilderness parks to explore, to get close to nature, and to enjoy a welcome measure of solitude. This is especially true when they're so close to civilization, in this case just a couple hours' drive from the Seattle metropolitan area. The park's companion national recreation areas offer striking views and entry-level trails into the wilderness of North Cascades. Consider longer hikes through the park for a genuine wilderness experience.

Olympic National Park

Washington | nps.gov/olym

Olympic National Park. Could there be a better name for this regal place? (In Greek mythology, Mount Olympus was the home of the twelve Olympians, or Greek gods.) Square in the middle of nearly million-acre Olympic National Park rises America's Mount Olympus, nearly 8,000 feet high and cloaked in the glaciers that helped shape the mountains and this park. Follow these glaciers and their meltwater downstream toward the Pacific Ocean through subalpine meadows of wildflowers to find the park's emerald valleys, which hold some of the world's most impressive and beautiful old-growth rain forests of Sitka spruce, western hemlock, bigleaf maple, and western red cedar. Some trees are more than 300 feet tall and 70 feet around, and everything is covered in moss and lichens. Just a little farther west, walk along the park's more than 60 miles of wild Pacific Ocean coastline with its sea stacks, tide pools, and driftwood. All this is close to the Seattle metropolitan area. It's no wonder the park was named a World Heritage Site in 1981.

The underlying geology of the park is complicated, a mix of several of the conventional forces and processes that have shaped much of North America. Cracks in the floor of the Pacific Ocean west of the present-day park emitted magma that eventually formed a deep sea range of volcanoes (called seamounts) composed primarily of basalt. Later, the tectonic plate underlying these volcanoes—the relatively small Juan de Fuca Plate—moved east and collided with the much larger tectonic plate underlying the northwest portion of the continent. As these plates collided, the seamounts were pushed up to form the core of the present-day Olympic Mountains. Subsequently, water and glaciation eroded the landscape, forming the system of U-shaped valleys that radiate off the mountains.

Over deep time, luxuriant vegetation, including the ecologically significant rain forests that currently grow on the west side of the park, covered most of the area. The Hoh Rain Forest is an excellent example. This land receives more than 12 feet of rain annually and has a rich understory of ferns as well as a large population of epiphytes (plants that grow on trees). Higher elevations receive less rain and are dominated by forests of subalpine firs and meadows. The highest elevations in the park are above tree line and vegetation is sparse and low-growing. The wide variation in the park's habitats supports many species of wildlife, including Roosevelt elk, cougars, black bears, bobcats, black-tailed deer, beavers, and marmots. Mountain goats are also present but are nonnative. Marine

(above) Prodigious rain—an average of 12 feet annually—has created luxuriant rain forests on the western side of the park; Hoh Rain Forest is a premier example.

(opposite) The Olympic Mountains dominate the geographic center of this large and diverse park.

Walk along the park's more than 60 miles of wild Pacific Ocean coastline with its sea stacks, tide pools, and driftwood.

mammals include sea lions, seals, sea otters, porpoises, and gray whales. Notable birds include bald eagles, red-tailed hawks, ospreys, and great horned owls.

A large Native American presence on the Olympic Peninsula has been traced back 12,000 years and was focused on hunting and fishing, particularly salmon and marine mammals. Sadly, diseases introduced by European Americans decimated most of the tribes that inhabited the area; the present-day Olympic Peninsula includes several small Indian reservations. Explorer Juan de Fuca recorded seeing the Olympic Peninsula in 1592, but because of its isolation and ruggedness, it was approximately 400 years before serious European exploration of the area began in the late nineteenth century; logging became a primary economic activity, but clear-cutting proved devastating and drew growing opposition. President Theodore Roosevelt established Mount Olympus National Monument to help protect the area in 1907; an additional level of protection was provided with establishment of Olympic National Park in 1938.

Walking Olympic

This is a large and highly diverse park and it has a trail system to match: nearly 600 miles of maintained trails. Hike through the rain forests, along high ridgelines, around mountain meadows, and along the Pacific Ocean coast. Many trails can be walked as day hikes, but consider a backpacking trip as well; nearly all the park is designated wilderness. The following hikes will give you a good sense of this glorious park.

Hurricane Ridge

Hurricane Ridge is a large elevated area that's served by the 17-mile steep and winding Hurricane Ridge Road; it's the most heavily visited area in the park. Here you'll find a network of short trails that feature the most outstanding views in the park (including the Olympic Mountains and glacier-capped Mount Olympus; the Strait of Juan de Fuca, Vancouver Island and Victoria, British Columbia), lush meadows filled with wildflowers, subalpine forests, and wildlife such as black-tailed deer. Depending on the time you have available, pick one or more of these short trails, including Big Meadow Loop, Cirque Rim Trail, High Ridge Loop, and Sunrise Point Spur Trail. Most of these trails are less than a mile or so, and some are interconnected, allowing you to fashion your own route. Check with rangers at the Hurricane Ridge Visitor Center for advice and a map of the area, and consider joining a ranger-led hike. There are many ways to enjoy walking dramatic Hurricane Ridge.

Hoh Rain Forest

The extensive and luxuriant rain forests on the west side of the park are a dominant feature of Olympic; Hoh Rain Forest, perhaps the finest example, is readily accessible to hikers. As noted earlier, this ecologically significant area receives copious rain annually, and this generous precipitation supports a large old-growth forest. A lush understory of younger trees, tall shrubs, and ferns carpets the area, and dramatic spikemoss hangs from the branches of many trees. Look for older trees that stand on massive stilted roots, evidence that these trees sprouted on fallen "nurse logs" that have since rotted away. Two short nature trails start from the visitor center that serves this area. The Spruce Nature Trail (1.3-mile loop) and Hall of Mosses Nature Trail (0.8-mile loop) wander through the forest, and each features a series of interpretive signs. You may see the Roosevelt elk that inhabit this area. If you'd like a longer hike, consider the 17-mile Hoh River Trail, which follows the Hoh River and then climbs steeply to Glacier Meadows on Mount Olympus. We enjoyed walking the first few miles of this trail from the visitor center and feel it would make an excellent but challenging backpacking trip.

Rialto Beach

Its more than 60 miles of wild Pacific Ocean coastline are a signature feature of the park and demand at least one epic hike. Our favorite begins at Rialto Beach and travels north along the rocky coast for about 2 miles to Hole in the Wall, a massive sea arch. Along the way you'll see dramatic sea stacks, large accumulations of driftwood, pristine beaches, extensive tide pools (the best are just north of Hole in the Wall), and lots of wildlife, including seabirds, eagles, and many marine mammals such as whales, sea lions, and sea otters. Do this walk at low tide.

(top) The park includes many species of iconic wildlife, including Roosevelt elk.

(bottom) The park's highest elevations are above tree line and are often carpeted with wildflowers.

(above) Olympic is a large national park with a trail system to match, offering nearly 600 miles of maintained trails.

(above right) Nearly all the park is designated wilderness that provides opportunities for solitude.

Sol Duc Falls

The Sol Duc Valley in the northwest portion of the park is a diverse area with old-growth forests, subalpine lakes, snowy peaks, and lots of wildlife. The valley is defined by the beautiful Sol Duc River, its name a Quileute term meaning "sparkling water." The trail to Sol Duc Falls, one of the most popular attractions in the park, is an easy out-and-back walk of 1.6 miles (round-trip) beneath a dense cover of forest and along the joyfully cascading river. You'll hear Sol Duc Falls long before you see it, a nearly 50-foot drop into a narrow rocky gorge. Enjoy great views and memorable photos of the falls from both up- and downstream.

Logistics

Olympic is a large park that dominates the Olympic Peninsula, south and west of the Seattle metropolitan area. Large wilderness areas of the adjacent Olympic National Forest surround the park and make it feel larger still. The park is open year-round, but winter can be severe in the upper elevations and rainy in the lower elevations; the primary visitor season is June through September. The park is encircled by US 101, with many side roads that lead into the mountainous and coastal regions of the park; no roads cross the park, and this has helped preserve it. There are three visitor centers—in the town of Port Angeles, on Hurricane Ridge, and in the Hoh Rain Forest. Displays and staff at these centers are very helpful. There are sixteen campgrounds in the park with nearly 1,000 campsites, as

Rivers fed from Pacific Ocean storms and glacial melt run through the park and out to sea.

well as four lodges. A range of lodging, commercial campgrounds, and other visitor facilities and services can be found in Port Angeles, Sequim, and some of the smaller villages in the vicinity of the park.

The Last Word

Mountains, glaciers, meadows full of wildflowers, old-growth rain forests, 60 miles of wild coastline, iconic wildlife. Olympic has all this and more. The surrounding roads offer great views of the park, but to really see it—to experience and appreciate it with all your senses—take to the trails.

Petrified Forest National Park

Arizona | nps.gov/pefo

Sometimes a name says it all, but that's definitely not the case at Petrified Forest National Park. Of course there's a prehistoric forest of remarkable and stunning petrified wood—many square miles of it, some of the wood huge, including logs more than 100 feet long and up to 10 feet in diameter. In fact, this may be the world's largest deposit of "mineralized" wood. But there's so much more here: important artifacts of the ancient indigenous people who lived here, including the remains of large pueblos and massive rock art panels; fossils of plants and animals from the Late Triassic period, the dawn of the dinosaurs; a striking and expansive painted desert, a badland cloaked in a palette of pastel colors; a wilderness of more than 50,000 acres where you can find wildness, beauty, and quiet; and a remnant of Historic Route 66 complete with a 1932 Studebaker! This is a place that will please and fascinate visitors, but it is also a remarkable scientific and educational resource that has been studied since the early 20th century.

Petrified Forest is in eastern Arizona, but this hasn't always been its address. Geologists tell us that when the 200-million-year-old supercontinent of Pangea was intact, the land that is now the park was near the equator. This was a warm, humid subtropical environment where trees of 200 feet or more grew and eventually fell. A great river carried many of these trees downstream, and they were buried in layers of sediment that contained silica from volcanic ash. The trees absorbed water and silica, which crystalized into quartz and replaced the tree's organic matter. The quartz took on a rainbow of colors depending on the minerals it contained. The remarkable results of this process of fossilization are stone replicas of the original trees, often accurate right down to the smallest detail, including growth rings and knotholes. At least nine species of trees have been identified, all now extinct. A similar process resulted in fossils of other plants and even animals, including giant crocodile-like reptiles and early dinosaurs.

The park's petrified trees and fossils are in the Chinle Formation, a geologic layer up to 800 feet thick composed of colorful bands of sedimentary rock that give the Painted Desert its name; the park includes an especially colorful portion of this desert. The Chinle Formation was deep within the earth, but the upper layers eroded away, partly as a result of the great upthrust of the Colorado Plateau some 60 million years ago; the elevation of the present-day park generally varies from about 5,000 to 6,000 feet.

(above) Petrified wood is actively eroding out of the park's hills and washes.

(opposite) This park features many square miles of petrified wood, but it holds other attractions as well.

Blue Mesa Loop Trail is a short but spectacular walk through dramatic, deeply eroded hills that feature layers of bluish bentonite clay.

There are three general types of habitats in the park—desert, grassland, and riparian—and these provide homes to a variety of plants and animals. Plants include more than one hundred species of grasses, yuccas, prickly pear cactus, and a variety of wildflowers that bloom when there has been adequate rain. The park, protected from development and grazing for many years, includes some of the finest natural grasslands in northern Arizona. Larger and otherwise interesting animals include mule deer, pronghorn, coyotes, badgers, jackrabbits, foxes, bobcats, and prairie dogs. Iconic birds include golden eagles, roadrunners, and ravens.

Prehistoric people in the Petrified Forest area left evidence of activity 10,000 years or more ago. Initially, nomadic people searched the area for food and water, but later settled here and adopted an agricultural lifestyle. They built pueblos of up to one hundred rooms (be sure to take the short walk to Puerco Pueblo), but had migrated away from the area by the end of the fourteenth century, perhaps because of prolonged drought. The contemporary Hopi believe these people moved northwest and joined them. These ancient people left a wealth of petroglyphs in the park, though much of their meaning remains a mystery. However, archaeologists believe some of the petroglyphs were solar calendars marking solstices and equinoxes. There are more than 650 petroglyphs on Newspaper Rock alone, some more than 2,000 years old. The present-day park lends itself to an east–west

transportation corridor that was used by Native Americans for centuries. In the mid-nineteenth century, the federal government surveyed the area for railroad routes, and the Atlantic and Pacific Railroad through the area was completed in the early 1880s (trains still run through the park). Many passengers laid over in the nearby towns of Holbrook and Adamana (now a ghost town) to visit the present-day park, then called Chalcedony Forest. In the 1920s Route 66 was opened from Chicago to Santa Monica, California, running along the railroad tracks in the park; the park includes a small section of the original road, dubbed the "mother of transcontinental highways," along with a period Studebaker. The road was ultimately superseded by I-40. Increasing commercial and tourist interest in the Petrified Forest area in the late nineteenth century, along with large-scale removal of petrified wood, caused the Territory of Arizona to petition the federal government to protect the resource. President Theodore Roosevelt used the provisions of the Antiquities Act to establish Petrified Forest National Monument in 1906; Congress upgraded the area to Petrified Forest National Park in 1962.

Walking Petrified Forest

Walking in Petrified Forest offers the best opportunity to see and appreciate the unexpected diversity of this park. While there are a limited number of maintained trails, we found three of them compelling. Moreover, there's a large wilderness portion of the park that's more accessible than in

(above) The spectacular collared lizard is the largest in the park.

(below) The park's celebration of Historic Route 66 includes a 1932 Studebaker.

most national parks. Given the relatively small number of visitors to the park, expect some welcome moments of solitude on these walks.

Long Logs Trail / Agate House Trail

The trailhead near Rainbow Forest Museum and Visitor Center leads to two destinations—the Long Logs area and Agate House—but a good choice is to combine them into one hike of about 2.5 miles. This easy route follows an old road for part of the way and gently undulates over the remaining path. Long Logs is a loop that winds through one of the largest concentrations of petrified wood in the park. This is the site of an ancient log jam where the original fallen trees were carried down a river. Many of the trunks are in their entirety or nearly so, and in some cases they are stacked on top of each other. The main trail continues to Agate House, a small ancient pueblo of eight rooms that was occupied about 700 years ago. Part of the pueblo was reconstructed by the Civilian Conservation Corps in the 1930s, but they used the same materials—large pieces of petrified wood—used in the original construction. Of course it makes sense to use local materials for building, but use of petrified wood makes the building take on a character we'd never seen (or even considered). This made us wonder about what the Ancestral Puebloan people thought about petrified wood, these trees made of stone.

Blue Mesa Loop Trail

Blue Mesa Loop is a mile-long spectacular walk through dramatic badlands hills that feature layers of bluish bentonite clay. Petrified wood is scattered about the area and is actively eroding out of the hills and ravines. Drive the 3-mile spur off the main park road to Blue Mesa (with wonderful views to the desert floor below) to find the trailhead. The trail descends steeply at first then levels off to make the circuit through the sharply striated hills and bluffs of this Triassic landscape. The distinctive "elephant skin" appearance of the surface of the badlands hills is caused by infrequent but often torrential rains that erode the surface of the soil in rills, gullies, and washes. The bentonite clay swells and then shrinks and cracks as it dries. We first hiked this trail in the afternoon and enjoyed it, but we hiked it again early the next day to see the blue colors light up during the morning "golden hour" and highly recommend this. We saw no one else on the trail that morning.

Onyx Bridge Route

In addition to the maintained trails, there are a series of innovative "Off the Beaten Path Hikes," routes that explore the park's vast wilderness and vary from a few miles to more than 8 miles. The park has developed a three-ring binder that describes these hikes in detail, including pictures of landmarks along the routes to make wayfinding easier. We chose the walk to Onyx Bridge, a 4-mile out-and-back route that starts at the Wilderness Access Trail beside the Painted Desert Inn, and this turned out to be our favorite hike in the park. Onyx Bridge is a large petrified log—a Triassic conifer tree—that forms a bridge over a small wash. While we enjoyed seeing this natural phenomenon, it was the walk through the Painted Desert that stole the show. We started our hike in the early morning, and the colors of the Painted Desert popped—we were astounded! We worked our way through hills of white, red, and orange; across large stretches of open land; along huge Lithodendron Wash (which was mostly dry but had some large pools of water); and up narrow canyons that required just a little scrambling to reach our destination. Large quantities of petrified wood were emerging from the landscape in what is called the Black Forest. This was the adventure we were looking for, and we relished it—we had it all to ourselves.

The Painted Desert shines in the morning light at Petrified Forest.

Logistics

The park is open year-round, though its short winters can be cold and its summers hot. Extended springs and falls are ideal times to visit and walk. There are entrances at both the north and south ends of the park, with a 28-mile scenic road connecting them. The Painted Desert Visitor Center is near the park's north entrance. Exhibits and information are also available at the park's Painted Desert Inn National Historic Landmark (a 1920s hotel that is now a museum) and the Rainbow Forest Museum near the south entrance. There is no campground or other lodging in the park, with the exception of backcountry camping, which requires a permit. Visitor facilities and services can be found in nearby communities, including Holbrook and Winslow. (Be sure to sing the Eagles famous song as you drive the streets of Winslow!)

The Last Word

As if the astounding, globally significant collection of petrified wood weren't enough, the additional attractions of other Triassic fossils, an extensive prehistoric Native American presence, the expansive and beautiful Painted Desert, and the wild wilderness portion of the park (to say nothing of the celebration of Historic Route 66) should be more than enough to convince you to visit and hike this underappreciated national park.

Pinnacles National Park

California | nps.gov/pinn

Even if you're a seasoned national park–goer, you may not be familiar with Pinnacles National Park, one of the country's newest, established in 2013 (though its predecessor, Pinnacles National Monument, boasted an early establishment date of 1908). This is a land where the word "pinnacles" has two meanings—one referring to the rocky spires, crags, and monoliths that dominate this distinctive landscape; the other suggesting that this is the zenith of this type of dramatic landform. We have no quarrel with either. However, full appreciation of the park requires a leap of geologic faith. The consensus among geologists is that the park had its origins in an 8-mile-long volcanic field named Neenach that was located nearly 200 miles to the southeast. After its eruption some 23 million years ago, the volcanic field was split by California's famous (infamous?) San Andreas Fault and its western half carried to its present location at a rate of about 3 to 6 centimeters per year (and this land is still moving!). Along the way, more tectonic movement, faulting, and erosion have shaped the land into the fantastic forms we enjoy so much today. The park is a treasure for both people and wildlife, and offers a remarkable wilderness retreat just a two-and-a-half-hour drive south of the San Francisco Bay area.

The park is part of the low-lying California Coast Range, and the highest peaks rise only a little over 3,000 feet. The climate is primarily Mediterranean with cool (sometimes cold) wet winters and hot, dry summers. Consequently, most of the park is covered in chaparral vegetation, including grasses, shrubs, and dwarf oaks. The rest of the landscape is a mix of distinctive oak woodlands with a dollop of pines, riparian habitat, and bare rock. If winter rains have been ample, spring wildflowers—more than a hundred species—carpet much of the park and draw large crowds. This is a fire-dependent environment, where periodic fires release seeds from many plant species and fertilize and prepare a natural seedbed. This environment supports diverse wildlife; notable mammals include mountain lions, black-tailed deer, bobcats, coyotes, and gray foxes. Nearly 200 species of birds are found here, including several species of nesting raptors, and the park is widely known for its recent successful reintroduction of California condors, one of the rarest birds in the world. With a wingspan of up to 10 feet, these birds weigh as much as 25 pounds and can fly up to 55 miles an hour and as high as 15,000 feet. Astounding! Other birds include prairie falcons, great horned owls, wild turkeys, golden eagles, and turkey vultures. A census of bees in the park found that the area supports more than 450 species, a greater variety per acre than anywhere else known in the world. The park

(above) Several series of carved stone steps with their accompanying iron handrails help hikers through the trail's steepest and narrowest sections.

(opposite) A dense network of trails winds through the park's iconic rock spires.

Lower-elevation trails run through California's distinctive oak forests.

includes large and steep talus slopes where boulders have fallen into narrow gorges to create several large cave-like structures (called talus caves) that support at least thirteen species of bats.

Like most national parks, the Pinnacles area was occupied by Native Americans, in this case the Chalon and Mutsun groups of the Ohlone people, who used the area seasonally for hunting and gathering. Spanish missionaries arrived in the 1700s, displacing many of the native people and inadvertently introducing diseases. By the 1880s Anglo settlers came for recreation and tourism. Influential politicians and government officials became interested in the area, in large part due to the promotional efforts of local homesteader Schuyler Hain. President Theodore Roosevelt proclaimed the area a national monument in 1908. The Civilian Conservation Corps constructed many of the park's recreation facilities in the 1930s. The federal government incrementally enlarged the monument over succeeding decades, and Congress ultimately elevated it to national park status in 2013. To help honor Hain, the unofficial "father of the park," most of the park is now the Hain Wilderness.

Walking Pinnacles

The park's trail system services most of the area's primary attractions but is limited in scope to only 32 miles; these trails range from easy to strenuous. Most of the trails form a dense network in the geographic and volcanic center of the park, with longer spur trails to the north and south. We can thank the Civilian Conservation Corps for many of these routes. Plan to stay in the park for several days to walk much of this diverse landscape and truly appreciate all the park has to offer.

Condor Gulch Trail / High Peaks Trail / Bear Gulch Trail

We opted to hike this grand loop in the counterclockwise direction, which required a moderate climb up the Condor Gulch Trail, with each switchback offering new views up into the park's High Peaks region. At mile 1.7 you join the High Peaks Trail, and the fun really begins as you wind among the park's iconic spires and massive rock walls. Soon a series of steps carved into the rock (with accompanying iron handrails) guides you through the steepest and narrowest sections of the trail, one of the highlights of hiking in the park. You're led out of the High Peaks and back down to your starting point at Bear Gulch via a short section of the Rim Trail. This hike is 5.3 miles long with about 1,300 feet of elevation gain, and we would rate it moderate to strenuous. You may be lucky enough to see condors soaring overhead or sunning themselves on rocks.

Moses Spring Trail / Bear Gulch Cave Trail / Rim Trail

This set of trails offers a pleasant and interesting lollipop route that features a set of the park's talus caves. The route begins at the popular Bear Gulch Day Use Area and follows the Moses Spring Trail to the Bear Gulch Cave Trail, an entertaining, head-ducking scramble through a string of talus caves;

a headlamp or good flashlight is a must. The trail emerges from the caves at the Bear Gulch Reservoir and returns to the starting point via the Rim Trail. This 2-mile hike is easy to moderate. If you hike the Condor Gulch Trail / High Peaks Trail Loop in the direction described in the previous hike, you can add the Moses Spring Trail / Bear Gulch Cave Trail / Rim Trail at the end of your route.

Old Pinnacles Trail / Balconies Cave Trail / Balconies Cliffs Trail

The Balconies Cave and Balconies Cliffs Trails are popular features of the park's hiking network, offering another talus cave experience and outstanding views of the park's iconic rocks and spires. Access both via the pleasant Old Pinnacles Trail, a nearly level route that follows the seasonal West Fork of Chalone Creek through a shallow wooded canyon. There are several creek crossings, but none are especially challenging given normal water levels. You soon reach the hiking route through Balconies Cave, requiring a headlamp or good flashlight and some scrambling among the large boulders. When you emerge from the cave you are technically on the west side of the park. Here, you double back on the Balconies Cliffs Trail, walking over the area of the caves you just scrambled through. The trail passes along the base of the Balconies Cliffs and their impressive canyon walls. Join the Old Pinnacles Trail again and return to the trailhead. This 5.2-mile lollipop route is easy to moderate. As an alternative when you emerge from Balconies Cave, you can continue west for about half a mile to reach the Chaparral parking area, which serves visitors who enter the park from the west.

North Chalone Peak Trail

Take this longer out-and-back hike into the park's southern wilderness to its highest peak and you'll be rewarded with the park's most wide-ranging views and a healthy dose of solitude that's good for the soul. The trail begins at Bear Gulch and follows the Moses Spring and Bear Gulch Cave Trails to Bear Gulch Reservoir, but then leaves the volcanic core of the park to enter the area's vast chaparral-covered hills. After a while you reach the wire "pig

Higher-elevation trails follow along the park's steep rock walls.

(above) The park includes large and steep talus slopes where boulders have fallen into narrow gorges to create several large cave-like structures (called talus caves) that support several species of bats.

(above right) Multicolored lichens decorate the rocks on many of the park's trails.

fence," erected to keep wild nonnative pigs out of the park. Here you negotiate two stiles over the fence and a gate and then follow a service road up to the summit of North Chalone Peak. You'll find 360-degree views that include the surrounding mountains, the San Andreas Fault, and agricultural valleys beyond the park that are trending toward vineyards. A fire tower (no longer in use) graces the summit. The round-trip hike is about 9 miles with a little more than 2,000 feet of elevation gain and is generally considered strenuous.

Logistics

The park is open year-round, but the winter months can be cold, including snow, and summers can be hot; the busiest season is mid-February through early June, when temperatures are mild and wildflowers are at their peak. Fall can also be busy. Consider visiting the park on weekdays during these peak periods. Pinnacles is a relatively small national park, about 27,000 acres, and is accessible on CA 146 (also called Pinnacles Parkway) from both the east and west entrances; however, the road does not continue through the park. This necessitates a 1- to 2-hour drive to connect the two roads along the south side of the park. The east side of the park includes the main visitor center and a campground (including some sites with RV hookups, showers, a small camp store, and even a swimming

pool!). Lodging, restaurants, gas, and other supplies and services can be found outside the park at nearby small towns. A shuttle bus runs on the east side of the park during the busiest weekends. The west side of the park is less visited, though it offers great views of the park's iconic pinnacles. The park's talus caves require scrambling and a light to negotiate, and they may be closed at times to protect resident bats or due to periodic flooding from winter rains and snows.

The Last Word

This recent addition to the National Park System offers a lot of bang for the buck, including a geologically unusual and remarkable landscape, interesting wildlife (including the rare California condor), a system of talus caves with resident bat populations, and a large wilderness easily accessible from the San Francisco Bay area that provides precious nature and moments of being alone in an otherwise urbanizing region. Hike the park's trails and see for yourself.

Redwood National and State Parks

California | nps.gov/redw

Like just about all the national parks, Redwood National and State Parks in northern California promises a lot and delivers even more. Of course it protects its namesake, the iconic old-growth coast redwood trees, the tallest living things on Earth. Some of these giants have been growing here for more than 2,000 years and can reach heights of 375 feet or more. Redwoods once covered 2 million acres of coastal California and Oregon, but indiscriminate logging through the latter half of the nineteenth century and continuing into the 1970s reduced the forest to just over 100,000 acres, nearly half of which is included in Redwood. But the surrounding land and sea of the park also protect the natural and cultural context of the redwood forest; there are nearly 40 miles of precious undeveloped coastline, the low-lying Coast Range of mountains, indigenous plant and animal life (including habitat for several threatened species), wild and scenic rivers (including the Smith River, the only free-flowing river remaining in California), prairie grasslands, and an area of sand dunes. The park also helps preserve the culture of the original inhabitants, the Native Americans who lived here for thousands of years and for whom the area is still home.

Management of the park is a fresh breath of administrative air, a cooperative venture between the NPS at the federal level and California State Parks. Officially known as Redwood National and State Parks, the area includes three state parks—Del Norte Coast Redwoods, Jedediah Smith Redwoods, and Prairie Creek Redwoods—and the federal Redwood National Park. In recognition of its international significance, the area was designated a World Heritage Site in 1980.

The park and its environs are geologically active, part of the massive "Ring of Fire" in the basin of the Pacific Ocean. But the star of the natural world at Redwood is its namesake tree. Redwoods are an ancient species, having evolved in the Age of Dinosaurs. Their scientific name is *Sequoia sempervirens*, the first word noting the genus (honoring the famous Cherokee) and the latter the species (meaning "ever-living"). But they're more commonly called simply "redwoods" and are closely related to the giant sequoias found in Sequoia/Kings Canyon and Yosemite National Parks. Redwoods grow taller than sequoias, but the latter have a greater mass. Redwoods grow only near the coastline of northern California and southern Oregon—not too close to the sea because they can be injured by salt spray, but close enough to be bathed by the fog common to the area in summer; this fog is absorbed by the leaves and provides the moisture needed to survive the area's hot, dry summers. The trees have bark up to a foot thick that protects them from insects, disease, and the

(opposite) Some of these redwoods have been growing here for more than 2,000 years.

(above) The Smith River, the only undammed river system in California, runs through the park.

(above right) A few of the largest and most majestic old-growth groves of redwoods are easily accessible on relatively short, well-maintained trails.

area's historic ground fires. Periodic ground fires clear the forest floor of competing species, and controlled burns are now used as a park management tool.

Old-growth coastal redwood forests are biologically rich, and when the park's other features are added in, including its range of elevations from below sea level (the park extends a quarter mile out from the shoreline) to nearly 3,300 feet, the park is important to many species of plants and animals. Other important forest trees include Douglas fir, Sitka spruce, Pacific madrone, and big-leaf maple. Understories of laurel, rhododendron, and ferns are common. Notable land mammals include black bears, mountain lions, Roosevelt elk, black-tail deer, and bobcats. Marine species include gray whales, seals, sea lions, dolphins, porpoises, and orca whales. Birds include pelicans, bald eagles, ospreys, and endangered northern spotted owls and marbled murrelets. Rivers provide habitat for salmon and steelhead.

Diverse groups of Native Americans lived along the coast for thousands of years, hunting, fishing, and gathering for subsistence and using fallen redwood trees for shelter and boats. Many of the descendants of these people still live in the area, on and off small reservations. In the 1800s the area experienced several economic boom periods, first for trapping, then for gold, and finally for logging the extensive groves of ancient trees. Logging continued into the twentieth century, powered by

Fern Canyon's steep walls are covered in ferns and other greenery.

the tools of the Industrial Revolution, including trains and bulldozers, and the lumber was used for building in San Francisco and other areas.

In the early twentieth century, conservationists became alarmed at the rapid disappearance of the redwoods and formed the Save the Redwoods League. In the 1920s the group successfully lobbied the State of California to set aside the three state parks that are such integral parts of the present-day system of protected areas. Over the years this group, along with the Sierra Club, National Geographic Society, and others, raised money and purchased land that was ultimately included in the park, and this process continues today. Some of this land has been logged but is now being restored, a process that will take centuries. The groups also worked for decades to create a national park to protect the area and finally succeeded in 1968. In 1994 the NPS joined with California State Parks to form Redwood National and State Parks, taking a coordinated approach to park management. The present-day park has grown to include a 40-mile stretch of northern California comprising 133,000 acres.

Walking Redwood

Walking is the best way to see, experience, and appreciate the national parks, and this may be especially true at Redwood. Only by walking through these ancient groves of trees can you fully sense

The park's 35-mile Coastal Trail can be walked in a series of day hikes or a multi-day thru-hike.

the seemingly impossible size of these trees and the centuries it takes to establish these old-growth forests. Redwood includes more than 200 miles of trails, some through the most iconic old-growth coast redwood groves, others along the Pacific coast and the streams that empty into the ocean.

The Ancient Redwood Groves (Tall Trees Trail, Lady Bird Johnson Grove Trail, Stout Memorial Grove Trail, Simpson-Reed Trail)

Though there are many huge redwood trees scattered through the park, a few of the largest and most majestic old-growth groves are easily accessible on relatively short, well-maintained trails. These are the heart of the park. Choose one, or, better yet, walk several, maybe even all of them; each seems more impressive than the last, and that's saying something. We've walked among these groves on several visits to the park and are still awestruck. The Tall Trees Grove has the longest trail (about 3.5 miles) and is thought by some to be the most magnificent, but maybe that's because it's the only one that requires a permit from the NPS to enter. Trails through the other groves are considerably shorter. Ferns and other greenery carpet all the groves, and interpretive signs posted along the trails enhance the quality of each walk.

Fern Canyon Trail

Fern Canyon is a magical place formed by the natural stone-cutting power of the waters of Home Creek. The result is a steep-sided canyon with 40-foot walls vegetated with ferns, mosses, and other rain forest plants. The canyon walls—nearly every square inch of them—are covered in this greenery, and the effect is enchanting. From the end of Davison Road, walk up the canyon about half a mile and then climb out of the canyon on a series of steps, returning to the trailhead along the canyon rim for a hike of about a mile. The trail through Fern Canyon is connected to a network of other trails in this area, offering opportunities for much longer hikes.

Enderts Beach

As impressive as the redwoods are, you should find time to walk at least one of the park's remarkable Pacific Ocean beaches, and scenic Enderts Beach is a good choice. A walk of just under a mile along the abandoned old Coast Highway brings you down to a crescent-shaped wild beach known for its waves, rocky shoreline, and opportunity for long walks, driftwood, and fascinating tide pools. Check the NPS website for ranger-guided walks here.

Redwood Creek Trail / Hiouchi Trail

These trails follow two of the most important streams in the park. Redwood Creek Trail is one of the most popular, though it's typically hiked only to a turnaround point about 1.5 miles from the trailhead—the point of the first major crossing of the creek on a footbridge. This and other bridges along the trail are only in place in the summer months, and fording the creek in high water can be dangerous. This first section of the trail is flat and well-maintained and is a delightful walk along the river and beside the rain forest composed of spruce, Douglas fir, maples, alders, and occasional redwoods. A resident elk herd adds to the excitement. The full length of the trail travels about 8 miles to the Tall Trees Grove noted above; it's best walked as a short backpacking trip, with camping opportunities anywhere along the usually wide creek bed (a permit is needed for this and other backpacking trips). The Hiouchi Trail is an out-and-back trail of 4.2 miles (round-trip) through expanses of redwoods and along the south bank of the Smith River (named for nineteenth-century explorer Jedediah Smith). Relish the tranquil scenery of the only undammed river system in California. The river's waters are a striking jade green derived from upstream deposits of serpentine (*Hiouchi* is a Native American word for "blue-green waters"). The trail ends at the magnificent Stout Memorial Grove noted above.

Coastal Trail

The park's epic long-distance trail traces its magical, largely undeveloped coastline almost continuously for 35 miles, and all of it can be walked, either in its entirety or in sections. This trail is part of the legendary 1,200-mile California Coastal Trail. Highlights include old-growth redwoods and Sitka spruce, migrating gray whales, secluded beaches, massive piles of driftwood, tide pools, Roosevelt elk, open prairies, off-shore sea stacks, thousands of seabirds, and sweeping ocean vistas. Check with the NPS on the status of backcountry camps along the trail; a permit is needed. Tide tables and the ability to read them are essential to safely navigate the trail.

Logistics

The park is open year-round, but winter tends to be rainy and summers can be hot and foggy; spring and fall are the best times to visit. Five visitor and information centers serve the park: Crescent City Information Center and Hiouchi, Jedediah Smith, Prairie Creek, and Thomas H. Kuchel Visitor

The park supports lots of wildlife, including Roosevelt elk.

(above) In addition to redwoods, the park also protects nearly 40 miles of precious undeveloped California coastline.

(above right) Every visitor should walk at least one of the park's remarkable Pacific Ocean beaches; scenic Enderts Beach is a good choice.

Centers. There are no lodgings in the park, but camping is available at the three state parks. Lodging and other services are available in the larger towns of Crescent City to the north and Arcata and Eureka to the south, as well as the villages that are strung out along the north–south orientation of the park, such as Klamath, Requa, and Orick.

The Last Word

The story of Redwood is complex, starting with the ancient trees that evolved here and the civilizations that lived in harmony with them for thousands of years. Then came an intense period of tragedy when native people were displaced and the vast majority of trees were destroyed. Now we're fortunate to be in a period of triumph, where many of the remaining redwood groves are protected and managed in concert with descendants of the original inhabitants. Of course much additional work is needed to more fully reestablish the ecological integrity of this area. But we should all celebrate the progress that's been made by walking among the groves and other features of these remarkable national and state parks and World Heritage Site.

Rocky Mountain National Park

Colorado | nps.gov/romo

The Rocky Mountains are one of the world's great mountain ranges, running from Alaska to New Mexico, the backbone of the western region of the North American continent. Rocky Mountain National Park straddles this mountain range in Colorado and is a microcosm of all that makes these mountains so famous. There are towering peaks—more than sixty mountains higher than 12,000 feet, including 14,259-foot Longs Peak—along with alpine lakes, deep forests, mountain streams, tundra, waterfalls, great meadows, and exciting wildlife. And all this is surprisingly accessible, just a couple hours' drive from Denver. The park's road system, including Trail Ridge Road—at over 12,000 feet, the highest paved through-road in the country—and an extensive system of trails offer outstanding opportunities to explore all aspects of the park. Though the park is not especially large by national park standards—265,000 acres—it's surrounded by another 253,000 acres of USDA Forest Service wilderness, making the area seem substantially larger. The vast majority of Rocky (that's what the locals call it) is designated wilderness.

Geologists suggest that the present-day Rocky Mountains are at least the third generation of mountains to occupy this area, the previous mountains having been nearly fully eroded. The mountains we now enjoy are relatively new in geologic terms, uplifted by tectonic forces between 70 and 40 million years ago and capped by the remains of older mountains, revealing rocks that are nearly 2 billion years old. The present-day mountains have been shaped by several periods of glaciation, lowering their original height and leaving behind deep canyons, streams, lakes, giant cirques, moraines, and grand meadows (often called "parks"). Rocky includes several small glaciers, but they're disappearing due to climate change. Climate change is affecting the park in many other ways as well. For example, winters are not as cold. This has allowed mountain pine beetle populations to explode, causing extensive die-off of lodgepole pines, and this in turn has made the park more susceptible to wildfires.

The nearly 6,500-foot variation in elevation, complemented by the dramatic differences in aspect and rainfall of the east and west sides of the park, results in a rich variety of plant and animal life. The montane portion of the park (below 9,000 feet) is found in the lowest band of

Rocky's 355 miles of trails access all the park's primary attractions.

mountains and includes great forests of ponderosa pine, aspens, Douglas fir, and lodgepole pine. The leaves of aspen turn bright yellow and gold in fall, and this glorious spectacle attracts many park visitors. Riparian areas and wetlands support willows and cottonwoods. The subalpine region generally ranges from 9,000 to 11,400 feet and is dominated by Engelmann spruce and firs. The alpine region, more than a quarter of the park, is generally found above 11,400 feet and is marked by extensive areas of tundra—a dense mat of low-growing vegetation, primarily herbs and mosses, that is well-adapted to extreme cold, short growing seasons, strong winds, and thin soils. Wildflowers abound, including blue columbine (Colorado's state flower) and range through all elevations.

The park is a favorite for spotting wildlife such as mule deer, elk, bighorn sheep, coyotes, and moose. You'll often see elk in the higher elevations in summer and in lower elevations during the fall, when males bugle in their pursuit of females. Note the black scars on aspen trees where elk and mule deer have grazed on the tree's soft bark. The Kawuneeche Valley is best for viewing moose. Mountain lions and black bears also inhabit the park, but their populations are low and they're seldom seen. Pikas and yellow-bellied marmots inhabit the higher elevations and are especially entertaining to watch. (Please don't feed them or any other wildlife.) Birders love Rocky; more than 270 species have been identified in the park area. Among the more interesting are white-tailed ptarmigan, which live in the tundra year-round, and American dippers in many of the park's rocky streams.

Given the high elevations and harsh climate of what is now Rocky, it's unlikely that Native Americans occupied much of the area year-round. However, the foothills and surrounding plains

Rocky includes towering peaks; more than sixty mountains are higher than 12,000 feet.

were used by Ute on the western side of the park and Arapaho and Cheyenne on the eastern side, and archaeologists suggest that this activity can be traced back some 6,000 years. The route over the Continental Divide that is now Trail Ridge Road was used by Paleo-Indians for hunting and foraging. However, things changed dramatically after the Louisiana Purchase in 1803, when many Native Americans were moved to reservations to make way for settlement. Steven Long, for whom Longs Peak is named, explored the area in 1820; settlers moved in the mid-1800s, and there was a short-lived gold rush in 1858. Local resident Enos Mills, inspired by John Muir, spent much of his adult life advocating for the establishment of a national park, finding allies in the Colorado Mountain Club and the Denver Chamber of Commerce, and the park was eventually established by Congress in 1915. The Civilian Conservation Corps built the park's remarkable Trail Ridge Road in the 1930s.

Walking Rocky

Rocky includes approximately 355 miles of trails that access all primary attractions, offering hikers ample opportunities to see, experience, and appreciate this spectacular, multidimensional park. Wander through lush meadows and across alpine tundra, hike through forests and around lakes, climb the high mountains, and walk along rivers and streams to find waterfalls. We suggest the following trails to enjoy the best of the diversity of this exceptional park.

Nymph Lake Trail / Dream Lake Trail / Emerald Lake Trail

This string of lakes is the most popular hike in the park, and for good reason. Lying high in the park's glacially carved Bear Lake Corridor, these iconic mountain lakes are an easy to moderate hike: half a mile to Nymph Lake, another six tenths of a mile on to Dream Lake, and seven tenths of a mile to Emerald Lake, for a 3.6-mile round-trip hike. Nymph Lake is named for its pond lilies (*Nymphaea polsepala*); the name Dream Lake will be obvious when you reach it. In our view, Emerald Lake is, indeed, the crown jewel—a green-tinted glacial lake hard against the towering cliffs of Hallett Peak. Embrace the fact that so many of your fellow hikers are enjoying this trail with you.

Ute Trail

More than a quarter of Rocky is alpine tundra (Russian for "land of no trees"), and the Ute Trail traverses a particularly dramatic stretch that follows an extended ridgeline. The trailhead is on Trail Ridge Road on the east side of the park. Centuries ago, Ute and Arapaho walked this area as they moved between their winter and summer hunting grounds. We followed the trail for 2 miles to where it reaches Timberline Pass, the point at which it descends sharply. We found the trail a dramatic mix

Rocky Mountain elk inhabit the park and are seen in the higher elevations in summer and lower elevations in the fall.

The Colorado River Trail takes hikers to the headwaters of this mighty river.

of the rich miniature forest that is the tundra, the stupendous views of the surrounding mountains and valleys, and the drama of the big sky and its powerful clouds. Many of the park's most impressive animals graze or live in this habitat, including elk (we marveled at a herd of nearly fifty), mule deer, bighorn sheep, and marmots and pikas (we heard many). Given the fragile character of the alpine plants, be sure to stay on the established trail.

Bridal Veil Falls Trail

This is a delightful 6-mile (round-trip) out-and-back hike in the northeast quadrant of the park. Yes, the trail leads to one of the nicest waterfalls in the park, but it was the walk itself that stole our hearts. The trailhead is at the historic McGraw Ranch, now a research station for the park. Walk right through the ranch and along lush Cow Creek all the way to the falls. You'll enjoy open meadows, big stands of Rocky Mountain aspens, and occasional old-growth ponderosa pines. The trail rises more than 1,000 feet, but it's all gentle until the last few hundred yards—a scramble over rocks to the falls. Parking is limited, so get to the trailhead early.

Colorado River Trail

The Colorado River Trail in the park's colorfully named Never Summer Range winds its way up the exquisite Kawuneeche Valley toward the headwaters of the Colorado River. This is the mighty

1,400-mile river that drains much of the southwestern United States, carved the Grand Canyon, and now provides water and power to millions of people in seven southwestern states. The Kawuneeche is a wide valley sculpted by one of the park's largest glaciers; here the nascent Colorado River meanders through lush meadows graced by great stands of lodgepole pines and the steep granite cliffs of the surrounding mountains, including the Continental Divide. The valley is steeped in history. Evidence suggests that the area was used by ancient people to hunt mastodons shortly after the glaciers retreated, some 13,000 years ago. In the early 1800s mountain men trapped plentiful beaver to near extinction. In the second half of the nineteenth century, the rush for gold and silver brought prospectors and miners who built Lulu City, a rough-and-tumble assemblage of some 500 people, along the river's headwaters. But the silver ore wasn't as rich as hoped, and the city went bust in 1884, melting back into the wilderness. The 7.4-mile (round-trip) out-and-back hike through the valley is a delight, offering insights into both natural and human history. Little evidence of Lulu City remains, but the wilderness that characterizes this area has proven infinitely more valuable than the silver it was thought to hold.

Yes, this trail leads to Bridal Veil Falls, one of the nicest waterfalls in the park, but it was the walk itself that stole our hearts.

Longs Peak

It's telling that the NPS website for Rocky emphatically states that the classic Keyhole Route up and down Longs Peak is not a hike—it's a climb! Our experience confirms this. Nevertheless, this 14,259-foot peak with its iconic profile calls to thousands who climb the mountain each year. The Keyhole Route (named for an opening in the ridge between Longs and Storm Peaks) is one of the most popular in Colorado and an extraordinary experience. The route begins on a trail through deep forest and across two streams, but the maintained trail ends in Boulder Field, a massive bowl of rocks that requires extensive scrambling. The Keyhole and the route beyond to the summit require much more scrambling, navigating narrow ledges and loose rocks, as well as careful attention to wayfinding. The view from the large summit is astounding, but take stock of the time and weather, and begin your descent as early as possible to avoid the dangers of afternoon thunderstorms and darkness. The

Fall brings many visitors to the park to see the transformation of Rocky's aspens from green to yellow and gold.

Keyhole Route is the easiest and most popular way to climb Longs Peak, as the many other climbers ascending and descending with you will testify. However, this is a very demanding climb, about 16 miles (round-trip) and nearly 5,000 feet of elevation gain and loss—and at very high altitude. You must start your climb *very* early—as early as 3:00 a.m.—to help ensure that you are off the mountain before thunderstorms materialize. We encourage you to read the page on the NPS website that addresses the climb, watch the helpful video posted on the website, and talk with rangers about local conditions. Think twice about climbing this mountain—there are many other wonderful and rewarding peaks to climb in Rocky. Above all, don't let a bout of "summit fever" suspend good judgment when you're on the mountain.

Logistics

The park has a generous five visitor centers—Beaver Meadows, Fall River, Moraine Park, Alpine, and Kawuneeche—where you can get good advice on how best to see and appreciate the park, including hiking trails and up-to-date local conditions. There are five campgrounds along with many backcountry camping opportunities in the wilderness portion of the park. Hotels, motels, B&Bs, and other accommodations and visitor facilities and services are available in the Estes Park region on the east side of the park and Grand Lake on the west side. The park is open year-round, though Trail Ridge Road is closed in winter and much of the early spring and late fall. Most trails are snow covered except in summer; the prime visitor and hiking season is June through September. Due to the popularity of the park and the Bear Lake and Moraine Park areas in particular, a free shuttle bus system serves these areas. Trailhead parking lots tend to fill early every day, and the shuttle is an excellent alternative.

The Last Word

Yes, Rocky is glorious, but it can also be crowded; in relative terms, the park is only one-eighth the size of Yellowstone, but it receives even more visits. We outline ways to deal with this in Part 3 of this book. But the best advice is to *hike*—get off the crowded roads and onto the trails, taking advantage of the inverse relationship between distance from the trailhead and number of other visitors you see. Most of all, be thankful that places like Rocky have been preserved for all of us to enjoy and appreciate.

Saguaro National Park

Arizona | nps.gov/sagu

Just 10 miles to both the east and west of downtown Tucson lie dense forests of the remarkable giant saguaro cactus, the symbol of much of the Sonoran Desert and the American Southwest. These tall cacti are sometimes called the "Monarch of the Sonoran Desert" and the "Redwood of the Desert." To the west of the city is the park's Tucson Mountain District; to the east is the larger Rincon Mountain District. Together they protect nearly 100,000 acres of Sonoran Desert and low-lying mountains, as well as the stunning cacti and other vegetation and associated wildlife that live here. Giant saguaros are instantly recognizable; they're large, graceful, tree-like plants with upward-thrusting branches or arms that suggest human figures. There are an estimated 1.6 million saguaros in the park, constituting one of the most specialized landscapes in the National Park System.

Saguaros are wonderfully adapted to their desert environment, finding water through their shallow root system that extends out as far as 50 feet. The plant soaks up much as 200 gallons of water in a single rainstorm—enough to last a year—and stores the water in its fleshy tissue that expands much like an accordion. Their waxy skin and "leaves" of needles help reduce moisture loss and protect the plants from animals. The tall cactus can weigh as much as 8 tons, and long woody ribs add internal structural support. Saguaros begin their life cycle as a seed the size of pinhead and grow slowly at first, perhaps only an inch or so in their first several years. They sprout branches or arms at around 70 years and reach full height—about 50 feet—at about age 150. The trees bloom with cream-colored flowers (Arizona's state flower) in early summer—there can be as many as one hundred flowers on a single cactus. Their deep red fruit ripens in July and is an important source of food for a number of desert animals, including doves, bats, javelinas, and foxes. Tohono O'odham people still harvest the fruit to make syrup, jam, and wine. Gila woodpeckers and gilded flickers make nest holes in the saguaro's trunk and branches.

The underlying geology of the park is labyrinthine and includes many of the major geologic processes, including volcanism, sedimentation, and plate tectonics. The latter has shaped the vast Basin and Range Province that extends from northern Mexico to southern Oregon and

Mighty giant saguaros can live for more than 150 years and reach an astonishing height of 50 feet.

is generally defined by north–south oriented mountains separated by wide plains. The mountains in the park's two units span a wide range of elevations, from about 2,000 to nearly 9,000 feet, offering a great range of habitats for plants and animals, including desert, grassland, and mountain forest ecosystems. Twenty-five species of cactus grow at lower elevations; higher elevations support forests of Douglas fir and ponderosa pine. These differing habitats support a range of mammals, including black bears, mule and white-tailed deer, bobcats, ringtails, coyotes, mountain lions, and javelinas. More than 200 species of birds have been recorded, including Gambel's quail, roadrunners, Mexican spotted owls, great horned owls, golden eagles, and cactus wrens. Reptiles include desert tortoises, diamondback rattlesnakes, and Gila monsters and several other species of lizards.

(above) The Civilian Conservation Corps built enduring visitor facilities in the park in 1934, including roads, trails, and picnic facilities.

(opposite) Spring offers lovely walks through Saguaro National Park's Cactus Forest.

The earliest visitors to the Tucson Basin were Paleo-Indians some 10,000 years ago. More recently, Hohokam people lived here in villages, hunting and gathering and creating irrigation systems for farming. Evidence of their presence is found in petroglyphs and broken pottery. Spanish explorers arrived in the mid-thirteenth century and founded the San Xavier Mission in 1692 and Presidio San Agustín del Tucson in 1775. However, wide-scale settlement of the area didn't begin until Arizona became part of the United States and after passage of the Homestead Act in 1862. Homesteaders farmed and ranched in the area, grazing cattle on public lands, and prospectors searched for gold and other minerals. In response to rapid urban and suburban expansion of the Tucson area, President Herbert Hoover used the Antiquities Act to protect the area as Saguaro National Monument in 1933. The monument was later expanded and established as a national park by Congress in 1994.

Walking Saguaro

The park's Tucson Mountain and Rincon Mountain Districts include a combined 165 miles of trails. These range from short nature trails to a section of the mighty 800-mile Arizona National Scenic Trail. The park is surprisingly diverse, ranging from low-lying Sonoran Desert to the tops of the park's nearly 9,000-foot mountains.

Desert Discovery Nature Trail / Cactus Garden Trail / Desert Ecology Trail

These three nature trails (the first two in the Tucson Mountain area and the last in the Rincon Mountain area) are short (each less than a mile), accessible walks that introduce visitors to the

(above) Saguaro seedlings survive in greater numbers when they're sheltered by other vegetation (in this case, a paloverde tree).

(above right) Walk the park's nature trails and enhance your appreciation of the evolution and resilience of the native vegetation.

specialized desert plants and wildlife that have adapted to the extremes of heat and aridity. Interpretive signage along these trails will help enhance your walks through the rest of the park. For example, did you know that saguaro seedlings thrive under the shelter of other desert plants, such as mesquite trees? Here, young saguaros are sheltered from heavy rains, cold nights, and extreme heat, and they benefit from added nutrients in the soil. Later, their extensive roots systems allow them to outcompete their nurse trees for vital water. Walk one or more of these trails and learn about these interesting ecological relationships.

Signal Hill Trail

This is another short trail (about a third of a mile round-trip) in the Tucson Mountain District, this one focusing on human occupation of the park. Ancient people visited the Tucson Basin beginning more than 10,000 years ago, and the Hohokam left rock art panels that mark their presence. See several of these panels at the end of this trail. These mysterious symbols (petroglyphs) were made by pecking away the natural desert "varnish," and may have had spiritual or cultural significance. Please stay on the maintained trail and do not touch or climb on the rocks. The picnic facilities at the trailhead feature ramadas, tables, benches, fireplaces, and bathrooms constructed by the Civilian Conservation Corps in 1934.

The Sonoran Desert in Saguaro National Park includes a rich diversity of life adapted to the area's hot and dry climate.

Cactus Forest Trail

This trail traverses the heart of the Rincon Mountains' famous Cactus Forest, a hub of the park's diverse desert vegetation, including many species of cactus, green-barked paloverde trees, and spiked ocotillos. But the stars of the show are the many giant saguaros. This a long trail; we recommend walking the 2.5-mile section that's enclosed within the Cactus Forest Loop Drive (the portion of the trail that connects the Cactus Forest North and Cactus Forest South Trailheads). In addition to the desert vegetation, you'll find the interesting remains of old limekilns along the trail. Since this portion of the trail connects two points on a one-way loop road, you'll have to be clever about returning to your original trailhead: (1) Leave a vehicle (or bikes) at the trailhead you're hiking toward, (2) split your group and leave vehicles at both trailheads, swapping keys when you pass on the hike, or (3) hike the trail (or some portion of it) as an out-and-back. This is an easy trail with some small rolling hills that offer good views of the surrounding park.

Tanque Verde Ridge Trail

This long trail (about 11 miles one way) in the Rincon Mountain District features a nearly full range of the park's elevations and a steady stream of outstanding views of the park and the Tucson metropolitan area. The trail serves as one of the primary access points to the park's large high-elevation

The park's trails offer insights into the diversity of life in the Sonoran Desert; examples shown here include giant saguaros, ocotillo, fishhook barrel cacti, chollas, and mesquite.

backcountry. The trail begins at the Javelina Picnic Area in the park's vast Cactus Forest and climbs onto the long Tanque Verde Ridge where it reaches the summit of Tanque Verde Peak after a 4,000-foot climb at just over 7,000 feet. Hikers can camp at nearby Juniper Basin Camp. The trail continues to historic Manning Camp at nearly 8,000 feet. Camping requires a permit. We day-hiked a portion of the trail, turning around after several miles and retracing our steps to the trailhead, and enjoyed the scenery and solitude the Tanque Verde Ridge Trail provided.

Wasson Peak (Sendero Esperanza Trail / Hugh Norris Trail)

At 4,687 feet, Wasson Peak is the highest in the Tucson Mountains and calls to many hikers. Several combinations of trails will take you there; we selected the Sendero Esperanza Trail (translated as "Trail of Hope") to the Hugh Norris Trail (named for a widely respected Tohono O'odham police chief) and up to the peak from there. We chose this route because of its varied terrain, diverse vegetation, and "superbloom" of wildflowers that was in full swing in early spring after an especially wet Arizona winter. The trail began with a sandy walk through a nice collection of saguaros and associated vegetation and then switchbacked to meet the Hugh Norris Trail. This is where the flowers began in earnest, lining the trail and flowing in great patches across much of the landscape; some of the showiest included Mexican poppies, lupines, and penstemons. Leaving the flowers, the trail followed the Hugh Norris Trail up a long ridge, eventually reaching Wasson Peak, where we enjoyed views of Tucson, the Santa Catalina Mountains, and nearly all of the Tucson Mountains. This is an 8-mile round-trip hike that we judge as moderately strenuous.

Logistics

The park is open year round, though summer is exceptionally hot and dry; the primary visitor season is November through April. If the winter has been relatively wet, spring can offer bountiful wildflowers. Each of the park's two districts has a visitor center and a loop road that provides access to many of the park's trailheads. There are no campgrounds or other lodging in the park; however, these and other commercial visitor facilities and services are plentiful in the Tucson metropolitan area. Backpacking is allowed in the Rincon Mountain Wilderness portion of the park; a permit is required.

The Last Word

Like all the national parks, Saguaro is special; it preserves a large section of the unique Sonoran Desert, much of it covered in dense stands of mighty saguaro cactuses. The park also protects other desert plants and animals—monuments of biological adaptation and evolution in the face of extreme heat and aridity. This large national park sits on the doorstep of a major American city, making it easily accessible. Take advantage of the opportunity to walk through the park's many highly specialized and strikingly beautiful landscapes.

The prehistoric Hohokam people left mysterious petroglyphs that may have spiritual or cultural meaning.

Sequoia and Kings Canyon National Parks

California | nps.gov/seki

Sequoia and Kings Canyon National Parks have the good fortune to lie end to end in the southern Sierra Nevada. Together they measure nearly 900,000 acres and constitute one of the largest protected areas in the nation; they seem even larger due to the national forest wilderness areas that surround them. Though Sequoia and Kings Canyon are separate national parks, they're managed as one. These are parks of superlatives, including cathedral-like groves of giant sequoias (the largest living things); the highest mountain in the continental United States (Mount Whitney at 14,494 feet); one of the country's deepest canyons (Kings Canyon is more than 1.5 miles deep); and a staggering range of elevations, from 1,500 to 14,500 feet.

Many observers liken Sequoia/Kings Canyon to Yosemite National Park, born of the same geology, biology, and history. However, Sequoia/Kings Canyon has the advantage of being relatively undeveloped and receives far fewer visitors. Both Sequoia and Kings Canyon have especially fine scenic roads, trails, campgrounds, etc., but these are essentially wilderness parks—indeed, 96 percent of the land contained within them is designated wilderness, best seen on foot over the parks' extensive trail systems.

This region of California is geologically active due to movement of underlying tectonic plates that manifest themselves in periodic earthquakes. These forces have created an arc of mountains that extends from Alaska through South America and includes the Sierra Nevada. Pushed up by tectonic forces, the Sierras are a relatively young mountain range, at least in geologic time—about 10 million years old. Much of the underlying rock is the characteristic gray granite that was formed by ancient volcanos in the Age of Dinosaurs. These mountains were heavily glaciated several times, creating steep-walled, U-shaped valleys. Another characteristic feature of the Sierras is its granite domes, which erode, or "exfoliate," like the skin of an onion. Moro Rock in Sequoia is a textbook example. The parks also include an extensive group of caves carved from marble.

The extreme range of elevations in the park present diverse habitats that support a wide spectrum of plants and animals. Blue oak woodlands and areas of chaparral and grasslands characterize the lower-elevation Sierra foothills; during the dry summers and fall, these are the "golden hills" of

(opposite) Zumwalt Meadow is surrounded by steep granite cliffs and the Kings River.

(above) The size and age of giant sequoias are truly staggering; they're the largest living things on Earth and among the oldest as well.

(above right) The park's characteristic granite domes erode, or "exfoliate," like the skin of an onion; Moro Rock is a classic example.

California. Higher elevations of about 5,500 to 9,000 feet are covered by a mixed coniferous forest, including ponderosa, Jeffrey, sugar, and lodgepole pines; incense cedar; and white fir. Cold mountain streams and tranquil meadows punctuate these forests. Most importantly, this is where the park's extensive groves of giant sequoias reside. Areas above 9,000 feet are generally treeless and constitute the "High Sierra," an area of tall peaks, exposed rock, and high-elevation lakes.

The namesake giant sequoias are one of the defining features of these parks. The size and age of these trees are truly staggering—they're the largest living things on Earth and among the oldest as well. There are more than seventy groves of giant sequoias in these parks; two of them—Giant Forest in Sequoia and General Grant Grove in Kings Canyon—are the most famous and accessible and include the very largest trees. The General Sherman Tree in Giant Forest is the largest in the world, measuring 270 feet high and more than 100 feet in circumference! Its first large branch is 130 feet from the ground and boasts a diameter of nearly 7 feet; the tree is estimated to be about 2,200 years old. Astonishingly, these trees germinate from a seed about the size of a pinhead. Giant sequoias (*Sequoiadendron giganteum*) should not be confused with their close relatives, the coast redwood trees (*Sequoia sempervirens*) that grow along the coast of northern California and southern Oregon; coast redwoods are the tallest in the world, but they lack the girth of giant sequoias. Fire plays an important role in sequoia ecology and reproduction. Their cones release seeds only when

The Kings River drains most of its namesake park.

subjected to the heat of a fire. Periodic ground fires help prepare the soil for seed germination, and the sequoia's thick bark—up to 2 feet—protects the trees from these fires. This was not understood until relatively recently. During the first decades of the parks, fires were quickly extinguished in the sequoia groves, unknowingly putting the trees at risk; now periodic ground fires are allowed to burn, and prescribed fires are used under the right natural conditions.

The diverse habitats of Sequoia/Kings Canyon support more than 1,000 species of plants and more than 250 species of vertebrate animals, including black bears, mule deer, bighorn sheep, bobcats, foxes, coyotes, ground squirrels, rattlesnakes, and rare mountain lions. The last California grizzly bear was killed in Sequoia in 1932. More than 200 species of birds have been documented in the parks.

Native Americans (the Monache) occupied the foothills of the parks; evidence shows these people traveled through the mountain passes in summer to trade with tribes to the east. Pictographs are found in the lower elevations of the park along with bedrock mortars used to grind acorns. Many of the native people died of smallpox and other diseases introduced by early explorers and settlers. The first European-American settler was Hale Tharp, who crafted a home from a fallen, hollowed-out sequoia in Giant Forest; this unique dwelling can still be seen in the park. Many sequoias were cut down for their lumber, and this continued until Sequoia National Park was established in 1890, the country's second national park. Former logger Walter Fry worked hard to save the remaining trees, as did John Muir and Susan Thew and many citizens of the nearby San Joaquin Valley. The park has

Ninety-six percent of these parks is designated wilderness and best seen on foot over their extensive trail systems.

been expanded several times since then, including the 1978 addition of the Mineral King Valley in the southern part of Sequoia, saved from a massive ski resort development proposed by the Walt Disney Corporation. Kings Canyon National Park was established in 1940.

Walking Sequoia/Kings Canyon

The parks' two main roads—Generals Highway and Kings Canyon Scenic Byway—compete as two of the most beautiful in the National Park System, but the most genuine and intimate way to see these parks is on foot. The parks' generous trail systems invite visitors to abandon their cars and hike. Some of these trails are short and easily accessible; others demand—and offer—more. The trails we describe below will leave you glad you experienced the diversity these parks offer.

Moro Rock Trail

Moro Rock is an outstanding example of the granite domes that are notable features of the Sierra Nevada, and climbing Moro Rock is a ritual for nearly all first-time visitors. This huge monolith hangs on the southwest side of the mountains near the south entrance to Sequoia. The trail is short—just half a mile round-trip—but it includes nearly 400 steps and some modest exposure to reach its 6,725-foot summit. The Civilian Conservation Corps constructed the trail in the 1930s, and it's now on the National Register of Historic Places. While you're catching your breath along the stairway, notice the characteristic exfoliation of the granite sheets that compose the dome. The summit offers exceptional views of the foothills below, the tops of giant sequoias, the Great Western Divide mountains in the heart of the park's wilderness, and a 100-mile or more view out over the great Central Valley of California all the way to the state's coastal mountains. Unfortunately, this view is now sometimes marred by California's infamous air pollution, which drifts into the park; this pollution not only affects the views but also harms the park's trees.

General Sherman Tree Trail / Congress Trail

All visitors must walk in Sequoia's Giant Forest. No matter how many times we've seen giant sequoias, they never fail to impress; indeed, they seem nearly otherworldly. But seeing one of these trees doesn't begin to compare to wandering through this 1,800-acre forest with dozens of these monoliths. Giant Forest is a maze of trails that can be confusing, but the 1-mile (round-trip) General Sherman Tree Trail leads to its namesake, the largest living thing on the planet. This is a must-do, and a shorter wheelchair-accessible route is available. The 2-mile (round-trip) Congress Trail that starts at the General Sherman Tree offers fewer visitors and a stroll through a whole forest of giant sequoias, including "young" ones that are a mere century or so old, ancient ones with fire scars that have accumulated over the centuries, and fallen ones that naturally resist rotting because of the tannins they contain. The trail includes several named trees, including groups known as The House and The Senate (thus the name "Congress Trail"), as well as The President. There's also a tree named Chief Sequoyah, which seems only fair.

Crescent Meadow Trail / Zumwalt Meadow Trail

We noted earlier that the forests of Sequoia/Kings Canyon are punctuated by lovely, lush meadows, and these have been one of our favorite features in these parks for many years. Crescent and Zumwalt Meadows are two of the finest and are easily accessible. Crescent Meadow is part of Sequoia's Giant Forest; a 3.2-mile circuit of trails will lead you around this extensive, tree-lined opening, full of flowers in summer and a rich golden color in fall. John Muir called Crescent Meadow the "Gem of the Sierras." The trail passes Tharp's Log and Chimney Tree as additional attractions. Zumwalt Meadow is in Kings Canyon near the eastern end of the park's scenic byway, and is one of the most memorable meadows in these parks. The one-and-a-half-mile loop trail around the meadow has the

Kings Canyon is one of the country's deepest.

There are more than seventy groves of giant sequoias in Sequoia/Kings Canyon; two of them—Giant Forest and General Grant—are the most famous and include the very largest trees.

advantage of being surrounded by steep, dramatic granite cliffs and the Kings River; part of the trail is an accessible boardwalk.

High Sierra Trail

Given the wilderness character of these parks, you should consider a longer, backpacking trip through this astonishing landscape. There's no better choice than the High Sierra Trail, a 72-mile adventure through the heart of the High Sierra. The trail starts at Crescent Meadow and is a roller-coaster walk up and over the Great Western Divide (through 10,700-foot Kaweah Gap), down through Kern River Canyon, then up to the summit of Mount Whitney, and finally down to Whitney Portal on the east side of the park. The trail joins the famous John Muir Trail and Pacific Crest Trail for the last couple of days of hiking. This is a challenging trail, but is truly a hike of a lifetime. You can sample this trail by walking the first 11 miles to Bearpaw Meadows, where you can camp or stay at the High Sierra Camp—a tent hotel and restaurant—and return to the trailhead the next day. A simpler option is to just walk an hour or so out and back along the trail.

Rae Lakes Loop Trail

Rae Lakes is the other glamour long-distance hike in these parks, starting and ending appropriately at Roads End in Kings Canyon. This is a 41-mile wilderness journey to a cluster of some of the most beautiful lakes in the High Sierra and includes deep evergreen forests, copses of cottonwoods and aspens, 12,000-foot Glen Pass, waterfalls, big mountain streams, lush meadows, and the treeless granite expanses of the High Sierra—much like it was when the last glaciers retreated. A portion of the route follows the famous John Muir and Pacific Crest Trails.

Logistics

Even though these are primarily wilderness parks, Sequoia/Kings Canyon is big enough to offer a full range of visitor facilities and services. The parks' two major roads, Generals Highway and Kings Canyon Scenic Byway, are spectacularly scenic and access many of the parks' major features. Automobile access is only from the west side of the parks; no roads cross the Sierra Nevada, helping preserve the wilderness character of the area. There are fourteen campgrounds, four lodges, and four visitor centers scattered along the parks' roads. In summer a free shuttle bus system serves some of the parks' major attractions. The High Sierra Trail and the Rae Lakes Loop Trail require a permit, which must be reserved as far in advance as possible.

The High Sierra Trail is a 72-mile adventure through the heart of the High Sierra; it's challenging, but truly a hike of a lifetime.

The Last Word

Sequoia/Kings Canyon protects the heart of the southern Sierra Nevada and all their richness—giant trees, high peaks, rushing rivers, lush meadows, deep forests, and iconic wildlife—all in a vast wilderness setting. Its ample trail system ranges from short nature trails to some of the most epic hikes in the National Park System. Walk these trails to take full advantage of these wilderness parks.

Shenandoah National Park

Virginia | nps.gov/shen

By the time the first national parks were being established on the vast public lands of the West, most of the land in the eastern United States was already developed or in private ownership. That's one of the things that made national parks in the East challenging to establish but so valuable as well: They're so close to so many people. Shenandoah National Park is a prime example, located just 75 miles from the Washington, DC, area. This long and narrow park of nearly 200,000 acres runs along the spine of the Blue Ridge Mountains of Virginia (the front range of the ancient Appalachian Mountains) for more than 100 miles, with the historic Shenandoah River and its valley on the west and the gentle, pleasing hills of the Virginia Piedmont on the east. Most visitors to Shenandoah know this park for its Skyline Drive, the scenic, winding road that runs its length, offering spectacular views from its dozens of overlooks. Less well-known are the more than 500 miles of trails that show off the behind-the-scenes version of the park to those who are willing to explore it on foot.

The geology of Shenandoah is a grand mix of land-making/shaping forces, including sedimentation, volcanism, tectonic folding and thrusting, and erosion. The resulting low-lying Blue Ridge Mountains rise as much as 3,000 feet above the adjacent Shenandoah River Valley and include rocks that are remnants of earlier mountains more than a billion years old. The range of elevations, latitude, and aspects, combined with lots of precipitation, support a very diverse collection of plants and animals.

Forests (almost all second-growth) cover most of the park and include a wide variety of hardwoods. American chestnuts were one of the dominant trees here, and in the Appalachian Mountains more broadly, but were devastated by introduction of chestnut blight in the 1930s; there is still no treatment. The park is widely known for the showy flowers of the mountain laurel that bloom in June and grace the Skyline Drive and many of the park's trails. Other notable flowering trees and

(above) Shenandoah includes more than 100 miles of the famous Appalachian Trail (note the white blaze, used to mark the trail over its 2,200-mile length).

(opposite) Hawksbill Mountain, the tallest in the park, offers classic Shenandoah views.

(above) Old Rag is the park's most iconic mountain and trail; note the mountain laurel and potholes in the granite.

(above right) President Herbert Hoover built his Rapidan Camp before the park was established, using it as the Summer Whitehouse.

shrubs include azalea, dogwood, and redbud. In fact, the park is home to more than 800 species of flowering plants, celebrated each May during Wildflower Weekend. Although mountain laurel is native to the park, the Civilian Conservation Corps planted much of it along the Skyline Drive in the 1930s. Notable park animals include several hundred black bears, coyotes, white-tailed deer, gray and red foxes, bobcats, a great diversity and number of amphibians, more than 200 species of birds, and 32 species of fish.

The park has a number of social and cultural stories to tell, many of them triumphant, but some contentious and controversial. Like most areas in the East, Native Americans hunted and gathered in these mountains but were eventually driven out as European-American settlers flowed across the land, displacing local tribes. *Shenandoah* is of unknown Native American origin, but a popular and romanticized belief is that it means "Beautiful Daughter of the Stars." In the early history of the region, extensive forests were cut for timber; other lands supported agricultural development, most of it small-scale family farms and rural hamlets. In the early twentieth century, interest developed in attracting visitors to the area for the purpose of economic development. The area's Skyland Resort had been attracting tourists for years, and President Herbert Hoover built his Rapidan Camp in what is now the park; it served as his Summer White House. A federal government study identified the Shenandoah area as having special potential for tourism development, and there was substantial support from local people and their representatives. Congress authorized establishment of a national park in 1926. However, nearly all the land to be included in the park was privately owned, with hundreds of families living within the proposed park boundaries; moreover, no federal funds were provided to purchase private lands. The State of Virginia began an aggressive program to acquire lands and employed its eminent domain/condemnation powers, requiring landowners to sell at fair market value. The program encountered a great deal of resistance from many inhabitants, whose families had lived and worked on this land for generations. A small number of older residents were granted life tenancy, allowing them to stay on their property until they died; the last such park resident passed away in 1979. By 1935 Virginia had acquired and transferred 1,088 parcels of land to the federal government, and the park was established. Even before the park's creation, 40 miles of the Skyline Drive had been completed, thanks in part to the mighty work of the Civilian Conservation Corps, employing more than 1,000 young men. The volunteer Potomac Appalachian Trail Club built the AT through the park and continues to help maintain it. Sadly, most of the park's visitor facilities and services, including lodges, campgrounds, picnic areas, and restrooms, were initially segregated; full integration was finally accomplished in 1950.

Walking Shenandoah

Most visitors to Shenandoah enjoy the park from their journey along the scenic Skyline Drive. But to have a more meaningful and authentic experience, we urge you to take to the trails. The expansive system of more than 500 miles of trails leads to many of the area's peaks and through its lush forests, follows its streams, reveals its many waterfalls, explores its quiet hollows, crosses meadows filled with wildflowers, hints at the park's human history, and offers opportunities to see its wildlife. Included in the trail system are more than 100 miles of the Appalachian National Scenic Trail; you're bound to walk part of it as you sample the park's trails. The NPS has developed free trail brochures that we found interesting and helpful; they're available at visitor centers and on the park's website.

Fox Hollow Trail

Shenandoah has an especially rich cultural history, including the period of settlement and the transition to national park status. The Fox Hollow Trail is a good introduction to this period. Begin this easy, 1.2-mile loop just outside the Dickey Ridge Visitor Center in the north of the park (Mile 4.6). Shortly you'll encounter several walls of large stones that the Fox family removed from the forest to establish their farm in 1856; try to imagine the work it took to fell the trees that stood much as they do today and to prepare the land for planting. Soon you'll reach the family cemetery. Perhaps giving up this farm and all its personal history to help create the national park was even more difficult for the Fox family than establishing and working the farm. Many families displaced by the park continue

(top) Taking a well-earned break at the park's Skyland Resort, Appalachian Trail thru-hikers rest their backpacks against the store's wall.

(bottom) Mountain laurel blooms in June, lighting up many of the park's trails.

Stone walls are dramatic manifestations of the hard work required to clear forests for agricultural uses.

to tend family cemeteries scattered across the land. The loop trail will bring you back to the visitor center, though you can continue the walk on the longer Snead Farm Loop Trail to see an example of the barns that served the area's farms.

Hawksbill Mountain Summit Trail

At 4,051 feet, Hawksbill Mountain is the highest in the park and demands to be summited. This is only a modest climb of less than 1,000 feet distributed over a 2.9-mile circuit, and the attractions along the way make the hike seem shorter than it is. Start at the trailhead on the northern end of the Hawksbill Gap Parking Area (Mile 45.6) and take a short spur trail to join the famous Appalachian Trail as it moves in a westerly direction. Note the white blazes on trees that mark the trail's 2,220-mile length; you're walking on a particularly beautiful stretch through a mature forest with an abundance of lichen-covered boulders, ferns, two large talus slopes, and lots of mountain laurel (at its peak bloom in June). Reach the summit of the mountain that affords commanding views, including Stony Man to the north, and a shelter named for Virginia's legendary US Senator Harry F. Byrd Sr. Be sure to look for peregrine falcons; park staff and partners have worked hard to restore these noble birds to the park. Complete the loop by walking downhill (steeply in places) on the Lower Hawksbill Trail.

Rose River Trail / Dark Hollow Falls Trail

Shenandoah is a well-watered park, and its many streams and waterfalls delight those who choose to find them. Start this 4-mile loop at Mile 49.4. After about a mile, you reach Rose River and enjoy a long series of cascades, pools, and waterfalls, each finer than the last. As Hogcamp Branch flows to meet the river, the falls increase in frequency and size. At a sharp bend, the trail begins its journey back to the trailhead via the Rose River Fire Road, a pleasant walk in the woods. As you make this bend, we recommend the short section of trail—less than a quarter mile—up Hogcamp Branch to reach Dark Hollow Falls, the largest and most dramatic of all the water features on this hike.

Rapidan Camp Trail / Laurel Prong Trail / Hazeltop Loop

In the late 1920s President Herbert Hoover established Rapidan Camp at one of the prettiest sites in what would become Shenandoah. This spot satisfied his interest in nature in general and fishing in particular, and he noted, "Here is peace and quietude." Visit this magical place and the surrounding countryside on this grand 7.4-mile loop. Start at Mile 53 and follow Mill Prong (locals often call streams "prongs") to Rapidan Camp, then follow Laurel Prong to the Appalachian Trail, where you'll walk along an especially pleasant section of this epic trail back to your car. Rapidan Camp includes three buildings that have been nicely preserved; the back of Brown House, where Hoover maintained his office, has the best views, and the back deck beckons hikers to sit a spell (we had our lunch here). Ranger-guided tours of the camp are offered periodically. If time doesn't allow a hike of the full loop, you can walk to the camp for an out-and-back distance of 4.2 miles.

Old Rag Mountain (Ridge Trail / Saddle Trail / Weakley Hollow Fire Road)

Many parks have a "glory hike," and at Shenandoah, it's Old Rag, a challenging walk to one of the park's higher peaks. The mountain's unusual name comes from the more formal, Old Ragged Mountain, referring to the rough rocks near its summit. The classic route starts outside the park and is a 9.2-mile loop trail that's defined by two long scrambles over billion-year-old granite boulders. The trail starts with a long but moderate climb through an attractive forest, but at about 3 miles, the action becomes more serious. The first long series of scrambles tested our ability to navigate this extreme terrain, reducing us to hands and knees in many places. A short stretch of trail was followed by a similar stretch of boulders, just a little easier than the first (or maybe we were just used to this type of terrain). Soon after, we reached the summit, where the views were glorious, the mountain laurel spectacular, and the sense of relief overwhelming. The descent was long but comparatively easy. Old Rag is the park's signature hike, so be prepared to share the experience with lots of other hikers. Also be prepared to accept the challenge of navigating the rough terrain.

Logistics

The park is open year-round, but winters can be cold and occasionally snowy. Spring through fall is the primary visitor season, with an especially heavy peak in October to view fall foliage. There are two visitor centers (Dickey Ridge and Harry F. Byrd Sr.), five developed campgrounds, and three concessionaire-operated lodge and cabin areas. The Potomac Appalachian Trail Club operates six cabins in the park's backcountry. Skyline Drive is a narrow, winding road built for sightseeing; through most of its 105-mile length it maintains a 35 mile-per-hour speed limit, sometimes slower. The road is marked with posts at every mile, starting with "1" at the northern terminus; this is a handy way to find trailheads and other facilities and services.

The Last Word

What a gift to have this glorious national park so close to so many people; it took hard work, lots of perseverance, and personal sacrifice to establish Shenandoah National Park. Travel the scenic Skyline Drive, but be sure to stop at some of the trailheads and walk a few of the park's many fine trails. We think you'll come away with a much better sense of the importance of this park; we sure did.

Dark Hollow Falls is one of the largest and showiest of the park's many waterfalls.

Theodore Roosevelt National Park

North Dakota | nps.gov/thro

While it may be common for people to shape the land, the reverse can also be true; Theodore Roosevelt National Park may be the ultimate manifestation of the latter. Roosevelt traveled to the rugged badlands of North Dakota as a 24-year-old refugee from New York City and decided to make this land his home away from home for several of his most formative years, owning and working on cattle ranches, including his beloved Elkhorn Ranch. He later wrote, "I would not have been President if it had not been for my experiences in North Dakota." As a result of his personal transformation, the American landscape was reshaped as well: While serving as the twenty-sixth president, he set aside 230 million acres of land that now serve as much of the foundation of the National Park System, as well as the National Forest and Fish and Wildlife Refuge systems. He's widely regarded as "the conservation president," but he was also a war hero (serving as a colonel in the Rough Riders during the Spanish-American War), an amateur scientist, and a prolific author. He also won the Nobel Peace Prize, helping negotiate the end of the Russo-Japanese War. It's fully deserving that this is the only national park named for a single individual.

Much of Theodore Roosevelt National Park is composed of rugged and dramatic badlands, deeply eroded over millions of years. Roosevelt scoffed at the term "badlands," describing the region as "the so-called Bad Lands." Debris eroded from the Rocky Mountains, ash from western volcanoes, and material deposited from ancient lakes formed many layers of soil. Later, the Little Missouri River and other streams cut through these geologic layers, forming elaborate multicolored cliffs, ravines, canyons, buttes, and other dramatic landforms. Grasses and wildflowers cover much of the park's prairie lands, while juniper trees occupy canyons, and cottonwood trees line stream courses. The area is rich in wildlife, including bison, elk, cougars, white-tailed and mule deer, coyotes, feral horses, bighorn sheep, pronghorn, and prairie dogs. Some of these species were decimated in the late 19th century under Roosevelt's critical eye but have successfully been reintroduced. For example, the now-flourishing herd of bison is a result of the animal's reintroduction in 1956. Prairie dogs, highly social animals that live in large "towns" in the park's grasslands, are a favorite of park visitors; Roosevelt called them "the most noisy and inquisitive animals imaginable." Visitors also enjoy a small herd of longhorn cattle maintained by the NPS as a living history exhibit. Regrettably, recent development of oil wells and related facilities and services on surrounding lands have intruded on the park's beauty, including its natural quiet and darkness.

(opposite) Theodore Roosevelt, twenty-sixth president, set aside 230 million acres of land that now serves as the foundation of much of the National Park System, as well as the National Forest and Fish and Wildlife Refuge systems. It's fully deserving that this is the only national park named for a single individual.

(above) Mysterious concretions erode from the badlands; the spherical ones are called cannonballs.

(above right) Much of Theodore Roosevelt National Park is composed of rugged and dramatic badlands, deeply eroded over millions of years.

Native Americans had a presence in the park going back thousands of years, but the rugged character of the area probably didn't support permanent occupation. Northern Plains tribes hunted the area's bison in historic times. The area became more accessible to settlement with the arrival of the railroad in the 1880s. Roosevelt made his first visit to the region in 1883, acquiring the first of his two cattle ranches, the Maltese Cross Ranch. The next year he suffered the death of both his mother and wife on the same day and retreated to North Dakota to live "the strenuous life" as a form of grieving. Shortly after arriving, he established the Elkhorn Ranch, which he considered his North Dakota home. In the 1930s and early 1940s, the Civilian Conservation Corps built much of the present-day park road system and other facilities that are still in use. Several efforts were made to preserve the area, culminating in establishment of a national memorial park in 1947; it was expanded and designated a national park in 1978–79. The park is divided into three discontinuous units: the large South Unit, a smaller North Unit, and the small, isolated Elkhorn Ranch Unit, which includes only a few remains of the Elkhorn Ranch. The three units are tied together by the Little Missouri River.

The park is rich in wildlife, including bison, elk, cougars, white-tailed and mule deer, coyotes, feral horses, bighorn sheep, pronghorn, and prairie dogs.

Walking Theodore Roosevelt

The park provides more than 100 miles of trails that showcase the area's finest features, including the deeply eroded badlands, expanses of prairie, colorful canyons, the Little Missouri River, and other rich riparian zones. Hiking offers the best opportunities to see park wildlife. We recommend trails in both the North and South Units.

Jones Creek Trail / Roundup Trail

The geographic center of the park's South Unit features a network of trails that can be combined to provide several good hiking options. We linked the lower section of the Jones Creek Trail with an extension onto the Roundup Trail. The Jones Creek Trail starts on the park's Scenic Loop Drive just north of Peaceful Valley Ranch and generally follows the creek due west for 1.8 miles; several creek crossings are required, but these are easy. We had a closer than intended encounter with a male bison that also wanted to use the trail. Walking in opposite directions, we briefly surprised each other at a blind curve; we were able to yield the right-of-way by quickly scrambling up a steep slope, and all ended well. Whew! At mile 1.8 the Jones Creek Trail meets the Roundup Trail; we turned north onto the latter, hiking 2.1 miles to a small parking area along the Scenic Loop Drive. This trail rises and falls along open territory, offering great views. The trail is marked with posts, and you must pay

Colorfully banded bluffs show the layers of sediments that have been deposited over geologic time.

attention to wayfinding. We were fortunate to have a ride back to the Jones Creek Trailhead, making for a pleasant hike of about 4 miles; otherwise, this would have been an out-and-back hike of twice that mileage.

Big Plateau Loop Trail

Another complex of trails is found in the northwestern part of the South Unit, west of the Little Missouri River. This location means that these trails are most directly accessible only by fording the river. The loop begins at Peaceful Valley Ranch and wanders half a mile through cottonwood trees to the river. It's wise to ask about river conditions at the South Unit Visitor Center to make sure the water is not too high and the current too fast for crossing. Hiking poles are highly recommended for added stability in the water. The Big Plateau Trail leads from the far shore of the river through small canyons and, as the name suggests, eventually climbs onto a very large plateau that includes expansive views and large prairie dog towns. At about 2 miles turn left onto the Maah Daah Hey Trail; this 144-mile trail (don't worry, you don't have to hike it all!) traverses the diverse landscape of northern North Dakota. The name comes from the Mandan Hidatsa Indians and generally means something that has been or will be around for a long time. Walk south on this romantic long-distance trail for 1.7 miles to the junction with the Ekblom Trail, where you'll travel east for a little over a mile back

to your original crossing of the Little Missouri River and then back half a mile to the Peaceful Valley Ranch. Much of this loop is generally open and offers commanding views of the surrounding park lands. We had read that feral horses could often be seen on this walk, and we were pleased to see several near the end of our hike; they had come down to the Little Missouri River to feed and drink. Though there is some disagreement about their origin, the NPS considers these horses as descended from the open-range grazing of early settlers; they are welcomed in the park as an important part of the area's cultural landscape.

Buckhorn Trail / Achenbach Trail

Although the park's North Unit is smaller than the South Unit, it offers two of the park's longest trails. The Buckhorn Trail, an 11.4-mile loop in the eastern part of the park, showcases much of the badlands portion of the park along with expanses of fragrant sagebrush flats. The trail is generally flat and offers easy walking, and there are several points where the trail can be accessed from the park's Scenic Drive, making the trail walkable in short sections. We recommend starting your walk at the parking area for the Caprock Coulee Nature Trail and joining the Buckhorn Trail after a short walk to the east. You'll walk alongside some deeply eroded bluffs; pause and admire the sculptural qualities of this landscape and the intricate detail of these erosional patterns. Shortly after the base

(above left) Roosevelt's cabin from his Maltese Cross Ranch has been preserved in the park; this is where he lived "the strenuous life."

(above) Posts mark most of the trails in the park, but bison sometimes use them for scratching posts and knock them over; pay close attention to wayfinding.

The NPS considers feral horses, descendants from the open-range grazing of early settlers, an important part of the park's cultural landscape.

of the bluffs, turn left (north) onto the Buckhorn Trail and follow it as far as you like. Two large prairie dog towns are about a mile and a quarter from the trail junction and make a good destination. The Achenbach Trail, a nearly 18-mile loop in the western part of the park, is more challenging; the southern portion of the trail descends from the Scenic Drive to the shores of the Little Missouri River and then rises again to the road. Much of the trail travels through the wilderness portion of the park and requires hikers to ford the Little Missouri River twice. These fords should not be attempted when water levels are high—check with park staff before hiking this portion of the trail. Like the Buckhorn Trail, the Achenbach can be accessed from several points along the Scenic Road and from other trails, making shorter hikes possible and very attractive. In particular, we recommend the 2.4-mile round-trip hike on the Achenbach Trail from the Oxbow Overlook at the end of the Scenic Drive to Sperati Point and its dramatic view of the Little Missouri River. The Buckhorn and Achenbach Trails can be combined into a great and grand loop that's well-suited to backpacking trips.

Logistics

The park is open year-round, but winters are typically cold and snowy and summers can be hot; spring offers lots of wildflowers. There are two campgrounds, one in the South Unit and one in the North Unit. There is no lodging in the park, but motels and other commercial facilities and services are available in surrounding towns, particularly tourist-friendly Medora (South Unit) and Watford City (North Unit). There are two visitor centers in the South Unit and one in the North Unit. The drive to the Elkhorn Ranch Unit of the park is long and rough; check with the NPS about road conditions. The park's North Unit in on Central Time, while the South Unit is on Mountain Time; the NPS likes to say that the Elkhorn Ranch Unit is timeless.

The Last Word

Come to North Dakota and celebrate the triumph of American conservation, including this off-the-beaten-track national park and all the good that has come from it. Pay your respects to the multitalented man who single-handedly helped shape the nation's extensive system of public conservation lands. Hike the park's trails and deepen your appreciation of the stark beauty and diversity of this part of the American landscape, just as Theodore Roosevelt did.

As the name suggests, Big Plateau Loop affords sweeping views of this region of the park.

Virgin Islands National Park

US Virgin Islands | nps.gov/viis

This park occupies much of the island of Saint John in the US Virgin Islands in the Caribbean Sea. Most of the park's land was donated by Laurance S. Rockefeller, and the park was established in 1956. The park features mountains, subtropical forests, beaches, mangroves, coral reefs, and colorful undersea life, and preserves much of the history and prehistory of the island. Several of the park's beaches, including Trunk Bay, Cinnamon Bay, Honeymoon Beach, Hawksnest Bay, Maho Bay, and Salt Pond Bay, are considered some of the most beautiful in the world. Popular recreation activities include boating, swimming, snorkeling, scuba diving, and hiking. The park's short trail system leads through tropical forests; to waterfalls, beaches, and observation points; and to historic areas such the ruins of sugar mills and petroglyph sites. There's even an underwater trail for snorkeling along the coral reef in Trunk Bay.

(above) The turquoise waters of Virgin Islands National Park attract visitors from around the world.

(right) Virgin Islands National Park was a gift to the American people by the Rockefeller family; the Rockefellers have helped create a number of national parks.

Voyageurs National Park

Minnesota | nps.gov/voya

Voyageurs National Park in far northern Minnesota commemorates the historic *voyageurs*, Canadian fur trappers of European descent who frequented the area from the late seventeenth to the early nineteenth century. The park was established in 1975. Nearly half the park is a series of lakes and rivers that supported travel by historic trappers and are now used primarily for recreation. Most visitors access the park by water, traveling by kayaks and canoes, though some rent houseboats or take a guided boat tour. The park includes a system of more than 50 miles of maintained hiking trails, but most are short and many accessible only by boat.

(top) A beaver must constantly work to keep its lodge strong and insulated, venturing out for materials even when the weather is less than ideal.

(bottom) Nearly 200 years ago, *voyageurs* paddled birch-bark canoes full of animal pelts and other goods through this area on their way to Lake Athabasca, Saskatchewan, Canada.

(left) Voyageurs is primarily a water-based park that is best appreciated by boat.

White Sands National Park

In the vast rural expanses of southern New Mexico lie the mountain-ringed Tularosa Basin and White Sands National Park. The park preserves much of the world's largest gypsum dunefield. Gypsum is a mineral (calcium sulfate) that was deposited at the bottom of an ancient sea that eventually evaporated and exposed the remaining gypsum to erosion and decomposition. The resulting sand-size

The grains of sand derived from gypsum give the resulting dunes their starkly beautiful white color.

A variety of specialized plants have colonized portions of the dunes.

grains of gypsum were blown by prevailing winds into extensive dunes, up to 50 feet high, and are notable for their bright white color. These sweeping sand dunes, seen in the context of the region's deep blue skies and surrounding mountains, are the park's primary attraction, and a stunning one at that. Historically, park lands have been used for many purposes, including subsistence by Native Americans, mining, ranching, and military research and testing. The park is surrounded by military facilities, including White Sands Missile Range and Holloman Air Force Base; the area includes the Trinity Site where the first atomic bomb was tested in 1945. White Sands National Monument was established in 1933 and elevated to national park status in 2019. The unusual landscape of White Sands must be seen to be believed, but hiking opportunities are limited by the inherently challenging steep topography of the dunes and the soft sand under foot. There are several maintained trails, but they total less than ten miles. Visitors are allowed to walk among the sand dunes, but wayfinding can be difficult, especially in windy conditions when blowing sand limits visibility.

Wind Cave National Park

South Dakota | nps.gov/wica

The names of national parks usually suggest why they're so important, but names can also be a little deceptive. Put Wind Cave National Park in this latter category. To be clear, there's nothing misleading about "Wind Cave"; in this park, you'll find the seventh longest cave in the world with more than 150 miles of explored passageways, a place worthy of preservation in its own right. In fact, it was America's first national park established to preserve a cave; it was also a very early national park, only the eighth in the country. But there's so much more to this park. Above ground, the park preserves one of the few remaining expanses of prairie, a glimpse of the open landscape that met westward-bound pioneers; the park helps visitors imagine the journey of exploration and settlement that is such an important part of American history. And on these lands graze herds of bison, elk, and pronghorn, adding to the drama and authenticity of this place. Thankfully, the park includes a well-developed trail system—below and above ground—to help visitors truly appreciate all it has to offer.

The geology of Wind Cave is complicated and the result is an unusual, multi-dimensional cave complex that includes several levels of passages; its three dimensional character is known as a "maze cave." As with just about all caves, the process started with a layer of limestone; in this case, the limestone was a layer of sediment on the floor of an ancient sea at least 320 million years ago. As precipitation eventually infiltrated the stone, it dissolved a network of passageways. About 60 million years ago, the area was uplifted by the same tectonic forces that raised the Rocky Mountains, fracturing and cracking the limestone, resulting in today's extensive three-dimensional network of passageways. The cave is known internationally for several of its uncommon features, especially "boxwork," thin layers of calcite that extend from the cave's walls and ceilings to form extensive honeycombs. Despite the large size of Wind Cave, scientists estimate that as little of 5 percent of the cave has so far been discovered.

The extensive prairies and forests in the mid-section of the park support diverse plant and animal populations that include elements of both eastern and western environments. For example, the park's ponderosa pines are characteristic of western lands, while American elms are more often found in the east. But the prairies are more characteristic of the nation's heartland and include many species of both short- and tallgrasses. Several of the area's celebrated wildlife species were extirpated from the area before the park was established but have now been successfully reintroduced.

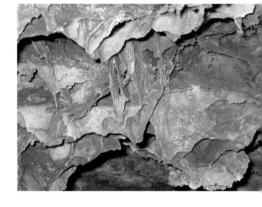

(top) Wind Cave is internationally famous for its boxwork—delicate formations of calcite.

(opposite) Wind Cave National Park includes the southern 6 miles of the 111-mile Centennial Trail celebrating the 100th anniversary of South Dakota statehood.

(above) Wind Cave includes many forms of decorative cave structures, such as these stalactites.

(above right) The trail along Rankin Ridge offers pleasing views of the park's mix of ponderosa pines and extensive prairies.

The Bronx Zoo donated fourteen bison to the park in 1913; the herd now numbers in the hundreds. Other reintroduced animals include elk, pronghorn, and black-footed ferrets. Prairie dogs are a favorite of many visitors.

Anthropologists report that the Lakota knew of the cave for centuries and considered it the sacred place where bison emerged from the underworld. The Bingham brothers "discovered" the cave in 1881 when they heard wind rushing from the cave's small opening. The wind was blowing so hard that it knocked the hat off Jesse Bingham when he attempted to peer down into the opening (at least, that's the local legend). All caves "breathe" to normalize air pressure between the cave's interior and the outside barometric pressure; Wind Cave's huge size and small opening magnify this exchange of air, thus its name. Tours began in the 1890s. Because people living near the cave broke off pieces of the cave's formations to sell to visitors, Wind Cave National Park was established in 1903 to protect the integrity of the cave.

Walking Wind Cave

Wind Cave is a relatively small national park—a little less than 35,000 acres—and at a little over 30 miles, its trail system is also modest. That mileage doesn't include the underground cave network, and you should be sure to take at least one of the ranger-guided cave tours. Then take advantage of the park's more conventional trails that wander across the prairie and through canyons and forests, offering opportunities to see the park's gentle landscape and entertaining wildlife.

Cave Tours (Fairgrounds Tour, Candlelight Tour, Wild Cave Tour)

All visits into the cave are conducted as ranger-guided tours, and the park offers five tours to choose from; we're especially enthusiastic about three of them. The Fairgrounds Tour travels through portions of the upper and middle levels of the cave. The former includes large rooms along with popcorn and frostwork formations; the latter features extensive areas of the boxwork formations for which this cave is internationally famous. The tour lasts 90 minutes and includes 450 stairs, making it moderately challenging. The Candlelight Tour re-creates conditions of early cave exploration; each participant carries a candle that is the only source of illumination. This 2-hour tour requires some stair climbing and bending and stooping. The Wild Cave Tour is for budding spelunkers and adventurous visitors; participants must be physically fit. The tour lasts 3 to 4 hours and requires lots of crawling. These tours are a great way to experience and appreciate this world-famous cave; all three require a reservation and fee.

Rankin Ridge Trail

Of the three interpretive trails in the park, we found this one to be especially enjoyable, offering firsthand insights into the park's natural history. The trail climbs gently to 5,013 feet, the highest point in the park, and offers striking views—all the way to Badlands National Park, 40 miles to the east. Rankin Ridge roughly defines the southern extent of the Black Hills and is marked by the interface of forests and prairies. This 1-mile loop trail rises about 250 feet through a ponderosa pine forest and makes its way along a series of fourteen stations keyed to an especially engaging brochure that explains much of the area's natural history. For example, many of the area's snags (dead and fallen trees) are a result of the periodic forest fires that naturally occur in the area at intervals of approximately eight to twelve years. These snags play an important ecological role, hosting insects that are food for many species of birds and serving as nesting sites for playful black-capped chickadees. (Listen for their characteristic *chick-a-dee-dee-dee* call.) Fire also helps maintain the dynamic balance between forests and prairies that characterizes the park and its surrounding region. Trees tend to expand their area over time, overtaking much of the prairie, but fire resets this balance. A nicely-crafted stone staircase carries hikers to the trail's summit, where you'll find a tall fire lookout tower. Even though the tower is closed to visitors, the open summit provides outstanding views of the landscape that met the European-American settlers of 200 years ago.

Lookout Point Trail / Centennial Trail Loop

The interior of the park, particularly on the western side, is laced with a network of trails that offer multiple hiking routes. We started our route at the trailhead that serves the Lookout Point Trail and the southern end of the Centennial Trail. We walked south and east along the former trail,

(above) Take advantage of the park's trail system that wanders across the prairie and through its canyons and forests.

(below) Large prairie dog towns invite walkers to pause and enjoy these endlessly entertaining animals.

(above) Afternoon thunderstorms in summer add an element of drama to the landscape.

(above right) The park's prairies are characteristic of the nation's heartland and include species of both short- and tallgrasses.

completing the approximately 4.5-mile loop by returning to the trailhead via the Centennial Trail; a short section of the Highland Creek Trail connects these trails. The first half of this loop was a stunning walk along a mix of ponderosa pine stands and rolling open grasslands with views in all directions, including Lookout Point. Animals were a highlight; there were large prairie dog towns and their entertaining occupants and several bison scattered along the trail. The former were so entertaining with their manic behavior and piercing warning calls that it was a challenge to maintain our forward progress. The latter required even more time for photos—and waiting for the animals to move far enough off the trail to safely allow our passage. The trail ultimately descended and joined the Centennial Trail, generally following sparkling Beaver Creek; this lively stream charts a course through some of the loveliest meadows in the National Park System (and showcased several more bison). What goes down must come up, and we ended our hike with a modest climb through a ponderosa pine forest and back to the trailhead. The 111-mile Centennial Trail opened in 1989 to help celebrate the one-hundredth anniversary of South Dakota's statehood. The trail showcases much of the natural diversity of the state, and the park includes the southernmost 6 miles of the trail.

Lovely Beaver Creek charts a course through some of the most beautiful meadows in the National Park System.

Logistics

The park is open year-round, but winters are cold, with occasional snow. The primary visitor season is spring through fall, though summer can be hot. The cave maintains a constant temperature of 54°F year-round. A visitor center and campground are located in the park, but there are no lodging or other commercial facilities or services. More visitor facilities and services are available in surrounding towns and parks. The park is located near several other national and state parks, including Custer State Park, Jewel Cave National Monument, Mount Rushmore National Memorial, and Badlands National Park.

The Last Word

Established in 1903, Wind Cave was one of the first national parks. However, it's been somewhat overshadowed by many other, much larger parks. But its world-famous cave, with dramatic prairie landscape and successful reintroduction of native wildlife, make it a worthwhile addition to your national park list. Consider combining a visit to Wind Cave with some of the surrounding national and state parks and forests for a more complete appreciation of this landscape.

Wrangell–St. Elias National Park and Preserve

Alaska | nps.gov/wrst

Established in 1980, Wrangell–St. Elias is the largest US national park, a staggering 13.2 million acres in south-central Alaska (six times the size of Yellowstone!). The park protects much of the

Wrangell-St. Elias National Park includes especially high mountains of volcanic origin.

Hiking routes in the park often require advanced wayfinding and backpacking skills.

St. Elias Mountains, which include most of the highest peaks in the United States, highlighted by 18,000-foot Mount St. Elias. These high mountains are the result of a massive manifestation of plate tectonics. Other features of the park include extensive glaciers, icefields, volcanoes, and coastline, as well as the remains of the early-twentieth-century boomtown of Kennecott, once one of the world's richest copper mines and now a National Historic Landmark. The park is a part of a vast World Heritage Site, a portion of which includes Kluane National Park and Reserve in Canada's Yukon Territory. Most of the park is difficult to access due to lack of roads, and most of its hiking trails are maintained for only the first few miles before becoming cross-country routes. Backpacking can be a rewarding experience, but hikers must be prepared to travel through rugged wildlands.

Yellowstone National Park

Wyoming, Montana, and Idaho | nps.gov/yell

How fortunate that our predecessors had sufficient foresight to establish this magnificent national park in 1872! Yellowstone was the first national park in the nation and, indeed, the world—the first time a nation set aside a large area of its land for the benefit of all its people, not just a privileged elite. Conservationist Wallace Stegner famously wrote that the national parks are "America's best idea," a manifestation of our foundational democratic ideals. Yellowstone led to creation of many other national parks, but it remains the most famous, and for good reason. More recently, the park was designated a World Heritage Site, a symbol of its importance to the world community.

And what a powerhouse of a national park! Yellowstone is large, even by national park standards; at more than 2 million acres, it's larger than the states of Rhode Island and Delaware combined. Much of the park sits in the caldera of an ancient and massive supervolcano, the largest on the North American continent; the caldera measures some 30 by 45 miles. Its most recent eruption, approximately 640,000 years ago, is estimated to have been 1,000 times more powerful than the eruption of Mount St. Helens in 1980, and emitted an estimated 240 cubic miles of debris. Ash from this explosion has been found at locations across the continent, and the eruption may have affected world weather patterns. Geologists think that Yellowstone has experienced several massive volcanic eruptions over the past 2 million years, and these eruptions have also deposited vast amounts of lava and ash in the park and beyond. The Grand Canyon of the Yellowstone River is a good place to see the resulting geologic debris layers that overlie most of the park.

The park's volcanic origin is plainly evident in its many geysers, fumaroles, mud pots, and boiling hot springs—the largest collection of such geothermal features in the world. Old Faithful geyser is the park's most famous geothermal feature, erupting approximately every 90 minutes. But the park includes many more natural attractions, including large canyons and associated rivers and waterfalls; world-famous megafauna; several mountain ranges that feature 10,000-plus-foot peaks; vast subalpine forests and meadows; the largest high-elevation lake in North America; and an extensive petrified forest. This is the national park that all Americans should see, and it offers more than 1,000 miles of trails so visitors can appreciate it in the most intimate and satisfying way.

Most of the park occupies a high plateau in northwest Wyoming, and it extends into portions of Montana and Idaho. The average elevation of the plateau is about 8,000 feet. The Continental Divide runs through the southwestern portion of the park. The park's variations in elevation

A herd of bison moves through the wildlife-rich Lamar Valley.

and geography have resulted in a great range of habitats that support highly diverse flora and fauna. Several species of evergreen trees are found in the park, although lodgepole pines make up 80 percent of the park's extensive forests. Quaking aspen and willows are the most common species of deciduous trees. Spring and summer bring diverse wildflowers, and unusual forms of bacteria grow in the park's geyser basins.

Yellowstone supports a variety of exciting wildlife, including grizzly and black bears, wolves, the largest herd of bison in the United States, elk, moose, mule and white-tailed deer, mountain goats, pronghorn, bighorn sheep, mountain lions, wolverines, 18 species of fish (including the famed Yellowstone cutthroat trout), and more than 300 species of birds. Wolves were extirpated from the park in the first half of the twentieth century because they preyed on the park's elk (as well as cattle on surrounding private lands) but were successfully reintroduced in the 1990s as a result of increasing ecological and environmental awareness. The howl of wolves, a marker of genuine wilderness, has been reestablished in the park.

Much of the park has experienced periodic wildfires, and many species of vegetation have evolved to be fire-dependent. For example, the cones of lodgepole pines open to disperse their seeds only when subject to very intense heat. In 1988 a conflagration burned more than a third of the park, and this opened a lively public discussion on how to manage fires in national parks and other protected areas. Prior to this, public policy was to extinguish wildfires as quickly as possible. However, this approach was ultimately found to be flawed because certain species of vegetation need periodic fires to reproduce. Additionally, suppression of natural fires can lead to denser growth of trees and other vegetation and accumulation of great amounts of dead and down wood that ultimately fuel infernos. Now wildfires are managed in Yellowstone and other national parks in ways that help allow fire to play its natural role. This management regime includes allowing natural fires to burn when they don't endanger people and their property—even setting controlled burns in places where they can be safely and appropriately managed.

In addition to its natural history, Yellowstone has a colorful human history dating back 11,000 years, when Native Americans used the area for hunting and fishing. These native people used volcanic deposits of obsidian to fashion projectile points and cutting tools, many of which have been found and dated. European-American explorers appeared in the nineteenth century; the first were trappers and colorful mountain men such as John Colter and Jim Bridger. Official government expeditions were mounted in 1870 and 1871, and the findings of these expeditions—in particular the geothermal character of the area and its natural beauty—were instrumental in convincing Congress to withdraw the area from development and establish a national park. Photographs by William Henry

Jackson and paintings by Thomas Moran, both of whom accompanied the 1871 Hayden Expedition to the park, provided visual documentation of the wonders of the Yellowstone territory. Support by the railroad industry, convinced the area would become a great tourist attraction, also helped spur establishment of the park. The 1872 act of Congress establishing the park stated that the area would be a public park "for the benefit and enjoyment of the people." These historic, democratic words were etched into the Roosevelt Arch that spans the northern entrance of Yellowstone, and President Theodore Roosevelt helped lay the arch's cornerstone.

However, simply establishing the park and its boundaries was inadequate to protect it, and poaching and illegal logging quickly caused damage. Since there was as yet no NPS, the US Army was called upon to bring order, occupying the park starting in 1886 and building Fort Yellowstone at Mammoth Hot Springs as their headquarters. Many of the original fort buildings are still in use as NPS offices and housing. Be sure to stop by the visitor center here for a good example of an early fort building; there's even an engaging historic walking tour. Congress established the NPS in 1916 to manage Yellowstone and the growing list of early national parks.

Walking Yellowstone

The size of Yellowstone and its rich natural and cultural history demand an equally grand system of trails, and the park doesn't disappoint. Encompassing all its diverse habitats and history, the park's trails extend more than 1,000 miles and range from short, informative nature trails to routes in wilderness that would take a human lifetime to fully explore and appreciate. We've pored over maps and trail guides, consulted resident rangers, hiked extensively, and are pleased to recommend a short list of author-tested-and-approved trails we feel are most representative of the park and accessible to most visitors.

Grand Canyon of the Yellowstone (North Rim Trail / South Rim Trail)

The colorful canyon carved by the Yellowstone River is one of the most recognized places in the park and simply shouldn't be missed; it's 20 miles long, more than a 1,000 feet deep, and includes two waterfalls that truly thunder. With walkers in mind, a network of trails has been developed to take visitors to all the most striking viewpoints; these trails can be sorted into networks on the south and north rims of the canyon. The south network extends 3.5 miles and features several highlights,

In a park with so many waterfalls, Tower Falls is among the most impressive.

Paintings of the Grand Canyon of the Yellowstone helped convince Congress to establish the park in 1872, the first national park in America and the world. Today, the canyon is one of Yellowstone's most photographed attractions.

including the Upper Falls Viewpoint, Uncle Tom's Trail, Artist Point (one of the most photographed views in the park), and Point Sublime. Uncle Tom's Trail, a steep, 500-foot descent into the canyon, is a favorite. The trails along the north rim extend 3 miles and include the Brink of the Upper Falls Trail, Brink of the Lower Falls Trail, Red Rock Trail, Grand View Overlook, and Inspiration Point. The Brink of the Lower Falls Trail drops 600 feet into the canyon, ending at a viewing platform that lives up to the trail's name; not for the faint of heart, this trail is especially popular. There are roads that more or less parallel the south and north rim trails, with parking lots that access several key viewpoints and the trails noted above. This makes it easy to walk only portions of the canyon trails if you're short on time. There is no public transportation along these roads, however, so the trails must be walked out and back. Walking the trails is a more peaceful way to experience this very heavily used portion of the park, offers a more or less continuous series of ever-changing views, and avoids the challenging issue of finding multiple parking places.

Upper Geyser Basin

Yellowstone's world-famous thermal features are scattered throughout the park, but most are concentrated in several major basins. The Upper Geyser Basin along the Firehole River is the most famous of these areas, including the majority of the world's active geysers and featuring Old Faithful, a real crowd pleaser. A large network of trails winds through the basin, allowing a range of walking opportunities from a short stroll to Old Faithful to a 5-mile ramble throughout the area. The visitor center that serves the Upper Geyser Basin predicts the time of the next eruption of Old Faithful; you'll need to be seated on the benches surrounding the geyser about 15 minutes before its eruption. After this up-close experience, walk a bit around the geyser basin and consider climbing Geyser Hill to Observation Point for a very different view of Old Faithful's next eruption. Don't forget to pay attention to the cultural components of this landscape (the area is a National Historic District), featuring the Old Faithful Inn (also a National Historic Landmark). Built in 1904, this is the largest log hotel in the world and a classic example of "parkitecture."

Fairy Falls Trail

While you're in the Upper Geyser Basin–Old Faithful area, you might enjoy this longer but easy hike to one of the park's prettiest waterfalls, graceful Fairy Falls, dropping nearly 200 feet. This is an out-and-back hike of 4.8 miles (round-trip). As you approach the falls, note how the forest is recovering from a fire and now includes pines of 30 feet or more. Be sure to take the short spur trail to an elevated view of world-famous Grand Prismatic Spring, its bright colors caused by a variety of algae and bacteria adapted to extremely high temperatures. It's possible to extend your hike from Fairy Falls just a little to see impressive Imperial Geyser.

Mount Washburn (Chittenden Road)

Mount Washburn is one of the most accessible high mountains in the park and one that offers a variety of attractions, including outstanding views, riotous wildflowers, and bighorn sheep. The shortest route to the top of this 10,243-foot peak is a pleasant walk up the old Chittenden Road; this well-graded gravel road is open only to official vehicles (this use is infrequent) and is used primarily by hikers and a smattering of mountain bikers—we saw one car and no bikes on our last hike. The walk ascends 3.1 miles and nearly 1,500 feet in elevation, making for a hike of only moderate challenge. Along the way you're likely to be dazzled by wildflowers, perhaps the best in the park; encounter snowdrifts that may last until August; and probably see bighorn sheep, either on the open slopes of the mountain or at its summit. (We did.) The mountain marks the northern edge of the giant caldera that defines much of Yellowstone. At the summit of the mountain, you'll find a fire lookout (one of several constructed in the early 1900s and still in use), a small visitor center, a telescope, restrooms, and expansive views—all the way south to the Teton Mountains on a clear day. A trail of similar length ascends Mount Washburn from Dunraven Pass, but it's a little longer and steeper in places. Ascending the mountain on one trail and descending on the other is ideal, but requires someone to provide a ride back to your car.

Upper Gallatin River Trail (Bighorn Pass Trail)

Most of the attractions and many of the finest trails in Yellowstone are heavily used, so it's refreshing to find some moments of solitude and quiet in the park. One place to look for these opportunities is in the relatively lightly visited northwestern corner of the park; here the famous Gallatin River rises and flows northwest out of the park and through its namesake national forest, which borders the park. Start your walk at Bighorn Pass Trailhead and travel upstream as far as you like; we're betting that, like we did, you'll walk farther than you originally envisioned up this broad, lush, meadow-filled valley. The trail (sometimes called the Bighorn Pass Trail) is mostly flat and roughly follows the river. We walked about 4 miles upstream and wished we'd had time for more; this would make a

(top) The trail along the Upper Gallatin River offers hikers solitude and quiet; we saw only two other hiking groups.

(bottom) Visitors can walk through many of the park's geyser basins on extended networks of boardwalks that help ensure their safety.

The view from the summit of Mount Washburn extends all the way to the Grand Tetons. Note the Grand Canyon of the Yellowstone River in the foreground and Yellowstone Lake in the background.

lovely short backpacking trip. We saw only two hiking groups and a lone angler on our hike.

Mary Mountain Trail (Nez Perce Trail)

We walked this trail more than a decade ago, and the experience has stayed with us ever since: the herds of bison we stopped to watch; the lush open meadows of the park; the challenge of this long day hike, including some wayfinding issues. It was such a memorable hike that we walked it again more recently as we prepared this book; this time we walked only a portion of the trail, and the good memories just came flooding back. We heartily recommend walking this trail (sometimes called the Mary Mountain Trail and sometimes the Nez Perce Trail) either in its entirety or just enough to get a lasting sense of why it's so representative of Yellowstone. This is a route through the geographic heart of the park, crossing much of the Hayden Valley, a place that mightily contributes to the park's reputation as the Serengeti of North America. The complete trail is just over 20 miles and must be done as a day hike—camping is not allowed due to the presence of grizzly bears. The trail isn't difficult, as there's little elevation change, but it's long, trails made by bison can confuse walkers, and bison often accidentally knock down poles placed to mark the trail in open meadows, either by scratching against the poles or by trampling them as they travel. The trail can also be boggy in places. The Hayden Valley is also prime grizzly habitat, so exercise all NPS-recommended precautions. Check with rangers about current, on-the-ground conditions before walking this trail. Most visitors will probably not want to walk the trail in its entirety; we recommend starting the hike at its eastern end just off the Grand Loop Road and walking as far as you like then retracing your steps, making this a glorious out-and-back day hike of whatever length you choose.

Logistics

A big park like Yellowstone can be complicated to negotiate, but it has an unusually large infrastructure to support its several million annual visits. There are ten visitor centers, information stations, and museums scattered across the park. Five park entrances connect to its historic 142-mile

figure-eight Grand Loop Road, which provides access to many of the park's most famous attractions and trailheads. There are twelve developed campgrounds in the park offering more than 2,000 campsites and nine hotels/lodges, including the historic Old Faithful Inn and the hotels at Mammoth Hot Springs and Lake Yellowstone. Backpacking is also popular at the more than 300 designated campsites in the park's vast backcountry (permit required). Many more campgrounds and hotels/motels are in the park's surrounding gateway towns. While the park is open year-round, winter is long and severe and includes deep snow; the primary visitor season is July and August, though June and September can offer some relief from crowding. Winter snows can take many weeks to melt, and snow usually starts again in mid-fall.

This trail along Slough Creek in the park's northeast quadrant is emblematic of the beauty and diversity of Yellowstone.

The Last Word

Contemporary conservationists are excited about the concept of landscape-scale conservation, and Yellowstone offers what may be the hopeful poster child. Even though the park is comparatively large, animals such as grizzly bears and bison wander in and out, protected in the former case but not the latter. Moreover, wildfires cross park boundaries indiscriminately. These are just two examples of why the geography of contemporary parks is often inadequately small; to be effective, environmental protection must be conducted on a grander scale. It's fortunate that Yellowstone is surrounded by other conservation-oriented lands—national and state parks and forests, fish and wildlife refuges, and protected areas managed by nonprofit groups—to form 20 million acres of land that's optimistically called the Greater Yellowstone Ecosystem. If these lands can be managed in a cooperative and coordinated manner, with Yellowstone National Park as is core, this presents an unusual opportunity to conduct a program of more effective conservation. Hike Yellowstone and appreciate the park for what it is and for what it and other parks ultimately could be.

Yosemite National Park

California | nps.gov/yose

Many people have at least passing knowledge of Yosemite Valley and its remarkable convergence of natural features: nearly sheer granite cliffs rising as much as 5,000 feet above the valley floor; the sparkling Merced River that meanders through the deep, old-growth valley forests; the internationally-recognized granite features of Half Dome and El Capitan; and some of the highest and most dramatic waterfalls in the world. Yosemite Valley may be the most strikingly beautiful place we've visited. (We had the good fortune to live in the park for a year as well.) But the valley is less than 1 percent of the park's 750,000 acres. There's a great deal of Yosemite beyond, including three groves of ancient sequoias, the vast High Sierra portion of the park with its 13,000-plus-foot mountains and lush meadows, two federally designated Wild and Scenic Rivers (the Merced and the Tuolumne), and the colorful history and philosophy of John Muir, the unofficial "father" of Yosemite and the National Park System more broadly. There's a lot to like about Yosemite.

Geology is the place to start in Yosemite—it's all there, right before your eyes. Tectonic forces in California's deep prehistory elevated the land into what we now call the Sierra Nevada, Muir's "Range of Light" and "gentle wilderness." But it's the glaciers that have given the current shape to these mountains by digging, scraping, and polishing. Yosemite and the other valleys in the park display the classic U shape associated with glacial action (flowing rivers tend to form V-shaped valleys). Actually, it was a series of glacial periods over the past 2 to 3 million years that shaped much of the park. At one point, it's estimated that Yosemite Valley was covered in 4,000 feet of "flowing" ice, plucking away at the granite walls of the valley and polishing the park's signature domes. The distinctive domes of the park are the result of plutons, igneous rock crystallized from pools of molten rock slowly cooling beneath the earth's surface. As erosion striped away the soil and other surface materials, the plutons began to cool and harden. The upper

(above) Some of the park's high-elevation lakes can remain ice-covered until midsummer.

(opposite) The strikingly beautiful Yosemite Valley is one of the most iconic views in all the National Parks.

The park includes portions of the John Muir and Pacific Crest National Scenic Trails.

layers of the plutons experienced this process first because they are the initial areas to be relieved of the weight and pressure of the surface materials. Consequently, they fracture or exfoliate, assuming a layered form much like an onion.

The park includes an especially wide range of elevations, from approximately 2,000 to more than 13,000 feet, and includes several vegetation zones. Many types of pines and firs occupy the park depending on elevation; deciduous trees include black oaks and canyon live oaks. Large meadows are found at elevations from about 4,000 to 8,000 feet, and the park is generally well-watered with many streams and lakes as a result of deep winter snows. Wildflowers put on exuberant displays in spring and summer. Three groves of giant sequoias are found in the park at an elevation of about 4,000 feet; these trees are the largest living things on the planet, many living 2,000 or more years. Yosemite's habitats support many species of wildlife; notable examples include mountain lions, black bears, bighorn sheep, coyotes, bobcats, red foxes, mule deer, spotted owls, pikas, and yellow-bellied marmots. More than 250 species of birds have been documented in the park.

The park's forests are highly susceptible to periodic wildfires, a natural and integral part of much of the Yosemite ecosystem. As with other national parks, the especially large fires Yosemite has recently been experiencing are partly due to the historic NPS policy of extinguishing all wildfires as quickly as possible. This policy left many forests with much dead and down wood, making them highly susceptible to conflagrations. Climate change is also an important cause, creating unusually hot and dry conditions and allowing explosive populations of forest insects that kill many trees. Research has found that the park's ancient sequoias are serotinous, meaning their cones open to disperse seeds with the heat of a fire; it's ironic that extinguishing fires for many decades has endangered the reproduction of sequoias, and the NPS is now allowing some natural wildfires (e.g., those started by lightning) to burn when they don't threaten people or their property, even setting periodic controlled burns under appropriate conditions. Yosemite is an exemplar of this evolving approach to managing wildfire in the national parks.

Establishment and management of Yosemite tells a number of important stories in the nation's conservation history. Sadly, it begins with the horrific treatment of indigenous people who visited and occupied the area for thousands of years. To deal with skirmishes between the area's Paiute and Miwok Indians and California gold rush miners, the Mariposa Battalion of the US Army was sent to the Yosemite region, where they "discovered" Yosemite Valley. The Indian village in the valley was burned and the occupants removed. This made way for a nascent, mostly tacky tourist industry, including a host of inappropriate visitor attractions. Early conservationists were appalled at the damage that was being done to the area and lobbied Congress to grant Yosemite Valley and the Mariposa Grove of sequoias to California to be protected by the state, which it did in 1864.

Later in the nineteenth century, John Muir found his way to Yosemite and devoted much of his adult life to exploring and protecting the area, as well as other places that would eventually become national parks. His powerful writing and speaking helped convince Congress to establish Yosemite National Park in 1890. In 1903, Muir famously hosted President Theodore Roosevelt on a three-day camping trip at Yosemite's Glacier Point and convinced him to help arrange the transfer of Yosemite Valley and the Mariposa Grove of giant sequoias from the state of California back to the federal government and incorporate them into Yosemite National Park. Soon after the park was established, the US Army was directed to protect it (the NPS was not created until 1916). Among the troops stationed in the park was the African-American 9th Cavalry, known as the Buffalo Soldiers, who helped protect several of the early national parks. It's both ironic and unfortunate that contemporary African Americans are substantially underrepresented as visitors to Yosemite and most other national parks.

Walking Yosemite

With more than 800 miles of trails in this world-renowned park, how do you decide where to hike? We've been privileged to spend a lot of time in Yosemite (including a year in residence) and have hiked extensively, including trails that follow great rivers, climb to the top of waterfalls and granite domes, and wander through groves of ancient forests and lush meadows, and have thru-hiked the John Muir Trail. We're especially enthusiastic to recommend the following trails.

Vernal Fall / Nevada Fall (John Muir Trail/Mist Trail/Panorama Trail)

This is *the* hike for every Yosemite visitor, a compact tour of so many of the features for which the park is internationally celebrated: granite spires and domes, a wild river, and world-class waterfalls. The park's trail system offers an appealing 5.8-mile lollipop route that gains 2,000 feet as it follows the rushing Merced River to Vernal Fall and then Nevada Fall. Start at the trailhead for the famed John Muir Trail, turn left on the Mist Trail to the top of Nevada Fall (bring a rain jacket to shield yourself from the spray of the waterfalls, especially in spring and early summer), and return on the John Muir Trail. A shorter alternative is to walk to the Vernal Fall Bridge and enjoy the very best

The park is known for some of the highest and most dramatic waterfalls in the world; this is Nevada Fall, a half-day hike from Yosemite Valley.

(above) Yosemite Falls peaks in spring and can be dry by the end of summer.

(above right) Lovely Lyell Canyon in the park's high country makes a great day hike.

view of its namesake waterfall, a 1.6-mile round-trip. For a longer alternative (but nearly all downhill), start your hike at Glacier Point and follow the aptly-named Panorama Trail 10.4 miles to the top of Nevada Fall; then descend to Yosemite Valley via the John Muir Trail for a hike of 13.7 miles. The only rub is that you'll need a ride to Glacier Point to start this hike; be creative.

Mariposa Grove (Grizzly Giant Loop Trail)

The Mariposa Grove is the largest collection of giant sequoias in the park, more than 500 mature trees, and the area is laced with trails. We recommend the Grizzly Giant Loop Trail, an easy walk of about 2 miles (round-trip) where you'll see several named trees, including the Grizzly Giant. Estimated to be more than 2,000 years old, this is the oldest and tallest sequoia in the park, standing more than 200 feet high with a diameter of more than 25 feet and circumference of more than 90 feet.

Lyell Canyon Trail

Let's switch our geographic focus and hike in Yosemite's vast High Sierra, and there's perhaps no better place to begin than Lyell Canyon, a sublime example of John Muir's "gentle wilderness." The trailhead is just off the Tioga Road near Tuolumne Meadows, and the hike follows the Lyell Fork of the Tuolumne River for 5.6 miles to the junction with the trail to Vogelsang Pass, making this an out-and-back hike of 11.2 miles (you can shorten the hike by simply turning around at any point).

This easy-to-moderate hike follows a sparkling river that pools and meanders through the area's extensive meadows with views to the surrounding mountains. There's no adequate way to describe the beauty of this place; you'll just have to see for yourself.

Half Dome

All serious hikers have heard of Half Dome, certainly one of the most widely known hikes in all the national parks. Half Dome is the scenic symbol of Yosemite, appearing on California's state quarter and driver's license, as well as on the logo of the Sierra Club. This is a challenging hike, especially if attempted as a day hike: 16 miles round-trip, nearly 5,000 feet of elevation gain, and an exposed section of cables that must be navigated to summit the dome. The first 3.5 miles are the same as the trail to the top of Nevada Fall (described above). Here you continue your hike around Little Yosemite Valley and then on to the junction with the Half Dome Trail at mile six. Follow this trail steeply up to the base of the dome, where you use fixed steel cables to reach the top of the dome. (Leather gloves help with this last pitch.) The rounded mass of rock you ascend falls steeply off on both sides; this is not a hike for the faint-hearted. The summit is flatter than it appears from the valley and allows hikers to rest and appreciate the truly remarkable 360-degree view of the park. If you're day hiking, you should start before dawn to help ensure that you're off the summit before afternoon thunderstorms develop. Perhaps a better plan is to make this a backpacking trip, staying a night or two at Little Yosemite Valley. This hike is so popular, it requires a permit, determined by lottery.

Half Dome is a classic example of the dramatic granite domes that grace the park; note the cables that lead hikers to the top.

High Sierra Camps Loop

This unusual and remarkable multiday route offers access to some of the most strikingly beautiful portions of the Yosemite wilderness. Here the park provides a series of six "camps"—clusters of large, semipermanent tents and common areas—spaced a day's hike apart. The camps are located in a way that offers a six-day loop that totals about 50 miles. Each tent has four to six dormitory-style beds with mattresses and pillows and a wood stove. Employees, mostly energetic young men and women, prepare family-style dinners and breakfasts and serve them in large canvas-sided dining halls. Showers are available at some of the camps, though a dip in one of the many (admittedly icy) lakes and streams along the trail may be an even better alternative. All camps have restroom facilities. By using the camps, one can backpack through the Yosemite wilderness without having to carry a heavy backpack! This system of camps offers a way of enjoying and appreciating the mountains that's more characteristic of Europe, with its extensive systems of huts. The landscape of the High

The Cathedral Peaks are some of the most dramatic and beautiful in the park.

Sierra Camps Loop is classic high-country Yosemite: mountains approaching 14,000 feet, smooth granite domes, spacious meadows that support a rich stock of wildflowers, deep pine forests, and a ready supply of inviting streams and lakes. It's not surprising that the High Sierra Camps are so popular that there's a lottery for their use. The camps are expensive, but you don't have to hike the whole circuit. You also can walk this same route on a more conventional backpacking trip (which requires a permit).

John Muir Trail / Pacific Crest Trail

We don't expect you to thru-hike these world-renowned long-distance trails, though it's definitely worth thinking about; the JMT was a life-changer for us. Both trails travel through Yosemite, where you can sample their power and magic. The park includes about 34 of the JMT's 211 miles and about 70 of the PCT's 2,650 miles. You walk portions of these trails on the way to Vernal and Nevada Falls, Half Dome, on the High Sierra Camps Loop, and in Lyell Canyon (as described above).

Logistics

Visitor demand for Yosemite is high, but there is a relatively large infrastructure of facilities and services. There are thirteen campgrounds scattered along the park's road system, and the vast wilderness portion of the park (about 95 percent) offers lots of room for backpacking trips (a permit is required). There are also eight lodging options, including the famous Ahwahnee Hotel. The park also includes the High Sierra Camps described above. Commercial campgrounds and other lodgings are located outside the park, though sometimes at a distance. The park includes two visitor centers, one in Yosemite Valley and the other at Tuolumne Meadows, and three information stations. The park is open year-round, but long winters and deep snow limit the primary hiking season to May through September, with July and August especially popular. Waterfalls tend to peak in May, but high-elevation roads and trails may be snow-covered (and closed) until mid-June or even July. Yosemite Valley can be hot and dry in the summer months. A free shuttle bus system operates in parts of Yosemite Valley and along the Tioga Road near Tuolumne Meadows; this helps relieve traffic congestion and provides shuttles to and from trailheads.

The Last Word

Yosemite is legendary, a crown-jewel park by all measures, but it can be crowded. "Principle 5: Avoid the Crowds" in Part 3 of this book offers a number of strategies that can be used to address crowding. Everyone needs to see and appreciate Yosemite Valley, but this is such a small portion of the park. Find your way into the high country and channel your inner John Muir, spending as much time walking the park as possible.

Zion National Park

Utah | nps.gov/zion

"Zion" is a rich and powerful word in many cultures and religions. It means "a place of peace and refuge," and there just couldn't be a better name for this remarkable national park in the southwest corner of Utah. This is an arid landscape of great and colorful slickrock canyons, towering cliffs, and magical spires and arches. The main feature of the park is Zion Canyon, 15 miles long and up to half a mile deep, where the North Fork of the Virgin River flows and sometimes rages its way toward the Colorado River. Zion National Park is sometimes called "the desert Yosemite," and this analogy is intended as a compliment. There may be no park more glorious than Yosemite, but in our view, Zion stands on its own merits as one of the most exceptional in the National Park System. It's not an especially big park, just under 150,000 acres, but it's packed with enchanting views, varied visitor attractions and trails throughout.

The natural history of Zion is dominated by its geologic heritage, a millennia-long sequence of sediment deposition, uplift, and erosion. The park is part of the huge geographic region known as the Grand Staircase, a reference to the alternating layers of limestone (sediment collected at the bottom of freshwater and maritime seas) and sandstone (formed by vast sand dunes) that are exposed throughout the area. In more recent geologic time, the expansive Colorado Plateau region has been uplifted thousands of feet by tectonic forces, and rivers have carved it into a series of canyons, some broad like the lower reaches of Zion Canyon and some narrow "slot canyons" like the Virgin River Narrows. The Navajo Sandstone layer, up to 2,000 feet thick, dominates much of the park. Its naturally occurring iron has been dissolved and washed out of its upper layers, where the walls of the canyon are bone white, and the lower layers show off the iron's pleasing reddish, or rusty, color.

The natural variation of the park—its wide range of elevations along with scattered streams and springs—results in four major life zones: desert, riparian, woodland, and coniferous forest. These zones support a great variety of plant and animal life. Highlights include mule deer, ringtails, foxes, mountain lions, and a great variety of birds, including eagles. Exotic plants include night-blooming (and poisonous) sacred datura and, where water seeps from canyon walls, lush hanging gardens of ferns and monkey flowers.

Archaeologists estimate that human presence in the park goes back to the Basketmaker culture, some 10,000 years ago; these pre–Ancestral Puebloan people grew maize, squash, and beans on the floodplains, but little physical evidence remains of them or of subsequent Native American tribes.

A curtain of water falls into the Emerald Pools.

The area was explored by Spanish missionaries in the eighteenth century and settled by Mormons in the nineteenth century. Remnants of a brief ranching period are still visible in the park and the surrounding area. Following early attempts at settlement, it didn't take long for the public to recognize the area's remarkable and dramatic beauty, and it was established as Mukuntuweap National Monument in 1909, the name meaning "straight canyon" in the language of the Paiute Indians. The name was later changed to Zion to honor Mormon settlement of the area, and the monument was elevated to national park status in 1919.

Walking Zion

For a relatively small park, Zion is especially rich in walking opportunities, and some of the trails are among the most famous in the National Park System. Given the understandable popularity of the park, it can be crowded, but the overpowering scenery more than makes up for this inconvenience. As always, the farther you get off the roads and away from the trailheads, the more moments of solitude you're likely to enjoy.

Emerald Pools Trail

Let's start with a pleasant walk that incorporates many of the finest aspects of Zion—well-maintained trails, great views across spectacular Zion Canyon (including the Great White Throne), and a series of waterfalls and pools. The trailhead is at the Zion Lodge stop on the park's innovative

Zion includes many slot canyons, but the Virgin River Narrows is the granddaddy of them all—a 16-mile route where staying dry isn't an option.

shuttle bus system, across the road from the lodge. There are three falls/pools to visit, each with its own character. It's 1.2 miles to Lower Pool, 1.9 miles to Middle Pool, and 2.5 miles to Upper Pool, all round-trip distances. At Lower and Middle Pools, you can walk behind their sheer curtains of water falling from above. The trail is paved to Middle Pool and is wheelchair accessible (with some assistance) to Lower Pool; it's rocky and steep to Upper Pool.

Virgin River Narrows

Zion includes many slot canyons (narrow and sheer-walled), but the Virgin River Narrows is the granddaddy of them all—a 16-mile route through a canyon that narrows to 20 to 30 feet across, with near-vertical walls that rise 1,000 feet or more. The North Fork of the Virgin River runs through the canyon—sometimes from wall to wall—and staying dry isn't an option. The walk through the canyon can be done in two ways. The first option is a long day hike or short backpack from the top of the narrows section of the canyon to its mouth in Zion Canyon. This is a very slow and challenging hike that requires a permit. The walk begins with a drive (or, better, a shuttle) out of the park to the head of the canyon. Then follow the river as it enters the narrows. Frequent river crossings are necessary as the river moves from one side of the narrow canyon to the other. The characteristic steep walls of the narrows are intermittent at first, allowing for tall conifers and shrubby maples. Soon the steep canyon walls become nearly continuous, and a number of small nameless tributaries and a few larger ones flow into the canyon. You must wade (or even swim in high water) several deep pools. Big Spring marks the upper end of a 3-mile especially dramatic section of the narrows, where only a slice of sky can be seen between the canyon walls. As you approach the mouth of the canyon, the narrows section widens quickly, bringing you to a paved walkway on the left of the river that leads you to the Temple of Sinawava Trailhead and the associated shuttle bus stop.

The second and more popular way to experience this slot canyon is as a shorter day hike up the Virgin River Narrows from the head of Zion Canyon. From the shuttle bus stop at the Temple of Sinawava Trailhead, follow the paved Riverside Walk for a mile and then enter the river as it flows out of the narrows. Walk upstream, mostly in the water, for as little as a few minutes or as long as a few hours. You can walk as far as Big Springs, but day hikers are not allowed beyond this point. Outfitters in the gateway town of Springdale rent specialized water shoes, hiking poles, and other equipment that may be helpful.

Angels Landing

Angels Landing is one of the most famous routes in all the national parks. The last half mile of this route requires a white-knuckle scramble along the knife-edge of Angels Landing, where the margins of the trail drop off 1,500 feet in both directions. At the end, intrepid hikers are rewarded with sweeping views up and down dramatic Zion Canyon, including the Virgin River as it bends around

A series of switchbacks makes its way up the west wall of Zion Canyon.

Angels Landing, all this seen from the perspective of one of the park's eagles. The NPS has installed metal chains and handholds along strategic portions of the route. Is this hike worth it? Yes! Do we want to do it again? No! Reaching Angel's Landing requires a 5.4-mile (round-trip) hike up the West Rim Trail (described below), including about 1,500 feet of elevation gain. It's very popular—start early in the day.

West Rim Trail

This is yet another of Zion's epic hikes—a 16-mile walk that offers a special richness of features and views—and is one of our favorite hikes in the National Park System. With an early start, it can be done as a long day hike, but is often done as a two-day backpacking trip (try to get backcountry campsite #6). The hike begins at the 8,000-foot Lava Point Trailhead and rambles and rolls across the large Horse Pasture Plateau and associated forests, offering stunning views into a variety of colorful canyons showcasing some the park's most iconic geologic formations, including North and South Guardian Angels and a number of distinctive domes and beehives. As the trail approaches the steep descent into Zion Canyon, the action really begins. An expanse of slickrock leads to the base of Angels Landing near Scout Lookout, and the exposed side trail that leads out and over Angels Landing starts here (see Angels Landing above). If you choose to follow this route, stop at Scout Lookout to refresh yourself with food and water. Back on the West Rim Trail, you immediately go down Walter's Wiggles (named for the park's first superintendent), a series of twenty-one tight switchbacks descending a

(above) Walter's Wiggles (named for the park's first superintendent), a series of twenty-one tight switchbacks, is a triumph of trail-making.

(above right) Angels Landing is one of the most famous hikes in the National Park System; it's a white-knuckle scramble along the knife-edge that leads to top of this formation.

60-degree slope. Stop to admire this triumph of trail-making, one of the most artistic "crafted" trails in the National Park System. After descending gently through refreshing Refrigerator Canyon, the trail drops sharply on a paved path that leads to the floor of Zion Canyon. A bridge leads over the Virgin River to the Grotto Trailhead, from which you can take the park's free shuttle bus to the visitor center and/or Springdale. Outfitters in Springdale offer shuttle service to the West Rim Trailhead.

East Rim Trail

We've chosen to describe this approximately 10-mile hike in the easterly direction because of the possibility of combining it with the West Rim Trail in a grand traverse of the park. But of course it can be hiked in the opposite direction, requiring less elevation gain. The hike begins at Weeping Rock, one of the stops on the park's shuttle bus system. Begin the climb on the Observation Point Trail, which will lead you through Echo Canyon and up to the East Rim Trail. There are two attractive add-on options as you climb. The first is a relatively short side trip into magical Hidden Canyon, where you can scramble through the canyon as far as you like. Second, where the East Rim Trail branches off the Observation Point Trail, you can stay on the latter and continue up to Observation Point, where there are sweeping views—some of the best in the park—of Zion Canyon. The East Rim Trail is an undulating and varied hike to the park's east entrance that leads you through open areas of slickrock (where the trail is marked with cairns—pay attention to wayfinding here) and upper-elevation forests of pinyon and ponderosa pines and Utah junipers. As you approach the end of the trail, there are dramatic views of classic Zion "checkerboard" mesas, sandstone formations where geologic forces, weather, and temperature changes have fashioned distinctive crosshatched grooves in the rock. Despite being a wonderful walk over varied terrain, we saw only a few other hikers on the length of the East Rim Trail.

Zion Rim-to-Rim

Combining the West Rim and East Rim Trails across Zion Canyon offers walkers the unusual opportunity to trace a broad cross section of the park—an approximately 28-mile trek that connects the park's east and west rims. We suggest traveling from west to east to save about 1,500 feet of elevation gain and get the longest shuttle out of way first. The trails can be connected by walking or taking the shuttle bus from the Grotto stop (the end of the West Rim Trail) to the Weeping Rock stop (the beginning of the route to the East Rim). The ideal way to conduct this walk is on a multiday backpacking trip, spending one or two days on each trail (you'll need a permit to camp). Or you could give yourself a break when you reach the floor of Zion Canyon by taking the shuttle bus to the Zion Lodge or into Springdale and spending the night, reversing the process the next morning.

The West Rim Trail starts in the park's high country where hikers enjoy groves of aspens.

Logistics

Zion has two visitor centers, one at the southwest entrance and another in the semidetached Kolob section in the northwest region of the park. The park includes three campgrounds and the Zion Park Lodge; commercial campgrounds and other accommodations are available in the park's tourist-friendly gateway town of Springdale. Visitors must ride the park's free shuttle bus system to travel the Zion Canyon Scenic Drive, which includes many of the park's major attractions and trailheads (a bike is a good option, as well). Most visitors enjoy the shuttle bus system, which is likely to represent the future of visiting many national parks. Outfitters in Springdale offer shuttle service to both the East Rim and West Rim trailheads, making it more convenient to hike one way. It's best to have a reservation. The park is open year-round but can be quite cold in winter and very hot in summer; spring and fall are the best hiking seasons.

The Last Word

Zion offers some of the most iconic walks in all the national parks. They often ask a lot of hikers, but they return even more. Prepare for these walks by carefully planning when and how you're going to do them safely. Check the park website for details about permits and local conditions, and talk with rangers at the visitor centers. Walk this park and see for yourself why "Zion" is the perfect name for this increasingly popular national park.

Part 3
How to Visit and Walk the National Parks

Given the astonishing beauty and richness of the national parks, it's no wonder they're so popular. But this means visiting and walking in these parks can present some challenges. What parks should you visit and when? Given the tens of thousands of miles of trails in the national parks, which should you walk and why? What can you do to enhance your enjoyment of these hikes? What constitutes appropriate behavior in the national parks, including helping to protect the parks, respecting other visitors, and protecting your own well-being? How should you plan your trips to the national parks? What types of accommodations are available inside and outside the parks? We answer these and related questions in a series of principles we've developed over our years of visiting and walking in the national parks. These principles work for us; we're confident they'll work for you too.

Principle 1: Find Your Parks and Trails

Sound familiar? It might as it's a variation of the slogan Find Your Park used for the centennial of the National Park Service. The national parks feature many kinds of natural and cultural environments and attractions found across the country, and all these parks are addressed in this book. You may know which park you want to visit; this book will help you plan your trip, perhaps tempting you to other parks as well. But what if you don't know where to go? Thumb through the table of contents for a list of all the national parks and then look at the map of all the parks at the beginning of Part 2; these are good ways to stimulate your thinking about which national parks you'd like to visit. Then let Part 2 help you decide—there's a chapter that focuses on each park, including its natural and cultural history, representative photos, and descriptions of the trails that are our favorites, trails that best represent the distinctiveness and diversity of each park. We suggest you consider some of the lesser-known parks. You can't go wrong! And the map in Part 2 suggests national parks that can easily be visited together. For example, there are several national parks across southern Utah that nicely complement one another. So do the three national parks in the State of Washington, the three in the northern Rocky Mountains, the three in the Dakotas, the

Cairns (small piles of rocks) are often used to mark
Trails above tree line. (Canyonlands National Park)

three in Texas and New Mexico, the two Hawaiian national parks, Great Smoky Mountains and Shenandoah—you'll discover lots of appealing combinations. Just be sure to budget enough time in each park to fully appreciate it.

Of course there are other resources to help you find your parks and trails. The NPS website (nps.gov) includes a map of all the national parks. Each park has its own NPS website that offers a great deal of information; we've included the official website address for each national park in the chapters in Part 2. There are a number of good general guidebooks to the national parks; we've included what we think are the best in the References section of this book.

Consider visiting national parks close to home. Some national parks are remote and require a long drive to reach them; some even require a long ferry ride or airplane trip. However, many are relatively close to population centers. Cuyahoga Valley National Park, for example, sits between Cleveland and Akron, Ohio; Shenandoah National Park is near the Washington, DC, metropolitan area; Acadia National Park is a short day's drive from the Boston area; Everglades National Park is just outside Miami; and Mount Rainier National Park is close to the Seattle area. These are just examples.

Principle 2: Plan Ahead

It can be disappointing to arrive at a national park to find that all campgrounds and lodges are full, it's hard to find a parking spot, and there's even a line of cars to get into the park. Your visits to the parks will be more successful and enjoyable if you plan well in advance, making reservations when and where advisable, and using the other strategies we suggest in this part of the book. This can be done relatively painlessly, as we describe here. First, it's important to understand that campgrounds, lodgings, and other services *in* the parks are generally provided by either the NPS or private companies (called concessionaires) that have been contracted by the NPS. Most campgrounds, lodgings, and other services *outside* the national parks are provided by private businesses, although there may also be campgrounds outside the national parks in nearby public lands such as national forests and state parks. Here's how to get the campsites, lodging, and other services you'll need, organized by type of facility and service: camping, lodgings, and special services.

Camping

Camping is a common and much-loved form of accommodation in the national parks, and developed campgrounds are usually available both inside and outside the parks. Backcountry or wilderness camping is offered in most national parks. These options are briefly described below.

Campgrounds in the National Parks

Most campgrounds in the national parks are operated by the NPS; these campgrounds are often well-located (e.g., some are close to attractions, while others offer lots of solitude), and they're rustic. They generally don't provide hot water, showers, or electrical and other hookups for recreational vehicles. The names and locations of all NPS-managed campgrounds are listed and described on the park's official website. Go to the website and select "Planning Your Visit" then either "Eating and Sleeping" or "Camping." (Not all parks use exactly the same wording, but it will be similar to what we've outlined.) You'll also find information on how campsites are allocated (e.g., first-come, first-served or reservation). If campsites can be reserved, you'll also find how far in advance you can make reservations. Generally, a centralized reservation website (recreation.gov) can be used; there's a toll-free telephone number as well: (877) 444 6777. Campsite fees are typically nominal, and there's usually a liberal cancellation policy. If campsites are allocated only on a first-come, first-served basis, schedule your visit to arrive at the desired campground as early in the day as possible.

Camping is a traditional way of enjoying the national parks. (Denali National Park and Preserve)

NPS has contracted with private companies to manage some of their campgrounds, and these areas often provide services such as electrical hookups for recreational vehicles. (These campsites cost more as well.) If there are concession-operated campgrounds in the park, they'll be noted on the park website and there will be a link to the company that manages them. Campsites in these types of campgrounds can usually be reserved well in advance.

Campgrounds Outside the National Parks

There are often campgrounds outside the national parks. These campgrounds are usually managed by private companies, and information about them can be found using internet searches and/or apps designed for this purpose (e.g., AllStays Camp & RV and membership organizations such as KOA, Good Sam Club, and AAA). Chambers of commerce in towns just outside the parks are also good sources of information. There may also be campgrounds near national parks that are located in national forests, state parks, and other public lands. Search the internet for maps of public lands near national parks that interest you, and then visit the websites for those areas.

Backcountry/Wilderness Camping

Most national parks include backcountry or wilderness areas where visitors can camp and backpack. "Backcountry" is a general word that refers to the non-developed portions of many parks; "wilderness" is a more specific word that refers to non-developed portions of many parks that have been designated by Congress as wilderness areas under the provisions of the 1964 Wilderness Act. Many of the larger national parks may have as much as 90 percent or even more of their land as either backcountry or wilderness, and most of this land is open to backpacking. Although this kind of hiking and camping is a traditional way of enjoying and appreciating the national parks, it's also subject to special provisions to help ensure protection of these areas, and a permit is usually required. Pertinent information is available on park websites. In some especially popular parks, you may need to reserve permits well in advance or even participate in a lottery.

Lodgings

Most national parks include options for accommodations other than camping. These options include hotels (some of them historic), motels, and cabins, and these may be found inside and/or outside the parks.

Lodgings in the National Parks

Most lodging facilities in the parks are managed by private concessionaires (contracted by the NPS). Go to the individual park website and navigate to "Eating and Sleeping" and/or "Lodging." Here there'll be a link to the company (sometimes more than one) that manages lodging facilities in the park; use these links to get descriptions, pricing, reservation policies, etc. In some of the most popular national parks, these facilities can be reserved a year or more in advance. Some national parks include grand historic hotels that were built many years ago to attract visitors to the parks. Examples include the El Tovar Hotel at Grand Canyon, Old Faithful Inn at Yellowstone, and Paradise Inn at Mount Rainier. David and Kay Scott's *Complete Guide to the National Park Lodges* (see References) offers descriptions of these hotels, which are usually expensive and must be reserved well in advance. Because of the historic character of these properties, they may not meet contemporary standards of design and service, but they're often loved by those who use them.

Some national parks include historic hotels designed to attract visitors to the parks. (Old Faithful Inn, Yellowstone National Park)

Lodgings Outside the National Parks

There are all types of lodgings outside most of the national parks, nearly all of them provided by private companies. Often these facilities and related services are found in the park's "gateway towns," towns that have grown up on the borders of national parks primarily to provide visitor facilities and services. Classic examples include Bar Harbor, Maine (Acadia National Park); Gatlinburg, Tennessee (Great Smoky Mountains National Park); Jackson, Wyoming (Grand Teton National Park); Estes Park, Colorado (Rocky Mountain National Park); and Moab, Utah (Arches National Park). Information on these facilities and services is readily available on the internet, and though demand is typically not as high as for lodgings inside the parks, reservations should be made well in advance.

Should You Stay Inside or Outside the National Parks?

There are potentially important advantages to spending the night in a national park, as this can lead to a more immersive experience; for example, you may see and/or hear nocturnal wildlife, and stargazing can be great. It also may be more convenient and efficient, because you're likely to be substantially closer to trailheads and won't have to wait in the lines that sometimes form at park entrance stations. The cost of hotel rooms in the parks can be higher than outside the parks, though this is not generally true for campsites; weigh this against the potential convenience of staying inside the parks.

Specialized Services in the National Parks

Some national parks offer specialized services to visitors, such as ranger-guided tours of caves at Carlsbad Caverns National Park and cliff dwellings at Mesa Verde National Park. In addition, as previously noted, permits are usually required for backpacking in the large wilderness portions of most national parks. Permits are also required for some extremely popular day hikes, such as Half Dome in Yosemite National Park, or on trails in especially fragile areas. Up-to-date information on reservations and permits for such specialized services is usually available on each park's official website; the reservation process may be managed by the park or at recreation.gov.

Contacting the NPS

We've tried in this book to provide the information you'll need to plan your visits to the national parks and to choose the very best hikes. However, the National Park System is highly diverse, and you may want to contact parks directly for additional information or clarification. You'll find a phone number for each park near the bottom of the first page of its official website. Because the NPS is staffed very thinly, you may be connected to a phone tree, but there's usually a way to reach a staff member who will be able to answer your questions. Another good option is to use the electronic "Contact Us" option near the bottom of the first page of the park's website. This will allow you to e-mail your questions. We've had good luck using this electronic option, usually receiving a personal reply within a few days. As we plan our trips and hikes in the national parks, we often request an official park map and newspaper through this e-mail option. Park websites frequently have this information online as well. We can't imagine visiting a park without having a good plan fashioned from this type of information.

Principle 3: Prepare Yourself

Preparation is needed to get the most out of your visits and hikes in the national parks. You should prepare yourself physically, obtain the information you'll need, and be sure you have the necessary clothing and equipment. We outline these issues below; most of this is pretty straightforward, but it's important to your enjoyment and well-being.

Physical Preparation

We hope you'll want to walk the trails we recommend, and to get the most enjoyment from them, you should practice walking at home. If you're not a walker at the moment, then become one by integrating walking into your daily life. For example, try to walk more each day; if feasible, consider walking to and from work, to the market and back, around your neighborhood in the morning or evening, in your local parks on the weekends. Start walking a few extra miles each week, and build your walking program as your body allows. We've included a few of the better sources about how to improve your walking fitness in the References section. Electronic fitness trackers can be useful and don't have to be expensive. Include some hills in your walks, walk even when the weather is poor (the weather's not always good in the national parks!), and carry your pack to get used to it. Join one of the local walking/hiking clubs where you live, and participate actively. The ability to comfortably walk in the national parks will enhance your experience immeasurably.

The Information You Need

You'll need some basic information about each park to deepen your enjoyment and appreciation and prepare yourself for the situations you'll encounter. We offer much of this information in this book by providing background material on each park, including its natural and cultural history, descriptions of the hikes we recommend (all of which we've trail-tested), and logistical considerations. We recommend two other sources of information: detailed trail guidebooks and the NPS. The trail descriptions we provide in Part 2 are aspirational in character; they're designed to help you decide which hikes you might like best. Once you've chosen the trails you'll hike, a guidebook, map, and/or GPS unit or app will allow you to find and follow the trails; popular GPS apps include Avenza and Gaia. (In the Appendix: find GPS coordinates for the trailheads of all the trails we recommend.) Most national parks have good detailed trail guidebooks; we like Falcon Guides when

Great Basin National Park offers tours of Leyman Caves, but they must often be reserved. (Great Basin National Park)

they're available. National Geographic Trails Illustrated topographic maps are also very useful. Of course the NPS is the most authoritative and up-to-date source on the national parks. Take advantage of these three sources: (1) the official NPS website for each park, (2) free printed and/or online materials on each park developed by the NPS, and (3) helpful park staff at visitor centers. The websites for all the national parks are organized in a pretty standard format, so you'll quickly get good at finding what you need. The NPS also offers printed and online materials on all national parks, including a free park map and often a free seasonal newspaper; we suggest getting these materials well in advance of your visit. Once you've traveled to the parks, consult with staff at the visitor centers; rangers and knowledgeable volunteers will know local conditions and offer helpful advice.

It's important to stay safe in the national parks and protect your well-being. The National Park System is exceptionally diverse, from oceans to deserts to mountains, and from east to west to Alaska and beyond. Most national parks are relatively large (some vast), and much of their land is undeveloped and natural. Consequently, you need to be prepared for many types of environments and issues that you probably don't encounter in your day-to-day life. Much of what you need to know is available in the literature the NPS publishes, each park's website, and park visitor centers; you should familiarize yourself with this information. We've learned many lessons from our years of studying, hiking, and living in the national parks; below, we briefly present guidelines that have enhanced our visits and hikes and helped keep us happy and safe.

One of the most important decisions you can make to ensure a successful hike is to properly estimate your hiking ability and align it with the degree of challenge a trail may require. Take into account the length of the trail, the altitude at which you'll be hiking (there's less oxygen available at higher altitudes), elevation gain, and roughness of the trail; we provide much of this information in the chapters in Part 2. Consider how much weight you'll be carrying as well, and try and minimize this; see the "Clothing and Equipment" section below. Compare this to your ability and experience, and consult with staff at visitor centers if you need advice.

Some park attractions are so appealing and engaging that it's easy to lose track of personal safety. Visitors should be as mindful as possible while in any national park. For example, be careful at drop-offs such as at the tops of waterfalls and cliffs; these areas can be slippery and unstable. Don't enter abandoned mines or unmanaged caves. The earth's crust is often thin around geysers and other thermal features; stay on boardwalks and maintained trails. Water is another attraction that can distract visitors. Be mindful around rivers, lakes, and the ocean, where water can be cold and currents strong. Think twice about swimming, and don't ford streams when the water is high. Slot canyons of the Southwest can experience flash floods; never enter if there is a chance of rain anywhere in the watershed.

Stay hydrated. Many parks include arid, high-elevation, or other environments where dehydration can lead to safety concerns. Physical activity always demands additional water (and snacks); carry and drink lots of water. Untreated water from park streams or lakes is likely to be contaminated; if you must drink it, purify it first by boiling or using any of a number of products available at outdoor stores. You may want to carry extra water and snacks in your car as some trailheads are remote.

Be cognizant of altitude sickness at higher elevations; symptoms include severe headache, dizziness, nausea, and fatigue. Drink lots of water, and descend to a lower elevation to protect yourself if you're exhibiting any of these symptoms. Another way to protect yourself is to avoid too much sun exposure; use sunblock and wear a wide-brimmed hat and sunblock clothing.

Wild animals in national parks are, of course, wild. A general rule is: Don't approach wildlife close enough to disturb the animal or change its behavior; some parks have specific rules or guidelines to ensure that all encounters are positive for both the visitor and the animal. For example, Yellowstone recommends staying at least 25 yards from most wild animals and 100 yards from bears and bison. Learn how to identify the risks in the park(s) you choose, and behave accordingly. Even tiny animals such as mosquitoes and ticks may require some specific behavior on your part (e.g., using insect repellent, examining yourself for ticks at the end of the day). As always, NPS literature and rangers will have good up-to-date advice.

Many national parks encompass an especially wide range of altitudes and environments, and it's important to consider where you'll be traveling and to check the weather forecast. The weather may be drastically different at your hiking destination than at the trailhead; you'll be safer (and enjoy the hike more) if you're properly dressed and equipped. Carry rain gear and a warm layer of clothing if there's a chance of precipitation, high winds, or cold weather; hypothermia (symptoms include shivering, slurred speech, clumsiness, and confusion) can be life-threatening. Be wary of lightning, especially in exposed areas.

Pay attention to wayfinding when hiking. The trails we recommend are generally marked with blazes, posts, and/or cairns (small piles of rocks used above tree line and on rock surfaces). Study maps and read guidebooks carefully, and learn to use maps, a compass, and/or GPS. We've listed some helpful resources in References at the end of this book. Cell phone reception is often spotty in the parks and sometimes nonexistent. GPS units usually work but can't be relied on, as land features such as deep canyons and dense forest may block the satellite signal.

Be sure to drive carefully and defensively in the parks; park roads are often narrow and winding and may not be in good repair. Most drivers aren't familiar with the roads and may be distracted by the scenery as well. Wildlife (and bikers and pedestrians!) may be present on roads, and drivers may stop unexpectedly to watch wildlife (creating "bear jams"). Check with visitor center staff about the condition of unpaved roads, which may be unpassable by normal passenger vehicles or slippery due to recent rain or snow. And be sure to top off your vehicle's gas tank when you can; many parks don't have gas stations, and if they do they're likely few and far between. Consider using park shuttle buses when and where available. Though crime levels are low in most national parks, be sensitive to potential threats by locking your car at trailheads and not leaving valuables exposed. Report crime or suspicious behavior to park rangers.

Clothing and Equipment

You'll need some specialized clothing and equipment for your hikes. You've probably heard of dressing in layers, and we heartily endorse this. Base layers include underwear, socks, pants/shorts, and shirts. Supplement with warmer layers of vests and jackets, and have warm gloves and hats at the ready. Good-quality, breathable rain gear is a must if there is a chance of precipitation. Much of this clothing should be "high tech"—lightweight, quick drying, and sun resistant; we include wide-brimmed hats in this category. Nearly everything for hiking these days comes in lightweight versions: shoes/boots, packs, clothing, hiking poles, tents, stoves, etc. For all our hikes, we use lightweight hiking boots or trail-running shoes. Don't let anyone sell you old-fashioned, heavy, expeditionary-type leather hiking boots (unless you're going on an expedition!). Of course you'll need a pack, maybe two—one for day hikes and one for overnight hikes. An empty day pack needn't weigh more than 1 or 2 pounds (maybe even less!), and a pack for overnight use shouldn't weigh more than a few pounds (ours don't). Consider investing in a pair of collapsible hiking poles; they help with balance and lighten the load on knees on the downhill sections of trails. The trend toward wearing and carrying less weight helps extend how far you can hike and how much more enjoyable hiking can be. We've included a couple of good guidebooks to clothing, equipment, and related issues in the References section. Some of the lightest equipment may not yet be available in mainstream outdoor gear stores but can be found and ordered online.

Principle 4: Be Adaptable

Yes, Principles 2 and 3 stress the need to plan ahead to get the most out of your national park visits and hikes, and we stand by this advice. But national parks are often big, complicated places and sometimes your best-laid plans may go awry: Weather might not cooperate, trails can be closed for wildlife considerations or maintenance, road work can slow traffic, parking lots can be full, etc. So it's wise to have backup plans you can put into place quickly. For example, if the weather is bad at your target destination, many parks are large enough that you can find other locations where the weather is better. Many parks have hundreds of miles of trails, so if the trail you planned to hike is closed, ask at the visitor center for another trail that might offer a similar experience. Check the NPS website for the park you're visiting; alerts will be posted on the opening page of the website.

Principle 5: Avoid the Crowds

The national parks can be crowded, at least in some places and at some times. This is the inevitable consequence of their foundational importance in American society and their stunning beauty; the hundreds of millions of annual visits to the national parks should be celebrated. However, from a pragmatic standpoint, this can sometimes be problematic; fortunately, there are several strategies that can be employed to deal with crowding.

Visit Less Well-Known National Parks

While every national park–goer wants to visit Yellowstone, Yosemite, and Grand Canyon at some point, consider visiting some of the less well-known parks as well; examples include Great Sand Dunes National Park and Preserve (Colorado), Guadalupe Mountains National Park (Texas), North Cascades National Park (Washington), and Capitol Reef National Park (Utah). Look through the table of contents of this book and the map at the beginning of Part 2 for ideas; these parks are all worth visiting, and many of them are comparatively underutilized. As their descriptions in this book suggest, all the parks offer a great diversity of attractions that can be richly rewarding, and many are much less crowded!

Visit National Parks in the Off-Season

Try to visit parks in the off-season, though these shoulder seasons are growing shorter as more people are adopting this strategy. Many parks accommodate the majority of their visits in the three summer months, leaving the rest of the year relatively fallow. The waterfalls of Yosemite are typically at their peak in May, fall foliage at Acadia is at its most colorful in October, and wildflowers in Grand Canyon are usually most prolific in April. Use the shoulder seasons in these and other parks to your advantage.

Get Out of Your Car and Walk

You won't be surprised that we strongly suggest that once you reach the parks, leave your car behind and take to the trails. It's the natural law of the parks that the number of people you see decreases exponentially with each mile from the trailhead.

Use Public Transit When Available

Traffic congestion and lack of parking (after all, it shouldn't be the National *Parking* Service!) plague many parks. The NPS is responding with public transit systems, usually shuttle buses; poster children include Zion, Rocky Mountain, Yosemite, Acadia, Denali, and a growing list of others. Use these (often free) transit systems to avoid the traffic and parking headaches that too many of us face in our everyday lives.

Rise Early and/or Stay Late

Get to attraction sites and trailheads early in the day, and consider hikes late in the day. Parking spaces are more readily available at these times, and you'll experience the parks at the "golden hours" when the light is at its finest—soft and rich—for viewing and photographing and when wildlife is more likely to be seen.

Purchase Park Passes and Other Goods Before Entering a Park

Shuttle buses in a growing number of parks are helping to relieve automobile congestion and air pollution. (Yosemite National Park)

Nearly all the national parks require an entrance pass/fee. There are many types of passes, including a weeklong or annual pass to individual parks, an annual pass to all areas of the National Park System, and special passes for active duty military personnel, seniors, volunteers, and disabled visitors; some are discounted, some are free. Of course you can obtain passes when you visit, but this may require waiting in line at the park entrance station or visitor center. You can obtain passes in advance on several websites, including nps.gov/planyourvisit/passes.htm, recreation.gov, and store.usgs.gov/pass. Not all passes are available at all websites. Also, save time (and usually money) by purchasing the goods and services you'll need (e.g., food, fuel, camping supplies) before you enter the park. Many of these items are often available in the parks, but only at a few locations; you may have to wait behind other visitors to make your purchases (wouldn't you rather be on the trail?) and pay high prices.

Welcome Other Visitors

Finally, welcome other visitors to the parks; it's a wonderful thing that so many like-minded people are interested in the parks. The national parks have become such an important component of our society at least partly because so many people visit and appreciate them. Yes, large numbers of visitors can sometimes cause crowding and congestion, but in the material above we offer a number of ways to overcome this. A wise NPS ranger once said that appreciation of the parks leads to their protection, and the parks need all the stakeholders they can get. Be especially welcoming of visitors from historically underrepresented groups.

Principle 6: Allow Adequate Time to See, Walk, and Appreciate the National Parks

Most of the national parks are pretty big—though they're not big enough to include all the critical wildlife habitat that's needed; to escape the air, water, light, and noise pollution that flow into them; or to shelter them from the advancing impacts of climate change. Don't underestimate the distances you'll need to travel to and through the parks and the number and diversity of inspiring trails that await you. Don't get caught in the ultimately frustrating "ten parks in two weeks" vacation trap. We give ourselves at least several days in each park. (We've sometimes spent a week or more in some of the largest and most diverse parks and when we've decided to take longer, multiday hikes.) Over the years we've substantially added to that time with return (and more return) visits. There's a story in national park lore about all this. A visitor once approached a park ranger in Yosemite and exclaimed, "I've only got 4 hours to spend in the park. What should I do?" The ranger, who had spent most of her professional life in Yosemite, replied, "Sir, if I were you, I'd sit down under that tree over there and cry." Don't disappoint yourself by budgeting too little time in each park.

Principle 7: Appreciate the Richness and Diversity of Each National Park

All the national parks are much more diverse and interesting than is generally appreciated. This is sometimes related to park names, which often emphasize only one feature. Let's take just one example: Petrified Forest National Park in eastern Arizona. As the name suggests, the park contains a remarkable collection of petrified wood (tens of square miles of it, some of the logs more than 100 feet long and several feet in diameter). But it also contains the impressive remains of dwellings and petroglyphs from a flourishing Native American civilization abandoned at the end of the thirteenth century, fossils of plants and animals from the Late Triassic period (the dawn of dinosaurs), the most colorful section of the vast Painted Desert, and the only section of Historic Route 66 protected in a national park. All the national parks are so much richer than their names might suggest.

Principle 8: Respect the National Parks and Your Fellow Visitors/Hikers

There's concern that we may be "loving our parks to death"; when we visit them, we can inadvertently trample sensitive vegetation, compact and erode soil, disturb wildlife, contribute to crowding, etc. Research suggests that many of these impacts are caused by visitors who are careless rather than by the sheer number of visitors. It's important that we all limit our potential impacts by staying on maintained trails, especially in the developed portions of parks; appreciating wildlife without feeding or disturbing the animals; being quiet and courteous so as not to disturb other visitors; and following rules and regulations established at each park. Make yourself aware of desirable outdoor recreation practices by looking at each park's official NPS website, examining the park map and newspaper that visitors are given at most parks, and learning and following Leave No Trace (LNT) principles. The following seven general LNT principles have been established by the nonprofit Leave No Trace Center for Outdoor Ethics: (1) plan ahead; (2) travel and camp on durable surfaces; (3) dispose of waste properly; (4) leave what you find; (5) minimize campfire impacts; (6) respect wildlife; and (7) be considerate of other visitors. These practices have been developed in conjunction with the NPS and other public land management agencies and reflect the latest research. You can find expansive discussion of these principles and related information at LNT.org and in the books on this topic we've included in the References section.

While much of the above discussion addresses matters of environmental impacts, visitors and hikers should be respectful of one another as well. As hiking has become more popular in the national parks and related areas, a code of conduct is emerging designed to help minimize conflict among hikers and other trail users. There are three primary groups of trail users in the national parks: hikers, bikers, and equestrians. Equestrians are historically important trail users, but their numbers have dramatically declined. Nevertheless, because horses are large, can be cumbersome, and are sometimes easy to spook, hikers and bikers should yield to horses (i.e., give them the right-of-way by stepping off the trail and being quiet as they pass). Bikes are generally not allowed on national park trails. Where they are allowed, there is sometimes conflict with hikers, and both groups should do what they reasonably can to minimize this problem. It's generally accepted that bikers should yield to hikers, though it may be more pragmatic for hikers to yield to bikers in some situations (e.g., when bikers are climbing a steep slope and to build goodwill).

Signs implore hikers to stay on designated trails. (Indiana Dunes National Park)

Don't approach wildlife too closely, for your safety and theirs. (Grand Teton National Park)

When hikers meet along the trail, those traveling downhill should yield to those going uphill. This is because hiking uphill is generally harder than traveling downhill, and it may be more difficult for the former to have to break stride. Also, those traveling uphill often have a smaller field of vision and may not easily be able to see oncoming hikers to yield the right-of-way. Hikers who wish to pass other hikers from behind should gently call out "hello" or a greeting of some kind so as to avoid startling them. When a group of hikers meets a single hiker or a smaller group, it's polite for the individual or small group to yield so as to inconvenience the fewest hikers.

Generally, all trail users should refrain from loud behavior, allowing others to hear the sounds of nature and enjoy the sense of peacefulness the trail environment can provide. This includes use of cell phones and other technology.

Given the popularity of dogs, it's important to address associated rules and regulations. The National Park System is large and diverse, and policies on dogs and other pets vary from site to site. Dogs are allowed in most national parks, but in nearly all cases they're limited to the developed portions of the parks and are not allowed on trails (or at least are restricted to certain trails), especially trails in the wilderness or backcountry. Limitations on dogs in national parks are due to several issues. They can carry diseases that can be transmitted to wildlife, alter the behavior of wildlife by chasing or scaring animals, or make noise that disturbs or displaces wildlife. They may become prey to large predators like coyotes and bears or disturb sensitive sites such as historic structures and archaeological sites, and they can bother some hikers and other trail users. Some parks have instituted the B.A.R.K. Ranger Program to recognize people and their dogs who have pledged to (1) **B**ag your pet's waste, (2) **A**lways use a leash, (3) **R**espect wildlife, and (4) **K**now where you can go. Check the website of the national parks you plan to visit to learn more about policies related to dogs and other pets.

Finally, we encourage you to be friendly and kind to other visitors and hikers. Despite outward appearances that can sometimes drive us apart, all visitors share their love of the parks, and this binds us together. Greet others with a smile and, when appropriate, strike up a conversation. "Where do you live?" "What are your favorite parks and trails?" "Have you seen any wildlife yet?" We've enjoyed meeting lots of other visitors over the years, and this has created good memories. Be sure to extend your kindness to park staff when you see them at visitor centers, patrolling the park, and doing trail maintenance; thank them for helping to protect the national parks.

Principle 9: Walk Your Own Walk in the National Parks

This principle is derived from an old saying in the walking/hiking community; we've just applied it more specifically to the national parks. It's an idea that resonates with us more and more as the years and miles add up. There are many reasons to walk: to enhance physical well-being, pursue adventure, learn about the world, deepen relationships with family and friends, escape the grind of everyday life, think more deeply about the world and our place within it, pursue spirituality, and find solitude. There are many ways to walk/hike: day hikes, backpacking trips, leisurely strolls, guided nature walks, hikes designed to test endurance, etc. All of these reasons and types of walking are valid, and none trumps the others; they're very personal and shouldn't be imposed on us. Also, the reasons to walk and the types of walking you do can vary from trail to trail and from time to time. Walk *your* walk.

In this book, we've recommended the trails we think best represent the significance, diversity, and beauty of each of the national parks. Some of these trails are short and easy, others long and more challenging; most are somewhere in between. Choose the hikes that best meet your needs, modifying them as you wish. For example, we recommend a number of out-and-back trails (trails that lead to a destination and are then hiked back to the trailhead); these trails can be walked in their entirety or a shorter distance that meets your time constraints, ability, or inclination. For some trails we recommend how they can be extended into longer, even multiday hikes. The choice is always yours, and that's the way it should be.

Principle 10: Evolve from National Park Visitor/Hiker to National Park Steward

The national parks were established to protect vital natural and cultural resources and to offer outstanding recreation opportunities, but they need our help. We're fortunate to have a National Park System that includes more than 400 areas (e.g., national parks, national monuments, and national historic sites) totaling more than 84 million acres, but the NPS is a small agency of only about 20,000 employees (about the same size staff as Disney World!) and receives annual funding of less than one-tenth of 1 percent of the federal budget. This has led to an accumulating list of deferred maintenance in the parks that's in the billions of dollars. The parks face a host of issues, including loss of biodiversity, habitat fragmentation, intensive development on park borders, invasive species, crumbling infrastructure, and estrangement of many young people from nature.

Two of the most pressing issues are climate change and social change. As we continue to burn vast quantities of fossil fuels, the resulting warmer and less-stable climate fundamentally threatens the integrity of our National Park System. Greenhouse gases lead to a cascade of environmental consequences, including melting glaciers and ice packs, rising sea levels, more frequent weather extremes, more intense wildfires, and species extinctions. Climate models suggest that glaciers in Glacier National Park will disappear within the next few decades; namesake plants in Joshua Tree and Saguaro National Parks may soon be unsustainable; freshwater wetlands in Everglades National Park may be contaminated by massive saltwater intrusion; coral reefs at Virgin Islands National Park

Glaciers in most national parks are melting at an increasing rate due to climate change. (Mount Rainier National Park)

and others may die from bleaching; and wildfires in many national parks will increase in frequency and intensity.

We're also undergoing substantial social change. Our population continues to rise; just as important, it's becoming substantially more diverse, and the National Park System must adapt accordingly. Existing parks must be reinterpreted to tell more inclusive stories; for example, the role of the African-American Buffalo Soldiers in protecting the national parks in their formative years should be told throughout the National Park System. And new parks must be added that tell the stories of more culturally diverse people, including African Americans, Hispanics, Native Americans, youth, the LGBTQ community, and others. Society has also become more polarized and divisive, and national parks can help bring us back together. There's a long history of support for the national parks among the American people and across the aisles of Congress that can help combat growing bipartisanship and incivility. This is a function of the fundamental democratic character of the national park idea.

This is a big agenda, and the national parks and the NPS need our help to facilitate this work. Fortunately, there are a number of partner groups that help support the national parks, including friends groups, volunteers, concessioners, universities, and generous donors (we like to call these people and entities "parkners"). But ultimately, it's up to all of us who love the national parks to support them. Rachel Carson, author of *Silent Spring*, an exposé of the environmental impacts of DDT and other pesticides, wrote that "no carefree love of the planet is now possible." This message should resonate with all of us who love the national parks: If we love them, we must help care for them. There's a long and storied history of individual championship of national parks: Theodore Roosevelt using his presidential powers to create so many national parks, the Rockefeller family's gifts of land and money to form and expand a number of national parks, and more ordinary people like John Muir (who once described himself as "an unknown nobody") and his campaign to create Yosemite National Park, Enos Mills and his support for Rocky Mountain National Park, and Marjory Stoneman Douglas, whose book *River of Grass* was instrumental in establishing Everglades National Park. All of us can be national park heroes by volunteering to maintain trails or staff visitor centers; welcoming visitors from underrepresented racial and ethnic groups; participating in programs of citizen science by monitoring ecologically sensitive sites; joining friends groups and philanthropic organizations such as the National Park Foundation, National Parks Conservation Association, American Hiking Society, American Trails, and local equivalents; living our lives in ways that decrease the need for more and more natural resources; and considering the welfare of the national parks when voting in local, state, and national elections. More ways to support national parks are often posted on national park websites at "Get Involved." Think about how you can best support the national parks and exercise your responsibility as a national park steward.

HIkers can find on-the-ground conditions of trails and good advice at the visitors centers in all the national parks. (Yellowstone National Park)

Appendix: Table of Trails

We've gathered vital statistics on the trails we recommend in Part 2 of this book and arranged them into the table below in hopes that it will be useful to readers. The table includes the names of each national park, the names of the trails we recommend, trail length, degree of challenge, GPS coordinates of trailheads, and the best months to hike. If you use this table to find hikes or trails you're interested in, we encourage you to read about those trails in Part 2. We've included the page number for the descriptions of all trails in the last column of the table to help lead you to descriptions of the trails you're interested in. In many cases, you'll see how hikes can be modified to make them shorter, longer, or changed in other ways that might meet your needs.

Park	Trail	Length (round-trip in miles)	Degree of Challenge	GPS Coordinates	Best Months to Hike	Page
Acadia National Park						
	Ocean Path	4	Easy	44.329988, -68.183738	April–October	11
	Emery Path/Homans Path/Jesup Path	1	Easy	44.361570, -68.208488	April–October	11
	The Beehive Trail	2	Easy to Moderate	44.331763, -68.185314	April–October	12
	Cadillac Mountain (South Ridge Trail)	8	Moderate	44.313166, -68.214799	April–October	13
	Carriage Roads (Around Mountain Loop)	11	Moderate	44.329542, -68.293080	April–October	13
Arches National Park						
	Park Avenue Trail	2	Easy	38.624751, -109.599704	April–October	17
	Delicate Arch Trail	3	Moderate	38.735587, -109.520674	April–October	18
	Fiery Furnace	Variable	Moderate	38.744218, -109.561658	April–October	18
	Devils Garden Trail	Up to 7.2	Easy to Moderate	38.783196, -109.594879	April–October	18
	Tower Arch Trail	3.4	Moderate	38.792571, -109.675087	April–October	19
Badlands National Park						
	Fossil Exhibit Trail	<1	Easy	43.772814, -102.003080	April–October	23
	Window Trail	<1	Easy	43.760213, -101.928300	April–October	23
	Door Trail	<1	Easy	43.760213, -101.928300	April–October	23

Park	Trail	Length (round-trip in miles)	Degree of Challenge	GPS Coordinates	Best Months to Hike	Page
Badlands National Park (continued)						
	Notch Trail	1.5	Moderate	43.760213, -101.928300	April–October	23
	Saddle Pass Trail/ Medicine Root Trail/ Castle Trail Loop	4.5	Easy to Moderate	43.758195, -101.974386	April–October	23
	Sheep Mountain Trail	4	Easy	43.692804, -102.578994	April–October	24
Big Bend National Park						
	Santa Elena Canyon Trail	1.7	Moderate	29.167208, -103.610624	October–May	28
	Lost Mine Trail	4.8	Moderate	29.274488, -103.286478	October–May	29
	Emory Peak (Pinnacles Trail)	10	Moderate to Challenging	29.269906, -103.300115	October–May	29
Black Canyon of the Gunnison National Park						
	Oak Flat Loop Trail	2	Moderate	38.555000, -107.686505	May–September	35
	Warner Point Nature Trail	1.5	Moderate	38.562751, -107.742041	May–September	36
	North Vista Trail	7	Moderate	38.587287, -107.704876	May–September	36
	Gunnison Route	2	Very Challenging	38.555930, -107.690326	May–September	36
Bryce Canyon National Park						
	Rim Trail	5.5	Moderate	37.628578, -112.162945	May–September	40
	Bristlecone Loop Trail	1	Easy	37.488368, -112.239521	May–September	41
	Queen's Garden Trail/ Navajo Loop Trail	3	Moderate	37.628473, -112.162984	May–September	41
	Fairyland Loop Trail	8	Moderate	37.649549, -112.146990	May–September	42
Canyonlands National Park						
	Grand View Point Trail	2	Easy	38.323305, -109.863069	April–October	45
	Upheaval Dome Overlook Trail	1.6	Easy	38.426422, -109.926176	April–October	46
	Big Spring Canyon Trail/ Squaw Canyon Trail	7.5	Moderate	38.150011, -109.802101	April–October	46
	Chesler Park Trail	11	Moderate	38.145193, -109.833675	April–October	46
	Murphy Point Trail	3.6	Easy	38.355093, -109.863844	April–October	47
	Horseshoe Canyon/ Great Gallery	7	Moderate to Challenging	38.484747, -110.197918	April–October	47

Park	Trail	Length (round-trip in miles)	Degree of Challenge	GPS Coordinates	Best Months to Hike	Page
Capitol Reef National Park						
	Fruita Rural Historic District	Variable	Easy	38.286642, -111.246750	April–October	52
	Grand Wash Trail	4.4	Easy	38.256348, -111.232760	April–October	52
	Capitol Gorge Trail	Variable	Easy	38.208262, -111.194866	April–October	52
	Rim Overlook Trail	4.5/9	Moderate to Challenging	38.288721, -111.227652	April–October	53
	Pleasant Creek	Variable	Easy to Moderate	38.180133, -111.180661	April–October	53
	Halls Creek Narrows	22	Moderate to Challenging	37.622026, -110.893885	April–October	53
Carlsbad Caverns National Park						
	Cave Tours					
	Big Room Trail	1.25	Easy	32.186415, -104.441818	April–October	58
	Natural Entrance Trail	1.25	Easy	32.186415, -104.441818	April–October	58
	King's Palace Tour	1	Easy	32.186415, -104.441818	April–October	58
	Slaughter Canyon Cave	2	Moderate	32.110543, -104.562855	April–October	58
	Rattlesnake Canyon Trail	6	Moderate	32.165729, -104.503294	April–October	58
Channel Islands National Park						
	Santa Cruz Island					
	Historic Ranch Trail	0.5	Easy	34.038802, -119.766918	April–November	63
	Potato Harbor Trail	5	Easy	34.038802, -119.766918	April–November	63
	Smugglers Cove Trail	8	Moderate	34.038802, -119.766918	April–November	63
	Anacapa Island	2	Easy	34.015653, -119.365013	April–November	63
	Santa Rosa Island	Variable	Variable	33.986411, -120.089822	April–November	64
	San Miguel Island	Variable	Variable	34.048216, -120.375119	April–November	64
	Santa Barbara Island	Variable	Variable	33.478770, -119.037237	April–November	64
Crater Lake National Park						
	Garfield Peak Trail	3.4	Moderate	42.909422, -122.140823	June–September	68
	Cleetwood Cove Trail	2.2	Moderate	42.979710, -122.083243	June–September	69
	Wizard Summit Trail	2	Moderate	42.979710, -122.083243	June–September	69
	Mount Scott Trail	5	Moderate	42.929235, -122.029936	June–September	70

Park	Trail	Length (round-trip in miles)	Degree of Challenge	GPS Coordinates	Best Months to Hike	Page
Cuyahoga Valley National Park						
	Blue Hen Falls Trail	0.5	Easy	41.257904, -81.572468	March–October	74
	Ledges Trail	2.2	Easy	41.226506, -81.511303	March–October	74
	Brandywine Gorge Trail/ Brandywine Falls Trail	1.4	Easy	41.276624, -81.540131	March–October	74
	Ohio & Erie Canal Towpath Trail	20 (point to point)	Easy to Moderate	41.281289, -81.562262	March–October	75
Death Valley National Park						
	Badwater Salt Flats Trail	Variable	Easy	36.229839, -116.767358	October–April	80
	Mesquite Flat Sand Dunes	Variable	Moderate	36.606635, -117.115977	October–April	80
	Salt Creek Interpretive Trail	<1 to 4	Easy to Moderate	36.590847, -116.990138	October–April	80
	Golden Canyon Trail/ Gower Gulch Loop Trail	2 to 4.7	Easy to Moderate	36.421316, -116.846876	October–April	81
	Ubehebe/Little Hebe Craters	Variable	Easy to Moderate	37.011338, -117.454815	October–April	81
	Wildrose Peak Trail	8.4	Moderate to Challenging	36.246702, -117.076265	October–April	81
Denali National Park and Preserve						
	Savage River Loop Trail	1.7	Easy	63.741414, -149.291644	May–September	86
	Savage River Alpine Trail	4 or 8	Moderate	63.741414, -149.291644	May–September	86
	Tundra Loop Trail	0.3	Easy	63.431049, -150.311435	May–September	87
	Eielson Alpine Trail	2	Moderate	63.431049, -150.311435	May–September	87
	McKinley Bar Trail	5	Easy	63.453564, -150.862747	May–September	87
Everglades National Park						
	Anhinga Trail	1	Easy	25.382700, -80.606461	December–April	94
	Pa-hay-okee Overlook Trail	<1	Easy	25.441182, -80.783708	December–April	94
	Mahogany Hammock Trail	<1	Easy	25.323828, -80.832049	December–April	95
	Shark Valley Trail	Variable	Easy	25.757077, -80.765334	December–April	95
	Slough Slogging	Variable	Moderate	Variable	December–April	95

Park	Trail	Length (round-trip in miles)	Degree of Challenge	GPS Coordinates	Best Months to Hike	Page
Glacier National Park						
	Saint Mary and Virginia Falls Trail	3.6	Moderate	48.674339, -113.608250	June–September	103
	Avalanche Lake Trail	6.2	Moderate	48.680235, -113.819441	June–September	103
	Grinnell Glacier Trail	11	Moderate to Challenging	48.797144, -113.668594	June–September	104
	Highline Trail/Garden Wall	11.6 (one way)	Moderate to Challenging	48.696599, -113.718158	June–September	104
Grand Canyon National Park						
	Grand Canyon Rim Trail	up to 14	Easy	36.062281, -112.109828	April–October	109
	Bright Angel Trail	20	Very Challenging	36.057795, -112.143537	April–October	109
	South Kaibab Trail	14.5	Very Challenging	36.059579, -112.083579	April–October	110
	Colorado River via the South Kaibab and Bright Angel Trails	17.2	Very Challenging	36.059579, -112.083579	April–October	111
	Grand Canyon Rim-to-Rim	21	Very Challenging	36.217234, -112.056846	April–October	111
Grand Teton National Park						
	String Lake Trail	3.4	Easy	43.785635, -110.727850	June–October	116
	Historic Districts					
	Mormon Row	Variable	Easy	43.666465, -110.664333	June–October	116
	Menor's Ferry	Variable	Easy	43.659594, -110.712589	June–October	116
	Murie Ranch	Variable	Easy	43.650330, -110.728580	June–October	116
	Phelps Lake Loop Trail	7	Moderate	43.626468, -110.773433	June–October	117
	Cascade Canyon Trail	8.8/14.2	Moderate to Challenging	43.750817, -110.724173	June–October	117
	Teton Crest Trail	up to 35	Very Challenging	43.587360, -110.827970	June–October	118
Great Basin National Park						
	Lehman Caves (Grand Palace Tour)	<1	Easy	39.005686, -114.219864	May–October	122
	Bristlecone Trail/Glacier Trail	3.4/4.6	Moderate	39.010054, -114.307091	June–September	123
	Wheeler Peak Summit Trail	8.6	Very Challenging	39.017057, -114.303260	June–September	123

Park	Trail	Length (round-trip in miles)	Degree of Challenge	GPS Coordinates	Best Months to Hike	Page
Great Sand Dunes National Park and Preserve						
	The Dunes	Variable	Easy to Challenging	37.740041, -104.517081	April–October	129
	Dune Overlook Trail	2	Easy	37.747665, -105.503520	April–October	129
	Mosca Pass Trail	7	Moderate	37.735023, -105.508456	May–September	129
	Medano-Zapata Ranch	1	Easy	37.652995, -105.593636	April–October	129
Great Smoky Mountains National Park						
	Clingmans Dome Trail	2	Moderate	35.556951, -83.495688	April–October	134
	Laurel Falls Trail	2.6	Easy	35.673543, -83.580971	April–October	134
	Charlies Bunion Trail	8	Moderate	35.612606, -83.425552	April–October	135
	Ramsey Cascades Trail	8	Moderate	35.702841, -83.357726	April–October	135
	Mount LeConte (Alum Cave Trail)	10	Challenging	35.629317, -83.450777	April–October	135
	Quiet Walkways	Variable	Easy	Variable	April–October	136
Guadalupe Mountains National Park						
	McKittrick Canyon Trail	6.8 to 10.8	Moderate to Challenging	31.978030, -104.752227	April–October	139
	Devil's Hall Trail	4.2	Moderate	31.896837, -104.828083	April–October	140
	Guadalupe Peak Trail	8.4	Challenging	31.896837, -104.828083	April–October	141
Haleakalā National Park						
	Leleiwi Overlook Trail	<1	Easy	20.744176, -156.230189	Year-round	145
	Keonehe'ehe'e (Sliding Sands Trail)/Halemau'u Trail	Variable	Easy to Challenging	20.714610, -156.250917	Year-round	145
	Kūloa Point Loop Trail	<1	Easy	20.661910, -156.044925	Year-round	145
	Pīpīwai Trail	3.7	Moderate to Challenging	20.661910, -156.044925	Year-round	146
Hawai'i Volcanoes National Park						
	Crater Rim Trail	up to 11	Easy to Moderate	19.416656, -155.242889	Year-round	150
	Kīlauea Iki Trail	2.5	Moderate	19.416656, -155.242889	Year-round	150
	Pu'u Loa Petroglyphs Trail	1.4	Easy	19.289073, -155.129866	Year-round	150
	Nāpau Trail	2.5 to 7	Moderate to Challenging	19.365054, -155.215551	Year-round	150

Park	Trail	Length (round-trip in miles)	Degree of Challenge	GPS Coordinates	Best Months to Hike	Page
Indiana Dunes National Park						
	Dune Succession Trail	1	Easy	41.262504, -87.206242	April–October	156
	Chellberg Farm/Bailly Homestead	1.3	Easy	41.624822, -87.088529	April–October	156
	Miller Woods Trail	3.2	Easy	41.606783, -87.267645	April–October	156
	Mount Baldy Trail	1	Easy	41.706744, -86.930141	April–October	157
Isle Royale National Park						
	Stoll Trail	4.2	Easy	48.145908, -88.482056	April–October	161
	Lookout Louise Trail	2.2	Moderate	48.157430, -88.475226	April–October	162
	Greenstone Ridge Trail	up to 42.7	Challenging	48.163344, -88.481348	April–October	162
Joshua Tree National Park						
	Hidden Valley Nature Trail	1.5	Easy	34.012696, -116.168083	March–November	166
	Barker Dam Nature Trail	1.1	Easy	34.025170, -116.142012	March–November	167
	Ryan Mountain Trail	3.4/4.6	Moderate	34.002787, -116.135936	March–November	167
	Lost Horse Mine Trail	4	Moderate	33.951186, -116.159702	March–November	167
	Lost Palms Oasis Trail	8	Moderate	33.738158, -115.810703	March–November	168
Kenai Fjords National Park						
	Glacier View Loop Trail	1	Easy	60.191603, -149.631892	June–August	173
	Harding Icefield Trail	8	Challenging	60.191603, -149631892	June–August	173
Lassen Volcanic National Park						
	Manzanita Lake Trail	1.5	Easy	40.531783, -121.564410	June–September	180
	Cinder Cone Trail	5	Moderate to Challenging	40.564932, -121.302638	June–September	180
	Bumpass Hell Trail	Variable	Moderate	40.465697, -121.514551	June–September	181
	Lassen Peak Trail	5	Moderate to Challenging	40.474165, -121.505461	June–September	181
Mammoth Cave National Park						
	Mammoth Cave (Grand Avenue Cave Tour)	4	Moderate	37.187110, -86.101281	March–November	186
	River Styx Spring Trail/ Green River Bluffs Trail/ Heritage Trail	Variable	Moderate	37.187110, -86.101281	March–November	187

Park	Trail	Length (round-trip in miles)	Degree of Challenge	GPS Coordinates	Best Months to Hike	Page
Mammoth Cave National Park (continued)						
	Cedar Sink Trail	1.6	Easy	37.158183, -86.159611	March–November	187
	Sal Hollow Trail/Buffalo Creek Trail/Turnhole Bend Trail	5.5	Easy	37.205763, -86.139435	March–November	188
Mesa Verde National Park						
	Cliff Dwellings					
	Cliff Palace	<1	Easy	37.167163, -108.464659	April–October	193
	Balcony House	<1	Moderate	37.161725, -108.464659	April–October	193
	Spruce Tree House	<1	Easy	37.184093, -108.486884	April–October	193
	Long House	2.2	Easy	37.187042, -108.535798	April–October	193
	Petroglyph Point Trail	2.4	Moderate	37.184614, -108.488534	April–October	194
	Soda Canyon Overlook Trail	1.2	Easy	37.167697, -108.469855	April–October	194
	Badger House Community Trail	2.5	Easy	37.189496, -106.534396	April–October	195
Mount Rainier National Park						
	Grove of the Patriarchs Trail	1.5	Easy	46.757994, -121.557620	June–September	199
	Comet Falls Trail/Van Trump Park Trail	7	Moderate	46.778813, -121.783612	June–September	199
	Skyline Loop Trail	6.8 to 10.8	Moderate to Challenging	46.787080, -121.734352	June–September	200
	Spray Park Trail	6 to 7	Moderate to Challenging	46.932833, -121.863553	June–September	200
	Wonderland Trail	93	Challenging	Variable (This is a long loop trail.	June–September	200
North Cascades National Park						
	Happy Creek Forest Walk/Happy Creek Falls Trail	2.9	Moderate	48.728681, -121.055643	May–September	208
	Cascade Pass Trail/Sahale Arm Trail	7.4/12	Moderate to Challenging	48.475495, -121.075021	May–September	208
Olympic National Park						
	Hurricane Ridge	Variable	Easy to Moderate	47.969295, -123.498376	June–September	213
	Hoh Rain Forest	Variable	Easy to Challenging	47.969295, -123.933026	June–September	213

Park	Trail	Length (round-trip in miles)	Degree of Challenge	GPS Coordinates	Best Months to Hike	Page
Olympic National Park (continued)						
	Rialto Beach	4	Moderate	47.921139, -124.638004	June–September	213
	Sol Duc Falls Trail	1.6	Easy	47.966982, -123.836043	June–September	214
Petrified Forest National Park						
	Long Logs Trail/Agate House Trail	2.5	Easy	34.814668, -109.866752	March–November	220
	Blue Mesa Loop Trail	1	Easy	34.940977, -109.756279	March–November	220
	Onyx Bridge Route	4	Moderate	35.084413, -109.788726	March–November	220
Pinnacles National Park						
	Condor Gulch Trail/High Peaks Trail/Bear Gulch Trail	5.3	Moderate	36.481579, -121.181385	February–October	224
	Moses Spring Trail/Bear Gulch Cave Trail/Rim Trail	2	Easy to Moderate	36.478486, -121.183586	February–October	224
	Old Pinnacles Trail/ Balconies Cave Trail/ Balconies Cliffs Trail	5.2	Easy to Moderate	36.495152, -121.173033	February–October	225
	North Chalone Peak Trail	9	Moderate to Challenging	36.455316, -121.198221	February–October	225
Redwood National and State Parks						
	The Ancient Redwood Groves					
	Tall Trees Trail	4	Easy to Moderate	41.208282, -123.993121	April–November	232
	Lady Bird Johnson Trail	1	Easy	41.303658, -124.018012	April–November	232
	Stout Memorial Grove Trail	1	Easy	41.788273, -124.085930	April–November	232
	Simpson-Reed Trail	1	Easy	41.813582, -124.108164	April–November	232
	Fern Canyon Trail	1	Easy to Moderate	41.401261, -124.065825	April–November	232
	Enderts Beach	1	Easy	41.718949, -124.145000	April–November	232
	Redwood Creek Trail	3 to 16	Easy to Challenging	41.304958, -124.032620	April–November	233
	Hiouchi Trail	4.2	Moderate	41.806651, -124.083362	April–November	233
	Coastal Trail	Up to 35	Moderate to Challenging	41.727321, -124.148790 and 41.547705, -124.071445	April–November	233

Park	Trail	Length (round-trip in miles)	Degree of Challenge	GPS Coordinates	Best Months to Hike	Page
Rocky Mountain National Park						
	Nymph Lake Trail/ Dream Lake Trail/ Emerald Lake Trail	3.6	Moderate	40.311939, -105.645545	June–September	239
	Ute Trail	4	Moderate	40.393443, -105.695093	June–September	239
	Bridal Veil Falls Trail	6	Moderate	40.431187, -105.500054	June–September	240
	Colorado River Trail	7.4	Moderate	40.401983, -105.848622	June–September	240
	Longs Peak	16	Very Challenging	40.271563, -105.556580	July–September	241
Saguaro National Park						
	Nature Trails					
	Desert Discovery Nature Trail	<1	Easy	32.254520, -111.197248	November–April	245
	Cactus Garden Trail	<1	Easy	32.254520, -111.197248	November–April	245
	Desert Ecology Trail	<1	Easy	32.203457, -110.725014	November–April	245
	Signal Hill Trail	<1	Easy	32.290115, -111.208958	November–April	246
	Cactus Forest Trail	2.5	Easy	32.199523, -110.721554	November–April	247
	Tanque Verde Ridge Trail	Up to 22	Moderate to Challenging	32.165653, -110.723945	November–April	247
	Wasson Peak (Sendero Esperanza Trail/Hugh Norris Trail)	8	Moderate	32.285412, -111.167157	November–April	248
Sequoia and Kings Canyon National Parks						
	Moro Rock Trail	<1	Moderate	36.546974, -118.765571	May–September	254
	General Sherman Tree Trail/Congress Trail	3	Easy	36.584874, -118.749715	May–September	255
	Crescent Meadow Trail	3.2	Easy	36.554181, -118.750208	May–September	255
	Zumwalt Meadow Trail	1.5	Easy	36.794455, -118.598250	May–September	255
	High Sierra Trail	Up to 72	Easy to Challenging	36.554926, -118.749008	May–September	256
	Rae Lakes Loop Trail	Up to 41	Moderate to Challenging	36.794792, -118.582746	May–September	256
Shenandoah National Park						
	Fox Hollow Trail	1.2	Easy	38.871846, -78.203595	April–October	261
	Hawksbill Mountain Summit Trail	2.9	Moderate	38.556473, -78.386746	April–October	262

Park	Trail	Length (round-trip in miles)	Degree of Challenge	GPS Coordinates	Best Months to Hike	Page
Shenandoah National Park (continued)						
	Rose River Trail/Dark Hollow Falls Trail	4	Moderate	38.514848, -78.366041	April–October	262
	Rapidan Camp Trail/ Laurel Prong Trail/ Hazeltop Loop	7.4	Moderate	38.499633, -78.445639	April–October	262
	Old Rag Mountain (Ridge Trail/Saddle Trail/Weakley Hollow Fire Road)	9.2	Challenging	38.571386, -78.286512	April–October	263
Theodore Roosevelt National Park						
	Jones Creek Trail/ Roundup Trail	4	Moderate	46.966320, -103.487006	April–October	267
	Big Plateau Loop Trail	5.7	Moderate	46.959475, -103.502957	April–October	268
	Buckhorn Trail/ Achenbach Trail	Variable	Moderate to Challenging	47.609865, -103.355918 and 47.603124, -103.441829	April–October	269
Wind Cave National Park						
	Cave Tours					
	Fairgrounds Tour	<1	Easy	43.556611, -103.478264	April–October	279
	Candlelight Tour	<1	Moderate	43.556611, -103.478264	April–October	279
	Wild Cave Tour	<1	Challenging	43.556611, -103.478264	April–October	279
	Rankin Ridge Trail	1	Easy	43.622761, -103.486044	April–October	279
	Lookout Point Trail/ Centennial Trail Loop	4.5	Moderate	43.581477, -103.483811	April–October	279
Yellowstone National Park						
	Grand Canyon of the Yellowstone					
	North Rim Trail	Up to 3.5 (one way)	Easy to Moderate	44.707977, -110.500274	June–September	287
	South Rim Trail	Up to 3 (one way)	Easy to Moderate	44.707977, -110.500274	June–September	287
	Upper Geyser Basin	Up to 5	Easy to Moderate	44.458743, -110.828238	June–September	288
	Fairy Falls Trail	4.8	Easy to Moderate	44.515475, -110.832538	June–September	289
	Mount Washburn (Chittenden Road)	6.2	Moderate	44.840438, -110.438846	June–September	289

Park	Trail	Length (round-trip in miles)	Degree of Challenge	GPS Coordinates	Best Months to Hike	Page
Yellowstone National Park (continued)						
	Upper Gallatin River Trail (Bighorn Pass Trail)	Variable	Easy to Moderate	44.928375, -111.049352	June–September	289
	Mary Mountain Trail (Nez Perce Trail)	Up to 20 (one way)	Moderate	44.678057, -110.487374	June–September	290
Yosemite National Park						
	Vernal Fall/Nevada Fall (John Muir Trail/Mist Trail/Panorama Trail)	1.6 to 5.8	Easy to Moderate	37.734554, -119.557807	May–September	295
	Mariposa Grove (Grizzly Giant Loop Trail)	2	Easy	37.503617, -119.600655	May–September	296
	Lyell Canyon Trail	Up to 11.2	Easy to Moderate	37.877791, -119.338525	June–September	296
	Half Dome	16	Very Challenging	37.738693, -119.557631	June–September	297
	High Sierra Camps Loop	Up to 50	Moderate to Challenging	37.911184, -119.419052	July–September	297
	John Muir Trail	211 (34 in park)	Challenging	37.734554, -119.557807	July–September	298
	Pacific Crest Trail	2650 (70 in park)	Challenging	37.854965, -119.296917	July–September	298
Zion National Park						
	Emerald Pools Trail	2.5	Easy to Moderate	37.250979, -112.958050	April–October	301
	Virgin River Narrows	up to 16	Moderate to Challenging	37.369821, -112.913399 and 37.285314, -112.947720	April–October	302
	Angels Landing	5.4	Very Challenging	37.272310, -112.950032	April–October	302
	West Rim Trail	16.5 (one way)	Moderate to Challenging	37.382087, -113.022847	April–October	303
	East Rim Trail	10 (one way)	Moderate	37.274174, -112.928402	April–October	304
	Zion Rim-to-Rim	28	Moderate to Challenging	37.382087, -113.022847 and 37.274174, -112.928402	April–October	305

References

Books

Abbey, E. 1985. *Desert Solitaire.* New York: Ballantine Books (original work published 1968-)

Alvarez, T. 2016. *The National Parks Coast to Coast.* Guilford, CT: Falcon.

Amato, J. 2004. *On Foot: A History of Walking.* New York: New York University Press.

Berger, K. 2004. *Hiking Light Handbook: Carry Less, Enjoy More (Backpacker).* Seattle, WA: Mountaineers Books.

Bryson, B. 1998. *A Walk in the Woods: Rediscovering America on the Appalachian Trail.* New York: Broadway Books.

Chamberlin, S. 2016. *On the Trail: A History of American Hiking.* New Haven, CT: Yale University Press.

Cole, D., and R. Brame. 2011. *Soft Paths: Enjoying the Wilderness without Harming It.* Mechanicsburg, PA: Stackpole Books.

Duncan, D., and K. Burns. 2009. *The National Parks: America's Best Idea.* New York: Alfred A. Knopf.

Fletcher, C., and C. Rawlins. 2010. *The Complete Walker IV.* New York: Alfred A. Knopf.

Gros, F. 2014. *A Philosophy of Walking.* New York: Verso.

Harmon, D., F. McManamon, and D. Pitcaithley. 2006. *The Antiquities Act: A Century of American Archaeology, Historic Preservation, and Nature Conservation.* Tucson: University of Arizona Press.

Harvey, M. 1999. *The National Outdoor Leadership School's Wilderness Guide.* New York: Fireside.

Heacox, K. 2015. *The National Parks: An Illustrated History.* Washington, DC: National Geographic.

Keiter, R. 2013. *To Conserve Unimpaired: The Evolution of the National Park Idea.* Washington, DC: Island Press.

Macfarlane, R. 2012. *The Old Ways: A Journey on Foot.* New York: Viking Penguin.

Manning, R., R. Diamant, N. Mitchell, and D. Harmon. 2016. *A Thinking Person's Guide to America's National Parks.* New York: George Braziller Publishers.

Manning, R., and M. Manning. 2013. *Walking Distance: Extraordinary Hikes for Ordinary People.* Corvallis: Oregon State University Press.

———. 2017. *Walks of a Lifetime: Extraordinary Hikes from Around the World.* Guilford, CT: Falcon.

McGivney, A. 2003. *Leave No Trace: A Guide to the New Wilderness Etiquette.* Boulder, CO: Backpacker.

McKinney. 2005. *The Joy of Hiking.* Berkeley, CA: Wilderness Press.

Marion, J. 2014. *Leave No Trace in the Outdoors.* Mechanicsburg, PA: Stackpole Books.

Moor, Robert. 2016. *On Trails: An Exploration.* New York: Simon and Schuster.

Muir, J. 1901. *Our National Parks.* Boston: Houghton Mifflin.

Nash, R. 2014. *Wilderness and the American Mind,* 5th ed. New Haven, CT: Yale University Press.

National Geographic and P. Schermeister. 2016. *Guide to National Parks of the United States,* 8th ed. Washington, DC: National Geographic.

Nicholson, G. 2009. *The Lost Art of Walking.* New York: Riverhead Books.

Oswald, M. 2017. *Your Guide to the National Parks.* Whitelaw, WI: Stone Road Press.

Runte, A. 2010. *National Parks: The American Experience*, 4th ed. Boulder, CO: Taylor Trade Publishing.

Scott, D., and K. Scott. 2017. *Complete Guide to the National Park Lodges.* Guilford, CT: Globe Pequot Press.

Sellars, R. 1997. *Preserving Nature in the National Parks.* New Haven, CT: Yale University Press.

Skurka, Andrew. 2017. *The Ultimate Hiker's Gear Guide.* Washington, DC: National Geographic.

Solnit, R. 2001. *Wanderlust: A History of Walking.* New York: Penguin Books.

Strayed, C. 2013. *Wild: From Lost to Found on the Pacific Crest Trail.* New York: Vintage Books.

Thoreau, H. D. June, 1862. "Walking." *Atlantic Monthly.*

Townsend, C. 2011. *The Backpacker's Handbook*, 4th ed. Plano, TX: International Marine/Ragged Mountain Press.

Tweed, W. 2010. *Uncertain Path: A Search for the Future of National Parks.* Berkeley: University of California Press.

Film

Burns, K. 2009. *The National Parks: America's Best Idea.* A documentary film. Florentine Films and WETA Television.

Websites

backpacker.com/skills/how-to-get-in-shape-for-hiking

backpackinglight.com

heart.org/en/healthyliving/fitness/walking

lnt.org. (Leave No Trace Center for Outdoor Ethics)

mayoclinic.org/healthy-lifestyle/fitness/in-depth/walking/art
-20050972

rei.com/learn/c/hiking

Photo Credits

All photos by Robert Manning except where noted below:

p. 31 above—NPS/Shaun Wolfe; p. 31 left—NPS/Judd Patterson

p. 65 top—Wikimedia Commons/Jtmartin57;
p. 65 bottom—Wikimedia Commons/Fredlyfish4;
p. 65 left—NPS

p. 89 above—NPS; p. 89 left—NPS

p. 97 above—NPS/Christopher Houlette; p. 97 left—NPS

p. 98 above—NPS; p. 98 right—NPS

p. 99 top—NPS; p. 99 bottom—NPS; p. 99 left—NPS

p. 142—Wikimedia Commons/Michael Oswald

p. 143 top—Wikimedia Commons/Michael Oswald;
p. 143 bottom—Wikimedia Commons/Howcheng

p. 144 above—Wikimedia Commons/Forest Starr and Kim Starr;
p. 144 below—NPS

p. 145—Wikimedia Commons/Joe Parks

p. 146—Wikimedia Commons/Svein-Magne Tuni

p. 152 top—Wikimedia Commons/Brandon Rush;
p. 152 right—Wikimedia Commons/Niagara66

p. 169 above—NPS; p. 169 left—NPS

p. 176 top—NPS; p. 176 bottom—NPS; p. 176 right—NPS

p. 177 top—NPS/J. Pfeiffenberger; p. 177 bottom—NPS/K. Jalone;
p. 177 left—NPS

p. 203 top—NPS; p. 203 bottom—NPS; p. 203 left—NPS

p. 272 top—NPS; p. 272 right—Wikimedia Commons/Bradley
Furrow

p. 273 top—NPS; p. 273 bottom—NPS; p. 273 left—NPS

p. 274—Wikimedia Commons/Raul Diaz

p. 275—NPS

p. 277—NPS

p. 278 above—NPS

p. 282—NPS

p. 283—NPS/Bryan Petryl

About the Authors

Bob Manning is Steven Rubenstein Professor of Environment and Natural Resources (Emeritus) at the University of Vermont, where he taught the history, philosophy, and management of national parks and conducted a long-term program of research for the US National Park Service. Martha Manning is an artist whose work has been inspired by the out-of-doors and featured in national shows and publications. They are both Hiking Ambassadors for the American Hiking Society, have walked dozens of long-distance trails around the world, and have lived, worked, and hiked extensively in the US national parks. Their books include *Walking Distance: Extraordinary Hikes for Ordinary People* (Oregon State University Press), *Walks of a Lifetime: Extraordinary Hikes from Around the World* (Falcon), and *A Thinking Person's Guide to America's National Parks* (George Braziller Publishers). Their website is extraordinaryhikes.com.

The authors take a break at Rapidan Camp in Shenandoah National Park.